Economics

by Terry Hillman

A member of Penguin Group (USA) Inc.

ALPHA BOOKS

Published by Penguin Group (USA) Inc.

Penguin Group (USA) Inc., 375 Hudson Street, New York, New York 10014, USA • Penguin Group (Canada), 90 Eglinton Avenue East, Suite 700, Toronto, Ontario M4P 2Y3, Canada (a division of Pearson Penguin Canada Inc.) • Penguin Books Ltd., 80 Strand, London WC2R 0RL, England • Penguin Ireland, 25 St. Stephen's Green, Dublin 2, Ireland (a division of Penguin Books Ltd.) • Penguin Group (Australia), 250 Camberwell Road, Camberwell, Victoria 3124, Australia (a division of Pearson Australia Group Pty. Ltd.) • Penguin Books India Pvt. Ltd., 11 Community Centre, Panchsheel Park, New Delhi—110 017, India • Penguin Group (NZ), 67 Apollo Drive, Rosedale, North Shore, Auckland 1311, New Zealand (a division of Pearson New Zealand Ltd.) • Penguin Books (South Africa) (Pty.) Ltd., 24 Sturdee Avenue, Rosebank, Johannesburg 2196, South Africa • Penguin Books Ltd., Registered Offices: 80 Strand, London WC2R 0RL, England

IDIOT'S GUIDES and Design are trademarks of Penguin Group (USA) Inc.

International Standard Book Number: 978-1-61564-502-2
Library of Congress Catalog Card Number: 2013957750

16 15   8 7 6 5 4 3

Interpretation of the printing code: The rightmost number of the first series of numbers is the year of the book's printing; the rightmost number of the second series of numbers is the number of the book's printing. For example, a printing code of 14-1 shows that the first printing occurred in 2014.

Printed in the United States of America

Note: This publication contains the opinions and ideas of its author. It is intended to provide helpful and informative material on the subject matter covered. It is sold with the understanding that the author and publisher are not engaged in rendering professional services in the book. If the reader requires personal assistance or advice, a competent professional should be consulted.

The author and publisher specifically disclaim any responsibility for any liability, loss, or risk, personal or otherwise, which is incurred as a consequence, directly or indirectly, of the use and application of any of the contents of this book.

Most Alpha books are available at special quantity discounts for bulk purchases for sales promotions, premiums, fund-raising, or educational use. Special books, or book excerpts, can also be created to fit specific needs. For details, write: Special Markets, Alpha Books, 375 Hudson Street, New York, NY 10014.

Publisher: *Mike Sanders*
Executive Managing Editor: *Billy Fields*
Senior Acquisitions Editor: *Tom Stevens*
Development Editor: *John Etchison*
Production Editor: *Jana M. Stefanciosa*

Cover Designer: *Laura Merriman*
Book Designer: *William Thomas*
Indexer: *Brad Herriman*
Layout: *Brian Massey, Ayanna Lacey*
Proofreader: *Virginia Vasquez Vought*

Contents

Part 2: Microeconomics: Business and the Consumer 69

Appendixes

Introduction

In learning about economics, we're discovering how people share and make the best use of the scarce resources available to them. Economics is about people and their stories. The stories are of creativity and innovation. They are about the individual as well as the community. There are too many tales of booms and busts, greed and fear, rich and poor. Economics involves scholars who try to understand how the economy works.

From the earliest societies—when the population was small, and people lived simply off the land—to today's complex civilization, the driving force on the most basic level has been the need to sustain ourselves with food, clothing, and shelter. What we cannot make or sow ourselves, we must buy, and thus emerged the marketplace.

Microeconomics focuses on the study of the marketplace—the buyers and sellers. The central dynamic of the market is supply and demand. Drilling down, economists study the consumer and the firm. They are curious about consumer behavior and how consumers make choices. They also want to know at what price a business will be motivated to produce more goods. The ultimate goal of a business is to maximize its profit, and microeconomics describes how to achieve this goal.

Businesses come in all sizes, so economists look at business size and market structure. A marketplace with many competitors is better for the consumer, who gets the best deal. Businesses create all that we need and use, but some create pollution and other hazards. Economists try to come up with ideas to solve this dilemma.

The big economic picture is the domain of macroeconomics. Here is where the forces of the marketplace aggregate to affect entire economies. In macroeconomics money itself becomes a point of focus. Money facilitates trade, but it also increases and decreases in value.

The business cycle seems to be an inherent part of a capitalist economic system. The economy expands and contracts along a growth trend. These ups and downs can be long and painful, so macroeconomists try to find ways to moderate the fluctuations.

While macroeconomists work on this problem, they cannot seem to do the impossible: end wars and temper greed. We all pay for these excesses. Some economists try to pick up the pieces; others believe things will work out in the long run and are not concerned with the here and now. Nevertheless, unemployment and poverty, inflation and deflation are very real and have a devastating effect on society. They cannot be ignored if we are to live in a just community.

Economic theories may seem to the uninitiated to be so much boring self-indulgence on the part of economists. The fact is that these concepts are transmitted to policymakers, who act on the recommendations of these same economists. Since they usually have diametrically opposing ideas, it's important to pay attention. The choices made by policymakers will affect you directly in the pocketbook.

How This Book Is Organized

Idiot's Guides: Economics is organized into four parts.

Part 1, Understanding the Economic World We Live In, is an overview of the economy and the elements that will be in focus during our journey. We will take a look at the trade-offs made in all economic activities. The observations of Adam Smith—which formed the first fundamental analysis of the marketplace (the famous "invisible hand")—are too insightful to ignore. A heads up on some of the economic jargon you will encounter when reading this and other economics books, as well as a painless math review, are included in Chapter 6.

Part 2, Microeconomics: Business and the Consumer, covers the main principle of the marketplace: supply and demand. This concept underlies most economic activity. Consumer behavior—how consumers make choices—is of great interest to advertisers, Facebook, and Google, but should be to you as well because you will learn how to get the most for your money. Part 2 includes how businesses can maximize their profit. If you plan to start your own business, this part is for you.

Part 3, Microeconomics: Market Structure, analyzes the important role competition plays in a fluid economy. Markets that include many players are likely to be healthy and more beneficial to consumers than markets that are controlled by a monopolistic firm. Oligopolies, in which a few firms dominate an industry, are more common than you might imagine. You've probably never heard of monopolistic competition, which is characterized by a large number of small firms with similar products. Learn more about this in Part 3.

Part 4, Macroeconomics, describes the major topics of this vital and fascinating subject. In this part, we learn how the entire economy and its components are measured. We see how money, goods, and services flow through the major sectors of the economy—households, firms, the government, and the outside world.

Economists grapple with unemployment and inflation and how they relate. The causes of inflation and deflation and their extremes shed light on the power and limitations of government and central bank policy when it comes to money.

Part 4 also explains the business cycle, a term that sounds innocuous and rhythmical, but hides the brutal nature of the recessionary and inflationary periods. More detail on recessions shows how they can feed on themselves, causing great human suffering. The main macroeconomic theories on recessions, their causes, and whether or not policies should be enacted to head them off give much food for thought.

Everything you've ever wanted to know about money, gold, and the gold standard is covered in Part 4. This leads to the central bank's role in adjusting the money supply to mitigate inflation, deflation, and recessions. Many lessons were learned during the Great Depression of the 1930s, and the central banks have taken their cues from this historic event. The financial crisis that began in 2008 and the ensuing Great Recession have presented a global challenge to central banks. We explain what measures they are taking and what they consider to be a successful outcome of their unconventional policies.

Finally, we explore the role of government in stabilizing the economy as regulator and determining fiscal policy, including the significance of budget deficits and public debt.

Whether you bought this book because you're taking your first economics course in high school or college, or because you want to know more about the way our economy works, *Idiot's Guides: Economics* provides plenty of background information and explains complex ideas in simple language.

Extras

Scattered throughout this book are sidebars that shed light on the material covered in the text. Be on the lookout for points of interest, clarification, and a bit of easy math:

DEFINITION

Important terms are defined for you in these sidebars.

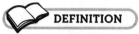

TAKE-AWAY MESSAGE

The key concept of a subject is summarized. If you didn't quite understand the information in a section, you can review this brief explanation.

DO THE MATH

Equations and other mathematical representations explaining ideas in the text are detailed here.

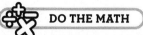

INTERESTING FACT

A bit of background, fun facts, and a look into the past, this information will broaden your understanding of the material.

Acknowledgments

I am grateful to Tom Stevens of Alpha Books, who had faith in me and offered me this project. I also thank the editors, who smoothed out the rough edges of my text.

This book is dedicated to the human factors of production in Bangladesh and elsewhere, whose lives were sacrificed to maximize the firms' profits.

I also dedicate the book to my mother and son, whose curiosity and love of art, music, and life show me the way.

Special Thanks to the Technical Reviewer

Idiot's Guides: Economics was reviewed by an expert who double-checked the accuracy of what you'll learn here, to help us ensure this book gives you everything you need to know about the principles of economics. Special thanks are extended to Andrea Lockhart.

Trademarks

All terms mentioned in this book that are known to be or are suspected of being trademarks or service marks have been appropriately capitalized. Alpha Books and Penguin Group (USA) Inc. cannot attest to the accuracy of this information. Use of a term in this book should not be regarded as affecting the validity of any trademark or service mark.

Understanding the Economic World We Live In

Imagine that you are a visitor to this planet, and you came here to understand how people live and organize their economic society. How would you describe your observations? You would find that businesses produce goods, and consumers buy them. To make these goods, producers might get a loan of some amount of money, or capital, at a certain interest rate from a bank. This capital is used to buy raw materials and equipment, to pay people who make the products, and to pay rent on the land and building where products are manufactured.

You would venture out to stores to see where these products are sold. Here you encounter the consumers who are busy comparing the products that meet their needs at the best price. They are able to buy the products because they earned money by working in the factory.

Picking up one of the products, you notice a trademark, a date, and the name of the owner. In turn, the trademark is issued by a department of the government because the government regulates business activities.

You get the picture.

Part 1 is an introduction to the market economy and the environment in which it functions. Adam Smith observed that the market was directed by what seemed to be an invisible hand—that it is self-regulated. The market economy is one in which there are trade-offs and gains from trade. Since the market economy exists in a larger society, attention must be paid to protect the public good.

All of this and more is explained in Part 1, including a review of graphing, which economists use to describe their ideas, and a vocabulary preview.

Welcome to the world of economics!

An Overview of Our Economic Society

The economies of most of the world are market economies. A market economy is an economic system in which economic decisions and the prices of goods and services are made by the interactions of consumers and businesses with minimal government intervention and little-to-no central planning. Only a few economies still use central planning as the basis of their economy, such as China, North Korea, and Cuba. Even these countries are beginning to introduce markets into their economies.

This chapter gives an overview of our economic world—just the highlights that will be discussed in detail throughout this book.

In This Chapter

- The long-term economic growth trend
- Business: providing the goods and services for society
- Understanding the consumer—the engine of demand
- Government's many hats: backstopping the economy, regulator, major buyer
- A brief look at the domestic and world financial system

Long-Run Economic Growth

The world economy has been following a steep growth trend since the market economy replaced feudalism in most of the world. A chart of the longer view is decidedly in an uptrend.

The technology developed in the 1600s through the 1900s was a start, but even 25 years ago, we could not have imagined conducting international business by having face-to-face conversations over the internet or carrying the internet in our pockets.

The world economy has made enormous progress in science and medicine—working with nanoparticles; having a good look at Mars; developing solar and wind energy, information technology, and computers that are now being groomed to think. The invention of the internet is changing our economic, social, and personal lives. Technological improvements in transportation speed and safety, and improved agricultural and manufacturing methods have spurred the world economy to continued progress.

A chart of long-term growth is impressive indeed. The accompanying figure, Gross World Product, shows the general trend in growth since about 1900.

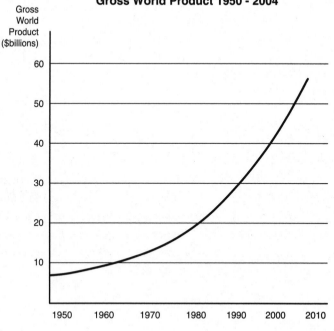

Gross World Product 1950 - 2004

Source: Worldwatch, IMF

Growth is measured by looking at the *real GDP per capita*. Real GDP is the gross domestic product, which is the total value of all final goods and services produced in the economy during a given year taking inflation into account. GDP per capita is the real GDP divided by the population.

Growth in manufacturing due to technological improvements has increased *productivity*, defined as output per worker. *Physical capital*, which includes the buildings and machines used in production, *human capital*, the educated workforce, and technology are the foundations of productivity growth.

DEFINITION

Real GDP per capita is the total value of all final goods and services produced in the economy during given year, taking inflation into account, divided by the population. **Productivity** is output per worker. **Human capital** is the educated workforce.

While world growth is in an uptrend, not every country experiences the same rate of growth. The "developed" economies emerged from the Middle Ages into an era of expansive trade and eventually capitalism. The "developing" economies remained in the early stages of economic formation, and some areas were subject to colonialism. We will never know how these civilizations would have evolved if left alone. Global growth at the present time is patchy, with some areas of the world making good progress while other areas struggle.

The Role of Business

Businesses are at the heart of a market economy.

Proprietorships, where a single individual is the owner of a small enterprise, and partnerships are at the low end of the size scale. Statistics from the Organization of Economic Co-operation and Development (OECD) from 2009 show a comparison of the percent of businesses that are self-employed in some OECD member countries: France, 9 percent; Germany, 12 percent; Italy, 26.4 percent; Sweden, 10.6 percent; United Kingdom, 13.8 percent; and United States, 7.2 percent. These include the small farms, the mom-and-pop retail stores, professional services—such as law firms, doctors, and accountants—some internet businesses, contractors to larger companies, film production companies, and so on. These firms plus businesses that are considered small, but are somewhat larger, employ a good portion of the workforce.

Percent of Businesses That are Self-Employed

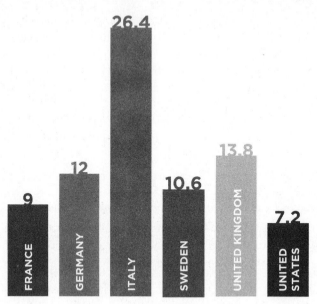

The large corporate enterprises produce the bulk of the sales generated in a market economy. Originating domestically, these businesses have become global in reach.

Let's see what makes a business tick.

Business Revenue

The goal of business is to maximize its profits, but it can't do that unless revenue exceeds costs. Generating revenue is a major activity in a business. Businesses guarantee to acquire revenue if they control a natural resource, such as oil, natural gas, base metals, telephone and electric utilities, and agriculture and food production. These are necessities for other businesses and for consumers.

Businesses also generate revenue by selling products that consumers need and want. It goes without saying that everything you own has been manufactured by a business somewhere in the world.

In order to sell products, businesses hire a sales force and back that up with advertising and public relations campaigns. They want to make sure that you know their product or service is the best. Their ideal would be for you to choose their brand and stick with it.

Business Expenditures

None of the products or services could be created without spending. The cost of production determines whether or not there are profits. Total revenues must exceed costs in order to take home a profit.

The expenditures include the labor necessary to do all the work required for information technology, manufacturing, construction, transportation, health care delivery, farming, providers of services, and the financial industry. Raw materials must be bought in most industries. Firms also have fixed costs, such as rent of land, office buildings, equipment, and utilities.

The Means of Production

The means of production to produce a commodity are labor, capital, and land—and some economists add entrepreneurship. Everything necessary to create a product or deliver a service is included in this category. Raw materials and energy are considered to be secondary.

Labor and capital are also called *factors of production*. These *inputs*, the resources used to create products, endure after the product or service is rendered; they are used continually for new products and services. Raw materials, on the other hand, are used up in the manufacturing process.

A well-functioning market and business will allocate factors of production efficiently.

Labor

Until the robots completely take over the world, labor will be the most important factor of production. Most of us either are or will be part of the workforce, unless we own a business or profession (doctor, lawyer, accountant, independent financial advisor). Labor does all the work necessary to make things and provide services, such as driving transportation vehicles, sanitation work, health care, farming, work on an oil rig, repair work, food service, hotel work, and more.

Labor is compensated with wages or salaries and other benefits. Classical economics considers labor to be supplied to the firm. When analyzing the labor market, economists identify labor as the supply and the firm as the demand. They use a standard supply and demand model to determine when demand for labor is in equilibrium, or balance, with the supply of labor. The supply of labor is a trade-off between leisure and work. The balance is subject to the wage rate—when the wage rate is high, labor will work more hours if the greater income generated by the high wage does not influence him or her to spend part of the income on leisure.

Labor is a unique input because it is composed of human beings. Human beings have needs and therefore don't behave as the other inputs to a commodity—land and capital. Workers try to meet their financial and welfare needs by negotiating with their employers for higher wages and better working conditions. Over the decades many workers have organized into labor unions to provide a unified voice to employers that can lead to negotiated contracts. The human dimension of labor raises questions about economic models. Differing approaches often spill over to the political realm.

Capital, Land, and Entrepreneurship

Capital refers to the equipment, building, and investment of money needed for production. Land is sometimes included as capital. These are considered fixed costs. Firms trade off more capital and less labor or the other way around, depending on the requirements of the production process.

Some economists consider entrepreneurship as an input to production. Without the entrepreneur, there would be no businesses. With talent, drive, and resources, an entrepreneur can turn a good idea into a thriving business.

The Role of Consumers

Consumers are the wellspring of the economy. The greater portion of real GDP is generated by consumer spending; without the consumer, businesses that produce goods and services would have no demand. Supply is not needed when there is no demand. Of course, this will never happen.

Understanding consumer behavior is crucial to businesses. Economists have therefore designed ways to measure a consumer's satisfaction. A consumer's satisfaction is also called a consumer's utility, and it is measured in utils. Utils are imaginary units of the degree of consumer satisfaction with consuming a good ... like an ice cream cone, a hamburger, or any other consumer good or service. Combinations of goods can also be measured. For instance, does Sara prefer to have 10 shrimps and a pound of noodles or 7 shrimps and half a pound of noodles?

Consumer Income

Since the consumer's spending is such a key factor in real GDP, an adequate income should be supported. This is not always the case, especially during a downturn in an economy. When consumers have more income, they will spend more, and this will help the economy grow.

Income can be spent or saved. Economists measure the choices consumers make by using the equation for the marginal propensity to consume (MPC). The MPC is the change in consumer spending divided by the disposable income. For example, if consumer spending in the economy rises by $4 billion, and disposable income is $10 billion, the MPC is $4 billion/$10 billion = 0.4. The portion of the income that is saved is called the marginal propensity to save (MPS). This is determined by subtracting MPC from 1 (1 − MPC = MPS). In our example, this would be 0.6. These measurements, MPC and MPS, are used by macroeconomists when estimating how the real GDP might grow with a given rise in consumer spending.

An increase or a decrease in income also affects the demand for a particular good or many goods. You will learn as we go on just how income affects demand using the supply and demand model.

The Role of Government in the Economy

Two lines of thought prevail in discussions about the role of government in the economy: yes and no, or more and less. Humor aside, this issue is among the most contentious and has been ever since capitalism and independent nations emerged.

Policy

This major rift in philosophy must be taken seriously because the implementation of policy based on one philosophy or the other has enormous impact on the economy.

Economists themselves are deeply divided. For example, the Classical school of economics and its modern iterations believe the government and central banks should not intervene in short-run periods of recession or depression. They think the short-run fluctuations of the business cycle reflect the economy at work and look to the long run, where the economy reaches equilibrium.

The Keynesian school of economic thought and schools that derive from Keynes's approach believe that the government can use fiscal policy to stimulate the economy. The central banks can use monetary policy to do the same by increasing the money supply. If necessary, more extraordinary measures can be taken. Quantitative easing has been used to mitigate the Great Recession of 2008 to the present. Both the Monetarist school and the Keynesian school believe that inflation can be contained by restricting the money supply, which can be accomplished by central banks' raising interest rates.

These economic philosophies are staunchly held by political actors in the government and their lobbyists. It is a global phenomenon—a deep philosophical divide. Entire administrations are elected and then thrown out of power largely as a result of the success or failure of the economy under its tenure.

Regulation

The government is charged with protecting its citizens in various ways. Of course, its defense department defends the country against foreign attack, but sometimes attack from within comes from the very industries that are the motor of an economy. We're referring to the excesses of large corporations and the financial industry. We can politely label some of their behaviors as "overenthusiastic," but, call it what you will, when the vast majority of the citizenry is injured by the actions of those with economic power, the government can step in with regulatory force.

Laws are enacted to regulate companies that pollute the environment or discriminate on the basis of race, gender, or sexual orientation. Laws are enacted in most countries against child labor, but child labor still thrives in some countries even with child labor laws.

Agencies are created by the central government to regulate certain industries. These include the financial industry, the food and drug industry, environmental protection, labor, and consumer protection. The specific agencies vary by country.

Government Expenditures

Governments have enormous spending budgets. The size depends on the size of the economy. The areas of appropriation depend on the country and its policies.

What does the government buy? Strictly speaking government expenditures cover goods and services, but not social security, Medicare, Medicaid, unemployment insurance, or other *transfer* payments (spending without receiving a good or service in return).

Governments spend for present as well as future needs. In countries that have a large welfare component, such as Sweden, Denmark, Luxembourg, and Finland, direct purchases are made from market producers that are given to individuals and households for current use. These expenditures are termed final consumption expenditures.

Acquisitions of goods and services that are used to create future benefit include such categories as infrastructure and spending on research. Economists classify this type of expenditure as government investment. It is usually the largest part of government spending.

Inevitably, elected officials debate about how big the government should be, translated to how much it should spend. Budget debates include what the final bill should be and how to allocate the budget according to departments. Transfers are also included in these debates, although they are excluded from National Income Accounting.

Government Revenue

Governments get revenue from taxes. They borrow money from the public by selling government bonds. In the United States (2010), 82% of revenue came from individual income tax (42%) and payroll tax (40%). Corporate tax accounted for 9% of revenues and excise taxes 3%. Each country has its own revenue structure, but taxes and bonds (government debt) are the primary sources of revenue.

The Financial System

The financial system, both domestically and globally, involves *financial intermediaries* that facilitate investments and loans for industry and loans to households and individuals. Financial intermediaries include such institutions as banks, pension funds, life insurance companies, and mutual funds.

DEFINITION

A **financial intermediary** is an institution that transforms the funds it gathers from individuals into financial assets.

Financial Intermediaries

In their most basic form, commercial and retail banks take deposits from savers and lend to borrowers. Banks allow individuals to put cash into depository accounts. The banks can use those funds to lend to other individuals or businesses. At the same time, the depositories have access to their funds. This is called fractional reserve banking. Fractional reserve banking is described in detail in Chapter 20.

While local banks still provide this service, large banks that have become global in scope have ventured into creating financial products that can be sold to investors. Instead of falling into the category of a traditional commercial or retail bank, companies such as J.P. Morgan, Bank of America, and Barclays have morphed into a hybrid of commercial banks/investment banks.

Investment banks specialize in large, complex financial transactions. They act as an intermediary between a securities issuer and the investing public. They attract and assist in obtaining investment for businesses, individuals, corporations, and governments. They also help companies merge to form one company, aid one firm to purchase another firm, and facilitate corporate reorganizations.

A *mutual fund* is a financial intermediary that creates a stock portfolio and sells shares of the portfolio to individual investors. The mutual fund is gradually being supplanted by *exchange traded funds (ETFs)*, which represent a market sector, commodity, or stock index, and trade like a stock. *Leveraged ETFs* enable short-term traders to place a directional bet on a market sector, commodity, or an entire index. The leverage is less than for options or futures markets.

DEFINITION

A **mutual fund** is a financial intermediary that creates a stock portfolio and sells shares of the portfolio to individual investors. An **exchange-traded fund (ETF)** is a security that represents a market sector, commodity, or stock index, and trades like a stock. **Leverage** is the use of various financial instruments or borrowed capital, such as margin, to increase the potential return of an investment.

The shadow banking system has become a major force in the world of finance. Financial intermediaries operating within the shadow banking system offer credit to corporations globally or domestically but fall through the cracks of regulators. They are not secret entities, but there are no laws at the present time to rein them in. Shadow banking also refers to unregulated activities by normally regulated institutions. Hedge funds and unlisted securities are included in the shadow banking system.

Regulators and Supervisors

Financial regulators are both global and domestic. Their job is to provide security, stability, market confidence, and consumer protection, and to reduce financial crime. These regulators supervise banks and other financial intermediaries to make sure they comply with existing laws and regulations.

Most large and medium-size countries have central banks that are tasked with overseeing the behavior of the financial institutions domestically. In addition, many countries have agencies that supervise the financial industry in their country.

Global regulators and agencies have been established by international agreement of the major nations. These include:

- The International Monetary Fund (IMF), whose stated purpose is to "work to foster global growth and economic stability. It provides policy advice and financing to members in economic difficulties and also works with developing nations to help them achieve macroeconomic stability and reduce poverty."

- The World Trade Organization (WTO) helps countries in need of financial assistance, but it also resolves disputes and assures that agreements are properly implemented.

- The European Central Bank also performs regulatory functions.

- The International Organization of Securities Commissions (IOSCO) coordinates the regulation of financial securities.

- The International Association of Insurance Supervisors (IAIS) promotes consistent insurance industry supervision.

The world economy has become tightly integrated. As we saw when a few U.S. investment banks collapsed in 2008, the dominoes rapidly fell throughout the world. Regulation within countries and internationally is being improved to prevent another catastrophe. Sound laws that deter unreasonable risk taking can protect the fragile balance in the financial system, which underpins the economy.

A Word About Globalization

Globalization has its strengths and weaknesses. One of the biggest impacts is on national labor markets. The manufacturing work goes where labor is least expensive, disrupting prior pockets of strength in a domestic workforce. Economists are grappling with the tide of globalization to better understand the best way to reap the benefits of trade and manufacture. A balanced approach, with the benefits of trade fairly dispersed, is necessary to assure the long-term growth of the world economy.

The Least You Need to Know

- The world economy has been on a growth trajectory since the market economy emerged.
- Businesses are at the heart of the capitalist economy. They produce the goods and services that consumers need and want.
- The means of production are labor, capital, and land; some economists add entrepreneurship. Labor and capital are the factors of production.
- Consumer spending accounts for more than 50 percent of real GDP in most countries. Consumers maximize their satisfaction, or utility, by choosing their favorite combination of goods and services.

- The government spends on investment and research. It derives income from taxes and borrows by selling bonds. The government protects its citizens by passing necessary laws and regulations.
- The financial system is composed of commercial and retail banks, where people and businesses deposit money; investment banks; pension funds; insurance companies; and the shadow banking system.

CHAPTER 2

Introducing the Market Economy

The market system that prevails throughout the world today is a far cry from the environment from which it emerged. We take for granted that there are small businesses and large corporations. People go to work every day to earn a living and, one hopes, to get some satisfaction from their labors. Advanced transportation and communication facilitates trade as businesses interact freely across the globe. They strive to gain profits by producing goods and services that they sell.

All these transactions can take place because there is a market system. The system has grown in size, and some economists question if it is qualitatively the same as the one Adam Smith studied. We can say that, even though population growth and technological improvements have changed the landscape, most of the market mechanisms he observed still play an important role in most economists' toolboxes.

This chapter will describe the underlying forces of the market system. These are the foundations for the models economists use to analyze current market conditions. The conclusions of the economists provide the guidance for policymakers to promote the welfare of society.

In This Chapter

- From feudalism to capitalism
- Adam Smith and the self-regulating market
- Opportunity costs: making choices with limited resources
- The benefits of trade
- The efficient market

The World Before Adam Smith

The economic landscape from the Middle Ages through the Renaissance and the Reformation in the sixteenth century could not have produced the market system so familiar to us today or even centuries ago. There were no markets during that historical period. Yes, there were market squares and traveling fairs, where some small quantity of goods could be bought and sold. Yet the fundamental requirements of production in a market system—land, labor, and capital—did not exist.

Land was owned by the nobles, but the nobleman had no notion of putting it up for sale. Neither was labor for sale. Instead, serfs, apprentices, and journeymen were the toilers. Peasants lived and worked on the estates of the noblemen; they were not free agents. The guilds regulated apprentices' pay and work hours as well as the length of the apprenticeship. Capital was equivalent to private wealth. It was not invested in an enterprise to produce goods.

The guilds of the sixteenth century might have sensed that their workshops would soon be threatened by change when the weaving trade in England developed mass production capabilities. The guilds protested to the King and were rewarded with a law to prevent the establishment of the protofactories.

Had Adam Smith been born in that epoch, his observations of the economic landscape would not have inspired him to envision the mechanism of a market system. It would take a jolting revolution that unfolded gradually to transform serfs and journeymen into independent workers and guild masters into capitalists. The entire feudal system had to be dismantled, and change never comes easily.

Over time, the wool from sheep became a commodity, and the noblemen fenced off their land that had previously been available to the general community for grazing animals. Private property was emerging. The wool industry was growing. The peasants were evicted from the land they had tilled for eons. There were few alternatives for work, as factories did not exist until later. These impoverished people were kept in workhouses even during Adam Smith's time in the eighteenth century. "Houses of terror" was the description of one clergyman.

Eventually, the former peasants and their children, born at the wrong time in economic history, became the workforce for production. The land of the noblemen, not without a fight, was broken out of the estates and combined with labor to provide the new emerging market economy with the means of production.

These changes took place alongside a trend toward centralized kingdoms. The monarchy provided some support to the new centers of production. At the same time, the church and religion were losing their grip on the movers in society. Scientific inquiry had some breathing room, and science and technology were able to progress. In time there were breakthrough inventions, including the mill, the windmill, the clock, and the map. Innovation grew into an attractive pursuit.

Towns multiplied, as did marketplaces. Merchants and their customers became accustomed to the use of money. Gradually, and simultaneous with traditional life, a new spirit filled the air. The concept of personal gain from the emerging economy was now permissible. Entrepreneurs in the vanguard were feeling their stride.

By the early eighteenth century, merchants and mercantilism legitimized the seeking of wealth. The new philosophy was to gain treasure and wealth through trade. Some mercantilist writers pondered how to keep the "poor, poor" in order to have enough cheap labor.

Not much later, some of the most creative thinkers were developing new visions of society. John Locke, Jean-Jacques Rousseau, Voltaire (born François-Marie Arouet), David Hume, and other leaders of the Enlightenment, as well as Benjamin Franklin, were important contributors to the zeitgeist. These were the times and influential figures of Adam Smith's life.

Adam Smith and *The Wealth of Nations*

Brilliant, forgetful, and distracted are all descriptions of Adam Smith. Dr. Smith taught at the University of Glasgow where he was first made Chair of Logic and Chair of Moral Philosophy, and then, in 1758, became dean.

In 1759 Smith published *The Theory of Moral Sentiments,* which included his early thinking on self-interest. After a brief stint as a tutor of the son of the British Chancellor of the Exchequer's wife (Charles Townsend, who imposed the tea tax on the American colonies), Smith returned to Scotland. He spent the next 10 years writing *An Inquiry into the Nature and Causes of the Wealth of Nations,* published in 1776.

The "Invisible Hand" of the Market

The basic concept put forth in *The Wealth of Nations* is that the market operates under simple laws. The behavior of individuals who are competing in the marketplace brings about predictable outcomes. Competition results in the provision of the goods that society wants. Furthermore, the goods will be provided in the *quantities* that society desires at the *prices* society will pay.

This regulatory mechanism begins with individual self-interest; it is self-interest that drives people to compete. Market participants will be ready to take advantage of a competitor who is too greedy: If he charges too much for his products, he will lose customers; if he refuses to pay a wage equal to the wage paid by other firms, he will lose workers. This feedback mechanism leads to social harmony.

TAKE-AWAY MESSAGE

The main points of Adam Smith's theory, explained in his major work, *An Inquiry into the Nature and Causes of the Wealth of Nations*, were:

- The market operates under simple laws.
- Competition results in the provision of the goods that society wants.
- Goods will be provided in the *quantities* that society desires at the *prices* society will pay.
- It is self-interest that drives people to compete.
- The "invisible hand" is the self-regulatory mechanism of the market. When the individual acts in his own self-interest, the effect is to benefit society.

"He [the individual] intends only his own gain, and he is in this, as in many other cases, led by an invisible hand to promote an end which was no part of his intention. Nor is it always the worse for society that it was no part of his intention. By pursuing his own interest he frequently promotes that of the society more effectually than when he really intends to promote it."

Smith describes a society in which the wages, profits, and rent are naturally regulated. The average rates at any given time and place are the *natural rates*, according to Smith. When there are buyers at the natural rate, the commodity is sold at a price equal to the cost, which includes the profit (*The Wealth of Nations*, Adam Smith, p. 55-57). The *market price* is the price at which the good is sold.

When there is not enough supply of a commodity to meet the demand, the market price will rise above the natural rate, according to Smith. For example, during a famine, the price of available food will rise acutely.

The laws of the market also regulate the *quantity produced*. When the supply is greater than the demand, the market price will be lower than the natural rate. If the producer manufactures more shirts than consumers need, he will have to lower the price of the shirts until there are willing buyers.

The degree to which the market price drops below the natural price depends on the need of the seller to dispose of his goods. Smith compares the need of the vendor who imports perishables, such as oranges, with the seller of iron. The vendor of oranges is liable to lose all of the oranges if he is not able to sell them before they rot. He might therefore be willing to take a low price for his goods. The seller of iron does not have this problem and can hold out for a better price.

Smith believed the labor market was also subject to the forces of supply and demand. In this case, the worker is attracted to a high wage and discouraged by a low wage. Higher wages result in a larger population of workers. When there is a surplus of workers, the wage decreases, and the population of workers decreases.

Rent is also determined by market forces, although to a lesser degree. The landlord lowers and raises the rent depending on the demand for land or workspace.

Price tends to revert to the natural rate eventually, according to Smith, although it can fluctuate around it. External events, such as natural catastrophes, can affect the market price as well.

This explains how the "invisible hand" of the market is a self-regulating mechanism: self-interest and competition form the foundation of Adam Smith's theory.

Long-Run Growth According to Smith

In the long run, growth will trend upward because society is dynamic. As wealth increases in society, more workers are added to the new factories. Division of labor is introduced, and there is greater productivity. Prices rise and fall according to the level of demand, but growth remains in a steady, upward climb.

Division of labor was an important concept for Smith. He believed division of labor to be the primary factor that would guarantee long-run economic growth and better the working class. He did not think that division of labor could be sustained indefinitely, though. He believed that long-run growth could not continue at the same pace. Smith projected that growth could only be sustained for 200 years, according to economist Robert L. Heilbroner (*The Worldly Philosophers*). At that point (which is about now), growth would stop, wages would stagnate or decline, and producers would make small profits in a stable market, but the landlord would do well because there would be a large population.

The Role of Government According to Smith

Smith is known for advocating that the market be allowed to regulate itself. Even in his day, this idea was used by industrialists to argue against government regulation. Some contemporary politicians also quote Smith's theory of a self-regulating market to show why the government should not enact regulations. Smith favored neither the capitalists nor labor. His main concern was that the consumer get the best deal.

Smith favored government protection of children at the workplace. In the eighteenth century, factory owners chained children to the machines. They fought the government's attempt to enact laws against whitewashing factories and to make shackling children illegal. Adam Smith wrote that the eighteenth century industrialists "generally have an interest to deceive and even to oppress the public."

Smith favored public investment in projects that cannot be accomplished by the private sector, such as roads and education. He was against any government intervention that restrained imports and exports, which would prevent industry from competing, and he did not favor government spending without a purpose.

Monopolies According to Smith

Smith was opposed to monopolies because they impede the workings of the market. An unfettered market, he believed, will increase the welfare of society because it is creating the greatest number of goods at the lowest possible prices. Any interference with the natural movements of the markets decreases the wealth of the nation.

The insights of Adam Smith provided structure and form to the understanding of the market economy just as it was emerging from the old economic order. Remarkably, his theory has remained largely accurate despite the centuries that have passed.

Individual Choice and the Dilemma of Scarcity

Many choices are made every day. Individuals, groups of individuals, and society as a whole have to decide which *resources* and how much of a resource to use. These choices must be made because resources are scarce. Resources can mean time (should I work or should I read a book?), land (should we keep the forest on our property or build a workshop?), labor (should we hire another person or should we buy a machine?), or capital (should we buy another truck for our fleet?).

 **DEFINITION**

Resources are sources or supplies from which benefit is produced.

You probably don't think about how many decisions and choices you make, whether during one day or one year. No doubt you make many choices that are trivial and some that are important: what to have for each meal; what to wear; what to buy at the grocery store; which television show to watch or website to visit; which movie to see; which apartment to rent; which car to buy. If you choose to have a hamburger for dinner, that means you are not having chicken. You're giving up one food choice for a different choice. If you decide to watch television, you are choosing not to go to the movies. If you choose the printed shirt, you won't wear the solid shirt.

Opportunity Cost

This discussion may seem obvious, so why are we *choosing* this topic instead of something more substantial? Well, actually, choosing to do one thing instead of something else is a fundamental part of economic analysis. There's a name for it—*opportunity cost.*

Opportunity cost is what you are giving up to do what you are doing. Said a different way, it is the benefits you could have received by taking an alternative action.

DEFINITION

Opportunity cost is the real cost of an item; what you must give up in order to do something else or get something else.

As an example, the opportunity cost of going to college is the salary you could have gotten if you had taken that job. Starting a business means you are giving up the opportunity to advance your studies. Eating a cookie when you are on a diet means you can't also have ice cream. These are all examples of the opportunity cost of *doing* one thing instead of another or *having* one thing and giving up something else in order to have what you choose.

Opportunity costs, as you can see from some of the examples, are not always costs paid in cash, and they are not always easy to measure. If you go to school to learn a skill for a better-paying, more rewarding job, you will have to pay cold, hard cash to get your diploma or degree. In addition, you are spending time in the classroom and studying at home. How do you total these costs? If you had to give up a job that paid you a salary of $35,000 per year, you know that you are giving up $35,000 per year. Your hope is that by advancing your education, you will eventually earn much more in salary, and if you're fortunate, you'll get more satisfaction from your new career. So you add it up:

- The cost in money for tuition—say, $25,000 per year.

- The salary you are giving up—$35,000 per year (the opportunity cost).

- This equals $60,000 per year.

Now estimate what you will be earning after you graduate. What do you think about your choice now?

This is an example of how economists consider cost. Cost is almost always opportunity cost. Opportunity cost will come up again and again as you learn economics, so it's important to internalize its meaning.

Measuring in Increments for Accurate Decision Making

Once you make your choice, the next question is how much? How many courses to take? Maybe you can get a part-time job. You choose ice cream over a cookie. How much ice cream should you eat? Maybe you can eat less ice cream so you can take a bite of a cookie.

Economists and other disciplines measure in increments, or additional units. This is called measuring "at the margin," or *marginal analysis*. Each decision, as you now know, involves trading off one thing for another or one action for another action. Marginal analysis measures the additional benefit versus the additional cost of doing something.

> **DEFINITION**
>
> **Marginal analysis** is measuring the additional benefits of an activity and comparing it to the additional costs of an activity.

Market Interaction and Efficiency

Traders in the financial markets know the importance of market interaction. There is almost always someone who takes the other side of a trade. That's because people disagree about the direction—up or down—of a stock or other asset. Without someone to buy what a trader wants to sell, the price will fall until another trader thinks it's a good value. When there are many traders in the stock, the seller will get a much better price. The market will be more efficient with many traders. Traders prefer not to trade when a market is *thin*, when there are few traders.

Efficiency is important in all markets. Since resources are scarce, operating inefficiently reduces the welfare of society. The market that uses resources efficiently is one in which no individual or group can be made better off while at the same time not making another individual or group worse off. Efficiency is also improved when goods are distributed optimally.

Efficiency and Fairness

When the children in the eighteenth-century factories were tied to their machines and their little fingers were able to make as many widgets as possible, that was operating efficiently from the point of view of the industrialist. True, but is this the kind of society we want? Your answer is probably "no." Yet the industrialists lobbied the government to prevent passage of laws against these working conditions.

INTERESTING FACT

In 1833 the English government passed The Mills and Factory Act to improve conditions for children working in factories. The Act can be summed up as follows:

- No child workers under nine years of age.
- Employers must have an age certificate for their child workers.
- Children of 9 to 13 years to work no more than 9 hours a day.
- Children of 13 to 18 years to work no more than 12 hours a day.
- Children are not to work at night.
- Two hours of schooling each day for children.
- Four factory inspectors appointed to enforce the law.

Policy issues like this one are not relegated to the bad old days. The choice between efficiency and fairness is a living reality in today's society. Just read the newspapers every day, and you will see another example.

Gains from Trade

Why do people trade? Why not just bake your own bread, fix your own car, and sew your own clothes? You laugh. Intuitively, we know that it is so much easier to buy what you aren't good at making yourself. Maybe you are a good cook or can sew. If you're not, think of the opportunity cost of making everything from scratch. Imagine the time and income you would lose by not seeing patients for $150 per hour or developing a new app for the smartphone. Gains are made when goods and services are traded.

When individuals in society specialize, they can trade their service or product for something they don't know how to do or make. Before money was used as a means of exchange, people traded their wares in the barter system. Money facilitates trade. These transactions improve society's welfare.

Markets Reach Equilibrium

The description by Adam Smith of how a market works: Producers respond to demand by increasing supply at higher prices until the product is too expensive for the consumer. Then, when there is oversupply, the price goes down until it is acceptable to the buyer. This adjustment of price and quantity demanded is what economists call reaching equilibrium. Markets tend toward equilibrium when there are many buyers and sellers, as Smith surmised. Equilibrium is achieved when no individual or group would be better off doing something different. There will be much more about equilibrium in the pages that follow.

When Markets Become Inefficient

Sometimes markets are inefficient. Adam Smith predicted one condition that would make a market inefficient—monopolies. He was against any entity—private or public—that would interfere with the smooth functioning of the markets. He was not against the government's preventing collusion to eradicate this inefficiency and harm to consumer welfare. In fact, he advocated that governments not give monopoly status to a firm.

Other inefficiencies in the market will be discussed in more detail in subsequent chapters.

The Least You Need to Know

- Adam Smith developed the concept of a self-regulating market, whereby competition results in the production of the quantity of goods needed at the price consumers want to pay.
- Smith was against any interference in the market, whether private (monopolies) or public (government). He was in favor of government regulation of abusive and other egregious behavior by industrialists.
- Individuals and groups must make choices because resources are scarce.
- Opportunity cost is the real cost of an item—what must be given up in order to do something else or get something else.
- Economists use marginal analysis to make accurate decisions.

CHAPTER 3

Comparative Advantage and Gains from Trade

Opportunity cost, efficiency, and gains from trade are fundamental concepts that were introduced in Chapter 2. They encompass much of the foundation of economic analysis in both microeconomics and macroeconomics.

This chapter will continue and expand the discussion of opportunity cost, efficiency, and gains from trade. Economists use graphic models to facilitate visualizing the trade-offs that take place during transactions by individuals and firms. These models also portray market efficiency and inefficiency as the trade-offs are made.

In This Chapter

- Introducing modeling in economics
- Using the concept of opportunity cost to make production decisions
- How the production possibility frontier illustrates the trade-offs needed for productive efficiency
- Comparative advantage and gains from trade
- How comparative advantage works in international trade

A Word About Economic Models

It is said that a picture is worth a thousand words. Economists use graphic representations of complex ideas to make them easier to understand. These models are not constructed solely to help students unfamiliar with economics; they are also shown at economics meetings when economists have an idea they are presenting.

Models are ideal forms of economists' visions of how the market or the economy functions. As you come across these concepts, you might think they don't make sense—not because you don't understand what has been said, but the idea doesn't seem to fit with your experience. It's important to realize that the models are very simplified and can never be completely realistic. Models are often modified when their predictions don't come to fruition. Such working models of modern economists are simply ideas put into graphic form that can work or not. The models we will be presenting in this book are used by the mainstream economists to understand, analyze, and recommend economic policy.

The first model we'll discuss is the production possibility frontier.

The Production Possibility Frontier

The *production possibility frontier* is a graph that is usually a curve but can be a straight line. It is used to illustrate a simple economy that produces only two goods. The concept of the model is that with two goods and limited resources, an economy cannot be efficient unless it produces each good at its maximum quantity, considering the needs and wants of the economy and its resources. In order to accomplish this, it's necessary to trade quantities of one good for the other. The combinations of goods are plotted on a graph with the preferred good on the *y* axis, and the secondary good on the *x* axis. As there is a trade-off of one good for the other, the plotted points create a curve or straight line on the graph. This curve is called the frontier.

 **DEFINITION**

A **production possibility frontier** is a graph, usually a curve, but it also can be a straight line, portraying the trade-offs facing an economy that produces only two goods. It shows the maximum quantity of one good that can be produced for any given quantity produced of the other.

For example, an economy that produces wheat and corn, but prefers to produce wheat, would begin with more quantities of wheat and less of corn. As more wheat is produced, the opportunity cost of producing wheat increases, and it becomes more profitable to produce more units of corn. In doing so, it must forego producing some units of wheat. The amount of wheat it chooses to stop producing depends on the needs and wants of the economy, or the producers. At all times, the most efficient production takes place on the curve of the production possibility frontier. It's not possible to produce in the greater quantities that lie beyond the production possibility frontier unless there is general growth in the economy. At the same time, production can take place below the production possibility frontier, but it is not efficient.

The explanation economists give for the increase in the opportunity cost for the first product—wheat, in our example—is that producers use the best land, or other resource depending on the industry, for the preferred product. When the best land has been depleted, it becomes more profitable to produce the alternate product.

The production possibility frontier (PPF) is used to explain a few related ideas. It is a simple way to show how the concept of *opportunity cost* is used by economists. As you might recall, opportunity cost is the real cost of an item—what you must give up in order to do something else or get something else.

The PPF can also illustrate *scarcity* because, as resources are scarce, products can't be produced beyond the production possibility frontier.

The PPF illustrates *efficiency* as well, which is when all opportunities are taken and resources are used with little or no waste. Efficiency can either be productive efficiency or allocative efficiency.

DEFINITION

Efficiency is defined in three ways: (1) When all opportunities are taken and resources are used with little or no waste. (2) When there is no way to make some people better off without making someone else worse off. (3) When there is no way to produce more of one good without producing less of another good.

Productive efficiency is shown on the PPF by the various combinations of two commodities in quantities that are restricted by the amount of fixed resources—land, labor, capital, and technology. Productive efficiency is achieved when the least amount of resources are used to produce a good.

Allocative efficiency occurs when the best use is made of resources. Producers will only produce goods that society wants and therefore are in high demand. Allocative efficiency is analyzed by economists and policymakers who are concerned with costs versus benefits for society as a whole. For example, economists measure the loss of benefits to society from price ceilings and price floors or the loss of welfare caused by pollution from a production process.

DEFINITION

Productive efficiency is when the least amount of resources are used to produce a good. **Allocative efficiency** is when capital is allocated so that all participants in a society benefit.

Now let's see what a production possibility frontier looks like and how it works.

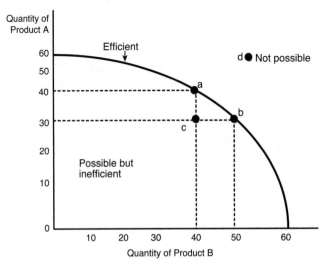

Production Possibility Frontier

The production possibility frontier (PPF) shows the maximum quantities that can be produced of each of two products, Product A and Product B, given the quantity produced of the other. The producer or the economy must trade quantities of one product for quantities of the other, given the total amount of resources available. All possible combinations of quantities of Product A and B that are efficiently produced are located on the production possibility frontier (PPF). At Point A, 40 units of Product A and 30 units of Product B can be produced. At Point B the quantity of Product A is reduced to 30 units, and the quantity produced of Product B is raised to 40 units. It's possible to produce at Point C, but it is not efficient. It's not possible to produce outside the PPF at Point D.

The figure, "Production Possibility Frontier," is an example of how trade-offs are made using the PPF model. The PPF shows the maximum quantities that can be produced of each of two products, Product A and Product B, with limited resources, given the quantity produced of the other.

The producer or the economy must trade quantities of one product for quantities of the other, given the total amount of resources available. All possible combinations of quantities of Product A and B that are efficiently produced are located on the production possibility frontier (PPF). At point **a** 40 units of Product A and 30 units of Product B can be produced. At point **b** the quantity of Product A is reduced to 30 units, and the quantity produced of Product **b** is raised to 40 units. It's possible to produce at point **c**, but it is not efficient. It's not possible to produce outside the PPF at point **d**.

Production is efficient at the point on the PPF where the maximum number of units of each product in combination is produced. If the point is below the PPF, production is possible, but inefficient. Production cannot occur outside the curve.

In the example above, the opportunity cost of producing 10 additional units of Product B means that 10 units of Product A must be given up. However, opportunity cost is related to the shape of the curve on the production possibility frontier. If the shape of the curve is a straight line, the opportunity cost of the goods is constant as production of different goods changes. The same amount of one product must be given up to produce each additional unit of the other product.

The figure, "Production Possibility Frontier: Opportunity Cost," gives another example of how trade-offs are made on the PPF. In order to produce 20 units of Product B, 4 units of Product A must not be produced at point **a**. Ten units of Product A must be given up in order to produce 40 units of Product B at point **b**.

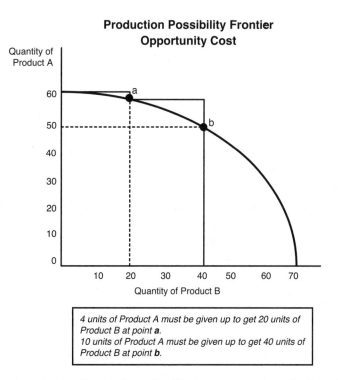

In order to produce 20 units of Product B, 4 units of Product A must not be produced at point **a**. Ten units of Product A must be given up in order to produce 40 units of Product B at point **b**.

Economic growth can also be illustrated on the PPF. Economic growth is shown by an outward shift of the PPF. The PPF indicates that quantities produced can increase all along the new PPF curve from producing 40 units of Product A and 30 units of Product B at point **a**, totaling 70 units, to producing 40 units of Product A and 45 units of Product B at point **e**, totaling 85 units. At point **f** 25 units of Product A and 60 units of Product B are produced, totaling 85 units.

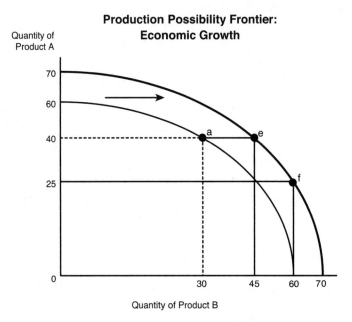

*Economic growth can be illustrated on a production possibility frontier by an outward shift of the frontier curve. All production combinations can be increased, as from point **a** to point **e**, and point **f**.*

Opportunity cost lays the basis for economic analysis of gains from trade. The idea is applied to trade in maintaining that the cost of a commodity is the amount of a second commodity that must be given up to release just enough resources to produce one additional unit of the first commodity.

When using the production possibility frontier to analyze trade, the shape of the PPF is a straight line for each nation. This indicates that opportunity costs are constant. They are in a one-to-one relationship. Each country has a unique production possibility frontier based on its opportunity cost. This means that countries don't produce at the same level of efficiency for individual products. The difference in efficiency of products as well as their opportunity cost provides the basis for trade.

Comparative Advantage

When there is no trade, a country can only consume what it produces. The production possibility frontier for a nation is therefore its consumption frontier. The PPF reflects the types of products that its consumers need and want.

More can be gained if countries trade. If each country produces more of the product that has a lower opportunity cost than its trading partner, it has a *comparative advantage* in that product. Opportunity costs for different products vary. Every country can identify a product it makes that has a comparatively low opportunity cost and that it can produce more efficiently than its trading partner. If this is true, then each country should produce more of the product having the least opportunity cost—which is the product in which it has a comparative advantage—and trade some of it with a country that has a different product reflecting *its* comparative advantage.

Comparative advantage is not the same as *absolute advantage*. An absolute advantage occurs when a country is the best at doing something, which is different from comparative advantage, where the opportunity costs and production efficiencies are compared. Adam Smith originally used the idea of absolute advantage to describe how international trade functions. David Ricardo later theorized that comparative advantage best explained how gains from trade could be made.

> **DEFINITION**
>
> **Comparative advantage** refers to producing a good with a lower opportunity cost than the opportunity cost of its trading partner for that good. **Absolute advantage** is when an individual or country is better at producing something than its trading partner.

Specialization

How does comparative advantage apply to the real world? If, for example, the United Kingdom has a comparative advantage in producing cotton, and it is trading with Portugal, which has a comparative advantage in producing wine, it makes sense for the U.K. to produce more cotton than it requires to satisfy the needs of its consumers, and to trade the remaining cotton production with Portugal for wine.

Portugal may also produce cotton, but its opportunity cost is higher for cotton than for wine. It is also higher than the U.K.'s opportunity cost for cotton. While the U.K. may also produce wine, its wine production carries a high opportunity cost, and its production is relatively inefficient. It makes more sense for each country to trade the products that have the least opportunity cost and are produced with the greatest efficiency. These are the products of its comparative advantage.

The exchanges between countries of the products of their respective comparative advantage are the *gains from trade* for both countries.

> **DEFINITION**
>
> **Gains from trade** refers to the increase in consumption in each nation resulting from specialization in production and trading.

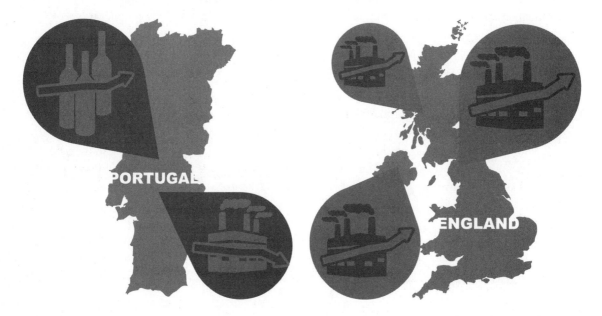

David Ricardo on Comparative Advantage and Gains from Trade

David Ricardo, one of the great British economists of the Classical school (1772–1823) developed the idea of comparative advantage in international trade. He concluded that countries should specialize in producing the good of their comparative advantage to an extreme level, even if it meant dismantling profitable national industries.

Ricardo used units of labor to compare which country had the comparative advantage in a product. Economists including Adam Smith, David Ricardo, and Karl Marx used some form of a labor theory of value.

Ricardo believed that there is mutual benefit from international trade even if one party has an absolute advantage over its trading counterpart, as proposed by Adam Smith. His idea was that nations would do better by trading to obtain those products in which it does *not* have a comparative advantage. He showed mathematically that this method would always yield positive results. Ricardo vehemently argued for free trade along with specialization.

Many economists took issue with his ideas, but with the exception of using labor as the basis for measuring costs, the theory is still in use. Austrian economist Gottfried Haberler developed the concept of using opportunity costs in place of labor.

Possible Negative Effects of Comparative Advantage

Here is some food for thought. An economic theory, even one that is in vogue during a good part of your lifetime, often has detractors. A few highly regarded economists disagreed with Ricardo's claim that comparative advantage is universally beneficial.

Joan Robinson, a student of John Maynard Keynes, took issue with Ricardo's idea that international trade is always beneficial. In 1978 she wrote that imposing free trade on Portugal ended the development of its nascent textile industry, while only a slow-growing wine industry remained. At the same time, exports of cotton cloth in England led to the mechanization of the cotton industry and ultimately booming growth during the industrial revolution.

Other economists also disagreed with Ricardo for a number of reasons. Concern still exists, especially in regard to the impact of international trade on developing nations. Some believe there is manipulation of currencies and taxes by powerful nations that prevents a level playing field.

On this and other issues you will come across in economics and policy based on economics, the best advice is to learn and understand the issues and make your own decisions.

The Least You Need to Know

- Models are used in economics to illustrate concepts.
- The production possibility frontier is a model that shows how economies face scarcity of resources and therefore must make choices between two goods to decide the most efficient use of its resources during the production of goods.
- Comparative advantage is a model that predicts there are gains in trade when a country specializes in the product in which it has a comparative advantage. The country has a comparative advantage when its opportunity cost of producing a product is lower than the opportunity cost of its trading partner for the same product.
- Absolute advantage is when a country or individual is the best at doing something.
- Not all economists agree with a model's theory. It is important to keep an open mind, as policy issues that affect everyone are designed using the prevailing economic models.

CHAPTER 4

How Economists Gauge the Economy

A major theme in economics is choice—consumer choice, which combination of products to produce, does a worker choose more work time or more leisure time, does a farmer plant wheat or corn, and so on.

Another important occupation of economists is measuring. They measure the size of the government, whether the economy is growing, what quantity of a good to produce will maximize profits, how much more a consumer wants of a product before he or she begins to tire of it, at what quantity of production labor becomes less productive, and much more.

This chapter gives an overview of the main sectors of an economy with an emphasis on measuring. All of these topics will be covered in more detail in the chapters that correspond with the topics covered here. This chapter is meant to give a broad picture of the economy and some of the issues that economists handle.

In This Chapter

* Measuring the health of the economy by the size and changes of the gross domestic product and its components
* The unemployment rate, consumer sentiment, consumer price index, and other indicators of economic health
* Quantifying the goals of business and the consumer
* Labor policy issues

Gross Domestic Product

The *gross domestic product (GDP)* is a measure of the total value of all the final goods and services that are produced in an economy during a given year or other time period. The GDP measures:

- Consumer expenditures
- Investment expenditures
- Government expenditures
- Net eXports (exports – imports)

The shorthand used to express the components of the gross domestic product is
GDP = C + I + G + NX.

It is called the *national income accounting identity.*

DEFINITION

Consumer expenditure is also called personal consumption expenditure. This includes spending on durable goods, such as cars and household appliances; nondurable goods, such as clothing, gasoline, and food; and services, such as transportation, financial services and insurance, and utilities.

Investment expenditure includes all the spending by businesses to produce goods and services. Examples are nonresidential structures and intellectual property products, as well as residential fixed investments.

Government expenditure includes federal government defense and non-defense consumption expenditures, gross investments, and state and local government expenditures.

Net exports includes all exports of domestic goods and services minus all imports of foreign goods and services.

As an example, in 2012, the percentage of each component of the U.S. GDP was: government (19.5 percent), investment (15.2 percent), consumer expenditures (68.6 percent), net exports (-3.4 percent). (*Source: Bureau of Economic Analysis.*)

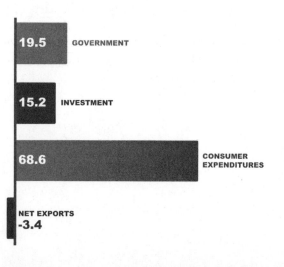

The GDP is the primary measure that economists use to take the temperature of the economy. Statistics on the trend of GDP growth are compared to see whether the economy is on the rise. Economists also want to know the rate of GDP growth. This information is used to determine if the economy is getting out of control to the upside or to the downside.

If growth is too fast, economists and policymakers might want to cool it off, because when the economy grows at an abnormal pace, inflation might develop. Inflation in a fast-growing economy could cause problems. (Inflation is discussed in greater detail in Chapter 17.) If growth is too slow, policymakers and economists will consider providing fiscal or monetary stimulus. Fiscal stimulus might include spending on infrastructure or lowering taxes. Monetary stimulus typically begins with the central banks lowering the interest rates. Other measures can be taken by central banks if necessary.

Evaluating the GDP numbers also lets economists know which sectors of the economy are doing well and which are doing poorly. This is another test to diagnose the health and allocative efficiency of the economy. For example, how is growth in consumer spending? Consumer spending makes up well over 50 percent of most economies. How are inventory levels? A pileup of inventory could be a sign that spending has slowed down to a crawl, or if it's a few months before the December holidays, it could just mean that businesses are preparing for the big rush on "black" Friday to buy presents for the holidays.

The GDP can be used to compare the economic size of countries. There are three ways to calculate the GDP:

1. The *official exchange rate (OER)*. The OER gives the GDP in terms of the domestic currency according to the national authorities or to the legally sanctioned exchange market, according to the World Bank.

2. *Purchasing power parity (PPP):* Purchasing power parity attempts to remove the effect of exchange rate fluctuations when comparing the cost of a basket of goods between countries by using a formula in the calculations. This makes for a more accurate assessment of the relative GDP of the countries being compared.

3. *Per capita GDP:* More information can be obtained by comparing the GDP of countries when the size of its population is taken into account. The GDP is divided by the population in each country. For example, when China's GDP is measured using the per capita GDP, the large size of its population will reduce its ranking in a list of countries' GDP.

The U.S. Central Intelligence Agency provides a listing of the GDP of countries using each of the above methods. It's interesting to see how each method changes the ranking of the countries. You can find these lists at the following web addresses:

- GDP using the official exchange rate: https://www.cia.gov/library/publications/the-world-factbook/fields/2195.html

- GDP using purchasing power parity: https://www.cia.gov/library/publications/the-world-factbook/rankorder/2001rank.html

- GDP using per capita GDP: https://www.cia.gov/library/publications/the-world-factbook/rankorder/2004rank.html

Other Measurements of the Economy

The unemployment rate is also a measure of the well-being of the economy. When the unemployment rate is going up, it usually means that workers are being laid off from their jobs. Alternatively, if the economy is already in a recession, an increase in the unemployment rate can mean that workers who had given up looking for a job and weren't counted as unemployed are once again sending out applications and filing for unemployment insurance until they get hired.

The unemployment rate includes the number of individuals who are willing to work but cannot get a job. These workers file for unemployment insurance. Another measure economists follow is the number of underemployed. These are workers who are working temporary jobs but would prefer a full-time job; *marginally attached workers*—those who are not looking for a job but have indicated they would be willing to work if a job were available; and *discouraged workers,* who have given up looking for a job.

DEFINITION

Marginally attached workers are not working nor looking for work but want a job and have looked in the past 12 months. **Discouraged workers** are a subset of marginally attached workers who are not looking for a job because of the unfriendly job market.

Consumer sentiment is a measure taken to get a general feel for the mood of the population. Consumer sentiment measures the confidence of consumers about the health of the economy. This index is important because if consumers are feeling comfortable with their income, they will spend. Spending boosts the overall economy. The Consumer Sentiment Index is included in the list of diagnostic measurements economists use to put together a picture of the health of the economy.

A list of other indicators includes …

- The Consumer Price Index and Producer Price Index, which measure inflation.

- Existing home sales and housing starts.

- Factory orders, industrial production, nonmanufacturing report, Purchasing Managers Index, durable goods report.

- Retail sales report, wholesale trade report.

- Trade balance report.

- The Federal Reserve (U.S.) Beige Book (anecdotal and discussion-based summaries of regional economic activity); the money supply.

These reports tell economists, policymakers, and the financial markets what they need to know to evaluate the condition of the economy. Once they have this information, they can proceed with policymaking and mapping out a trading strategy in the financial markets.

Government

The role of the government was presented in Chapter 1. Our focus here will be on taking the measure of government and the economy. Governments have a lot of expenses, including the direct expenses of purchases for the workings of administration and the agencies plus investment in long-term capital expenses, such as bridges, roads, and waterways. Transfer payments—welfare, Social Security, Medicare, Medicaid, and unemployment insurance—are not counted in the GDP. Despite the unofficial nature of transfer payments, the government has to come up with the money to pay for them. The accounting method—what counts as a government expenditure—was described in Chapter 1.

The government budget and the national debt are contentious topics among policymakers. Does government spending help or hurt the economy? Should there be a balanced budget? When does the debt burden and growth of the debt burden signal harm to the economy? What effect does tightening government's belt have on the economy? Economists disagree on these issues, but most believe that the best way to reduce long-term debt is by encouraging growth in the economy. The question, "Under what economic conditions is it appropriate to shrink the budget in the short run versus the long run?" is a policy and economic debate that falls along Keynesian/Classical economics lines. More on these topics will be detailed in Part 4 on macroeconomics.

Business

In a market economy, striving for profitable businesses while keeping the welfare of the greater community in mind is what supports economic growth. To that end, business owners have to be aware of how to produce efficiently in order to maximize their profits. They have to make the right choice about what products to produce if they are in the consumer discretionary market. For all sectors, businesses must produce just the right amount for just the right price, as Adam Smith would tell us.

Chapter 10 is all about the firm and describes in detail how economists believe businesses can go about maximizing their profits. The supply and demand model is fundamental to grasping how the mechanisms of the individual firm work. The supply and demand model is like the vocabulary for understanding how most economists look at the world.

Households

Businesses provide employment, and employees earn the income that, when cast as consumers, they spend. Businesses also pay rent, interest, and profits through stock sales to households. Households provide employees to businesses. Households also provide businesses with resources, such as land, labor, capital, and entrepreneurs, at least according to mainstream economists.

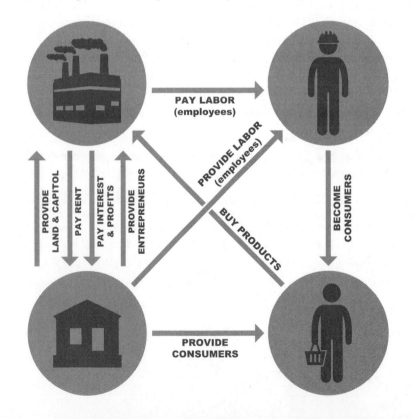

This circular flow of businesses, households, consumers, and resources is one way economists look at and measure the gross domestic product. They see the flow of money throughout the economy by way of these sectors.

Consumers

Economists want to know what makes consumers happy. They measure happiness or satisfaction, as was described in Chapter 1, in terms of utility. Trade-offs are made by consumers when they choose combinations of products and services that maximize their happiness given their budget constraints. This is accomplished in much the same way as the production choices illustrated by the production possibility frontier.

By quantifying the choices available to consumers under these conditions, it's possible to know which combination of goods or services will maximize the consumer's utility, or happiness. That is the essence of consumer theory.

Labor

Labor is the dominant factor in production. Despite automation, labor is still a major component of our economy. As such, the level of wages and unemployment has a great effect on the economy.

Economists monitor the unemployment rate because too much unemployment means lower spending, which affects the economy's growth. They are also concerned because there is an inverse correlation between unemployment and inflation under most economic circumstances. This relationship failed during the 1970s, when the supply of oil was sharply reduced because of political turmoil in the Middle East. Generally, when wages are rising, so is inflation, since higher wages filter into the prices of products.

The measure of labor productivity is an important metric for businesses and economists. Businesses want to get the most output for the labor they employ in order to maximize their profits.

Economists and politicians debate about policy as it affects workers. Some of the important policy issues regarding the labor force are …

- Should there be a minimum wage law, and how much it should be? Some economists believe the supply and demand model predicts that a minimum wage reduces hiring.

- How long unemployment insurance should last. Policymakers disagree about whether or not unemployment insurance takes away the incentive to find a job.

- What is causing unemployment? If it is caused by a slump in the economy (cyclical unemployment), some economists believe fiscal and monetary policy can reduce unemployment. If it is caused by a mismatch of jobs (structural unemployment), then other measures must be taken.

- Whether and how income might be more fairly distributed by a choice of tax structure or other means.

In sum, economists measure every part of the economy to make sure it is functioning as smoothly as possible.

The Least You Need to Know

- The entire economy is measured by evaluating the gross domestic product (GDP), which is the sum of all final goods and services produced in an economy per year.
- There are many ways to measure how the economy is functioning. Economists use a variety of indicators to know the health of the economy.
- Businesses want to maximize their profits. Consumers aim to maximize their happiness by choosing the best combination of products that is also affordable.
- Labor is the dominant factor in production. The level of wages and salaries affects productivity. The unemployment level is one of the factors in measuring the health of the economy.

CHAPTER 5

Public Policy and Microeconomics

Adam Smith showed us how firms, markets, and industries are efficient and can regulate themselves. He reasoned that competition gives market participants the incentive to produce the optimal quantity at a price that consumers are willing to pay. The producer benefits by realizing a profit, and the consumer benefits by getting a good price for a product he or she wants to buy.

There are instances when the markets do not operate efficiently, or it is not profitable for the markets to provide necessary and important goods and services to the public. When the private marketplace cannot provide goods and services efficiently, economists consider this to be a market failure.

There are a number of reasons why markets fail. This chapter briefly describes some of these, which are explained in greater depth throughout Part 2 on microeconomics. Here we explain a few specific instances of market inefficiencies— externalities and public goods. When markets fail to efficiently provide the goods and services needed by the public, the government must step in.

In This Chapter

- When markets are inefficient
- Externalities: negative and positive
- The Tragedy of the Commons
- When the government must provide public goods

Market Inefficiencies

If a firm controls the entire supply of a good or service, it can choose how much to produce rather than let the efficient market determine the quantity of output. The firm can then select a selling price that will maximize its profit. This type of firm is called a *monopoly*. Monopolies will be discussed in detail in Chapter 12.

Another cause of inefficiency in the marketplace is when there is incomplete information for the consumers and producers about market prices and product quality. This lack of information can result in the production of too little or too much of a good or service.

When external events—byproducts of production like pollution—result in unexpected costs or benefits, it is a case of market inefficiency. Since the costs or benefits are not initially included in the market price and quantity, the firm will not produce the optimal quantity of the good. Externalities will be covered in detail in this chapter.

Finally, markets are not always positioned to efficiently provide the goods and services necessary for the welfare of the general public. National defense is a requirement, but the cost of maintaining the armed forces and other parts of national defense is too high for private markets. National defense is considered a public good that must be provided by the government and paid for by taxes.

Sometimes it is not clear whether the market or the government would most efficiently provide a good or service. The factors that economists consider to make this determination are outlined here.

Market Failure and Social Welfare

Society benefits from a well-functioning economy that includes efficient markets, preservation of the environment and wildlife, and an educated and healthy population.

The market mechanism, by its nature, can't accommodate society's welfare in many cases. In fact, there are instances where society pays a cost for harmful side effects of industrial production, the most obvious being pollution. Not so obvious are the beneficial side effects from some types of industries, such as the beekeeping industry. Beekeepers can't control their bees. Bees fly into the fields of neighboring farms and pollinate the plants in the area. These side effects, both negative and positive, are called *externalities*.

DEFINITION

Externalities are costs or benefits to society of byproducts of consumption or production that are not factored into the original market price.

Public goods are not good candidates for markets. The social benefit of public property, such as lakes and parkland, is undeniable. Roads, bridges, sewers—the infrastructure—are necessary for everyone in the community. Police and fire departments, like national defense, are included here as well. Scientific research, with no immediate marketable products, provides clues to future breakthroughs in pharmaceuticals and technology. The public needs and wants these services, but the costs and other factors make these public goods unsuitable for generating profits.

Economists, policymakers, and the public decide which policies give the greatest benefits to society.

Externalities

An externality can be either negative or positive. *External* simply means that the cost or benefit of the consequence of consumption or production was not included in the original market price. The cost or benefit affects a third party, who had no say either on the supply side (the producer) or the demand side (the consumer) of a market. A negative externality is a cost that was not factored into the market price, and a positive externality is a benefit that was not factored into the market price.

Negative Externalities

Sometimes production or consumption causes negative side effects, such as industries emitting pollution, damages from oil spills, manufacture or use of nondegradable plastic bags, or livestock that produces large quantities of methane gas, cigarette smoking that negatively affects people in the vicinity, and other examples. When the byproduct of production or consumption has a negative effect on society, it is called a *negative externality.*

Most would agree that pollution causes harm to the environment, people, and animals. Some industries can't function, though, without creating some pollution. For example, power plants are needed to produce electricity, but they are polluters.

When we go grocery shopping, the store usually puts our groceries in plastic bags to make it easier to carry. Some people bring their own bag to the store, but there are still plenty who use plastic bags. These nonbiodegradable bags end up in rivers and parks and harm wildlife. It's unlikely, though, that we will stop using plastic bags.

Pollution and other negative externalities can't be completely eliminated if the industries we need are to survive. If that's the case, we have to be able to identify the amount of pollution that would satisfy the public's need for a clean environment as well as an industry's desire for profits.

Calculating the Costs of Negative Externalities

Economists have concluded that if they can determine the cost of the pollution, they can figure out a model for resolving this dilemma. They developed a measurement called the *marginal social cost of pollution (MSC)*. *Marginal* is the measurement of an additional unit of something. The marginal social cost of pollution is the additional cost imposed on society as a whole by one more unit of pollution. Each additional unit of pollution causes some harm to society.

The next variable to be measured is the benefit to society of the polluter's not spending money to revamp their plant. (Technology exists that could mitigate the pollution emitted, although it is costly.) Put that on the other side of the equation. This is called the *marginal social benefit of pollution (MSB)*. The idea is that another unit of pollution being emitted would make it unnecessary to spend the money to revamp the plant, making emission of pollution a social benefit.

Now we can compare the marginal social cost (MSC) with the marginal social benefit (MSB) of pollution. We can use an equation, or the numbers can be plotted on a graph. The result will give us the *socially optimal quantity of pollution*.

> **DEFINITION**
>
> The **marginal social cost of pollution (MSC)** is the additional cost imposed on society as a whole by one more unit of pollution. The **marginal social benefit of pollution (MSB)** is the benefit to society of the polluter's not spending money to revamp their plant. The **socially optimal quantity of pollution** is the quantity of pollution that is at the equilibrium of the MSC and MSB curves on a graph.

When a graph is drawn representing the MSC of pollution and the MSB of pollution, there is a point where the curves cross. This point is the socially optimal point and answers the questions "What is the socially optimal *quantity* of pollution?" and "What is the *cost* or *price* at that point?" In our example the optimal quantity is labeled Q^*, and the cost at that point is $100.

Now we know the precise cost to society of the socially optimal quantity of pollution. Unfortunately, the polluters have no incentive to compensate those affected by the pollution. They will continue producing even as the marginal social benefit (MSB) of pollution goes to zero and the marginal social cost of pollution (MSC) goes to $400. As a result, firms overproduce, which is inefficient. When a market is inefficient, economists say it is a *market failure*.

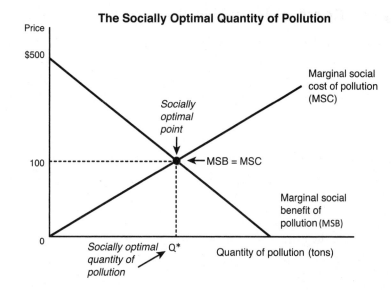

The marginal social cost of pollution (MSC) is represented by the upward-sloping curve, or line, on the graph. It crosses the marginal social benefit of pollution (MSB) curve at the cost of $100 and the socially optimal quantity of pollution quantity, Q*. This is where MSC = MSB.

Solutions for Negative Externalities

This is where the government can step in with a policy response. Economists have enough information to work with the numbers. When the quantity of pollution is reduced to Q* at a cost of $100, MSC = MSB. So $100 is the cost that must be offset.

What are the choices policymakers have to reduce pollution? One policy that has been tried is to set *environmental standards*. The outcome of the standards was effective; pollution was reduced. Economists believed they could design a more efficient way to reduce pollution using the type of analysis we calculated.

In our example, the quantity of pollution that must be reduced is known, as is the cost. One policy choice that can offset the cost imposed by the polluter onto society is to levy a tax of $100 per ton of emissions.

A tax that is equal to the marginal social cost of pollution at the socially optimal quantity of pollution is called a *Pigouvian tax*, named after Arthur Pigou, a British economist who, in 1920, wrote the book *The Economics of Welfare*, which addressed the problem of negative externalities.

Another solution is for the government to issue licenses that can be bought and sold by polluters, called *tradable emissions permits*. This is a more tailored approach, since some plants have more advanced equipment than others.

Private Deals Avoid Government Solutions

When damage caused by a negative externality is local, it is possible to avoid government policy by private negotiation between the affected party and the firm causing the damage. Ronald Coase, a Nobel laureate economist, developed a theorem that shows how private negotiations can work in these situations.

A private deal would negate the inefficiency of the market because the cost not originally included could be paid to the injured party, depending on who owns the rights to whatever is in question. Either way, the outcome will be efficient, but the exchange of money could go the other way. Coase's theorem terms taking external costs or benefits into account *internalizing the externality.*

When making a deal, the legal costs should also be considered, since they can be quite high. These legal costs, or other costs that might be incurred when a deal is made, are called *transaction costs.*

Pollution is a classic case of a negative externality. The actual cost of pollution has been established, and taxes or tradable emissions permits that can be bought and sold are now in use.

Steps to Compensate Society for Negative Externalities

A new technology for an old industry is now a big topic of debate and analysis—hydraulic fracturing for natural gas production. Economists are evaluating how to quantify the negative externalities of "fracking," as it's commonly called. There are certainly negative externalities, both global (greenhouse gas emissions that cause global climate change) and local. The local negative externalities include …

- Groundwater contamination in the immediate vicinity of wells.

- Contamination of aquifers on a wider, regional scale.

- Excessive use of fresh water.

- Health effects of undisclosed components of fracturing fluids.

- Spills and treatment of waste fluids.

- Blowouts, house explosions, and flaming kitchen faucets.

(Source and for more information: oilprice.com/Energy/Natural-Gas/An-Economic-Analysis-of-Fracking.html)

Following the steps economists take in preparation for a policy recommendation on hydraulic fracturing deepens our understanding of how policy is made.

Some of the factors that should be considered are …

1. What are the negative externalities of fracking?

2. What are their costs to society, both global and local?

3. How much specific information is needed before a policy can be designed and implemented?

4. What are the policy options? Who should be responsible and who should be compensated?

Some economic activities cause inadvertent social benefits. The market inefficiency of not factoring the social benefit into the market price can result in underproduction of a good or service. Let's see why this happens.

Positive Externalities

When the byproduct of an activity inadvertently benefits society, it is a *positive externality*. The benefit to the producer is less than the benefit to society.

Some examples of positive externalities are technology spillovers—the information about new techniques that is disseminated by employees of technology firms when they socialize. A beekeeper isn't compensated by the market price for the inadvertent benefit to farmers whose crops are pollinated by the bees.

Positive benefits for society can occur when a company moves into a run-down neighborhood. Maybe the firm gets a good price for buying the property and decides to plant several acres of trees and a large flower garden, beautifying the area. The result is that local housing prices rise, and homeowners are motivated to fix up their homes. This leads to an increase in home values in the neighborhood.

When the producer does not include the external benefit into the output quantity, she is undercompensated and produces a lower-than-optimal output quantity. The inefficiency caused by a positive externality is the underproduction of a good. This is a market failure.

The marginal social benefit (MSB) of a good or activity is equal to the marginal benefit (MB) that accrues to consumers plus its marginal external benefit (XB): $MSB = MB + XB$.

The following figure, Positive Externality, shows the market quantity (Q_{MKT}) and price (P_{MKT}) without the marginal external benefit and the new quantity (Q^*) and price (P^*) that includes the marginal social benefit. Notice that the optimal output quantity is higher than the market output quantity where the external benefit is not included.

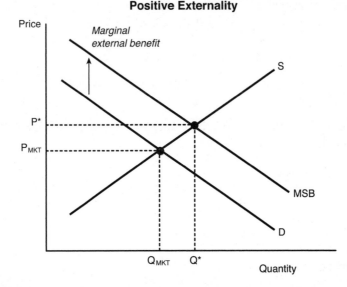

The market equilibrium, where the demand curve (D) and the supply curve (S) intersect and the market quantity produced is Q_{MKT} and price (P_{MKT}), does not include the social benefit of the good being produced. A marginal social benefit (MSB) curve is drawn, representing where the quantity produced would have been if the social benefit had been included. The optimal quantity of production is labeled Q* and price (P*).

The producer has no incentive to increase output. To increase production to the optimal quantity, the government could provide an incentive to the producer in the form of a subsidy equal to the benefit to society she did not previously receive. When a product is important to society, the government often subsidizes an industry.

Common Property Resources

Igor owns a small ranch in the Ukraine where he raises sheep. He takes excellent care of the sheep because he has a good business selling their wool. Igor plants the best grass seeds regularly so the sheep have fresh food.

Two kilometers down the road is a public area where everyone can bring their sheep to graze. The grass in the public area doesn't last very long because there's no incentive for people to plant seeds or protect the grazing area. Unless there is some form of regulation, using the common property is on a first come, first served basis. If Natasha doesn't get to the public area first, there will be no grass for her sheep. This depletion of common resources due to lack of care by those who use them has been called "The Tragedy of the Commons."

A common solution to preventing the destruction or depletion of common property resources, used also for fishing, hunting, swimming, and camping, is for the government to issue permits.

A private solution would be for the government to sell the public land to private companies. There would be little to no profit for a private firm unless the firm charged the public. This eliminates the public's ability to have free access to the land.

Public Goods

Sometimes whether a good or service should be provided by the government or the markets is a matter of opinion and philosophy. When economists refine the distinctions between public and private goods, they give a more objective view based on costs, benefits, and efficiency. Differences in philosophy and willingness to pay for the good or service make the choice debatable, and the public may ultimately decide in the voting booth.

Defining a Public Good

If a lighthouse is built by the local government, all ships may use the light to pass safely through the waters. No ships would be required to pay for the light, and no ship's use of the light could deny other ships its benefits. A lighthouse is considered a public good. This same concept can be extended to street lamps. Other examples are knowledge, flood control systems, a public sewer system, and fresh air. Markets are unable to efficiently provide this category of goods and services because there is no profit to be had.

Public goods have two characteristics: (1) the marginal cost of providing the good to an additional consumer is zero, called a *nonrival* good (example: the internet, national parks, roads); and (2) people cannot be excluded from consuming the good, called a *nonexclusive* good. It is difficult or impossible to charge for a good when no one can be excluded from consuming it (example: national defense).

What is the difference between a *rival* good and a *nonrival* good?

The market provides rival goods. These goods are consumed privately, and others cannot also consume them without the owner's permission. A donut would fall into this category, as would a private car. From an economist's point of view, they're called rival goods when the marginal cost increases as additional units of the good are produced. Marginal cost does not increase for nonrival goods, such as highways, because no matter how many cars drive on the highways, there is no additional cost. (Information from *Microeconomics,* 6th ed, Robert S. Pindyck/Daniel L. Rubinfeld.) When watching public television, no matter how many friends you invite to watch a football game on a public station, there is no additional cost.

What is the difference between an *exclusive* good and a *nonexclusive* good?

A refrigerator is an *exclusive* good. Once the refrigerator is sold to a consumer, he can't sell it to another consumer. If people can't be excluded from consuming the good, it is *nonexclusive*. A lighthouse is a nonexclusive good because once it's paid for, any boat sailing by can use it. National defense is used or benefitted by everyone; nobody is excluded. Street lights are nonexclusive because once they're paid for, anyone can use them.

Combinations of these characteristics further refine our understanding of the nuances in the differences between public goods and private goods.

A good can be nonexclusive and rival. The ocean is available to all, but there is an additional cost (this can be an opportunity cost) for a fisherman because when more fish are caught, there are less fish available to other fishermen. Fish are a limited resource.

A good can be exclusive and nonrival. An example is a television signal. It is nonrival because after the signal is generated, there is no additional marginal cost for another consumer. At the same time, it can be made exclusive by scrambling the signal so only people who pay for the content can get it.

A public good is nonrival and nonexclusive. Public goods provide benefits to the public at zero marginal cost, and nobody can be excluded from using them.

While national defense is a public good, not all government services are considered public goods. For example, education is mixed, since costs increase when additional students are added to a classroom. Education can therefore be rival (the marginal cost increases as additional consumers are added). Since public parks can sometimes have entrance fees, not everyone who would like to use a public park can afford it. Public parks that charge a fee are therefore exclusive.

TAKE-AWAY MESSAGE

A public good is nonrival and nonexclusive. Public goods provide benefits to the public at zero marginal cost, and nobody can be excluded from using them.

The Efficiency of Public Goods

Market efficiency, providing a private good, is achieved when the marginal cost (MC) equals the marginal benefit (MB). The efficiency of providing a public good is calculated by totaling the values each individual assigns to an additional unit of the good. This sum of benefits is the *marginal benefit to society (MSB)*. The MSB must equal the MC of production in order to be considered efficient.

- Efficient private good: **MC = MC**

- Efficient public good: Sum of individual MB = MSB = MC

The *free rider problem* is another market failure where the government can fill in to provide a good or service. This is a situation where a service, such as spraying insecticide to eliminate mosquitos, can't be limited to paying customers. Since the spray can't be contained, everyone in the neighborhood receives the benefit of mosquito reduction. The individuals who do not pay are called *free riders*. Since people who have not paid for the service reap the benefits anyway, the market is not efficient. If the service is to continue, the government would have to subsidize the provider.

Public Decisions About Public Goods

Individuals in a local community or on the national level don't always agree about which public good should be supported and how much to spend. The residents of a town might have different preferences about the number of days trash should be collected. On the national level, citizens might have a choice about education.

Decisions can be made at local community meetings or in larger settings in the voting booths. Calculating the most efficient solution by the willingness to pay, such as paying taxes, does not always result in the most efficient solution. In fact, economists have determined that under majority-rule voting, the preferred spending level of the median voter will always win an election against any other alternative. This is called the *median voter theorem*.

Evaluating Policy and Public Goods

Sometimes there is disagreement about whether or not a good or service qualifies as a public good that should be paid for by the government. What criteria are evaluated to guide this decision?

Let's take the example of health care in the United States. Even after the enactment of the Affordable Care Act in 2010, the United States has not officially identified health care as a public good. Private insurance companies paid for by private citizens, with some support from the government for low-income individuals, compete for customers.

Some economists believe that health care falls into the category of a public good and should therefore be paid for by the government. A blog post published October 8, 2009, at *The Economist* online examines the range of opinions about this issue (http://www.economist.com/blogs/democracyinamerica/2009/10/universal_health_insurance_is).

Everything we've described here is used to evaluate the policy issue of whether or not health care can be defined as a public good and whether the government should pay for it. The author's conclusion is that universal health insurance is a *common good*—nonexclusionary but rivalrous.

Economics is fundamental in forming policy. As you drill down into the details of the prevailing models of the workings of the economy, you will have a deeper understanding of policy issues as well.

The Least You Need to Know

- An inefficient market is a market failure.
- An externality can be either negative or positive. The externality is a social cost or benefit that was not included in the original market price.
- The government can offset the cost or benefit of the externality with a tax, when there is a negative externality, or a subsidy, when there is a positive externality.
- A public good is nonrival and nonexclusive. Public goods provide benefits to the public at zero marginal cost, and nobody can be excluded from using them.

CHAPTER 6

An Introduction to "Econospeak"

This chapter presents some of the essential vocabulary needed to understand the core principles of economics. Although definitions of unfamiliar words are included wherever they occur, a preview will prepare you for this new material.

If you haven't looked at a math book for a few years, this chapter will review two of the common tools used to analyze economic information: contructing graphs and identifying the slope of a line. Without these skills, it is difficult to work out problems based on the concepts presented in your economics studies.

You will also learn in this chapter how basic theories are explained using models, as well as their graphic representations. This background will help you grasp the fundamental ideas of economics and how they have changed over time.

In This Chapter

- Defining some important economic terms
- Brushing up your math skills: how to construct a graph
- Calculating the slope of a curve
- The role of models in economics

A Language of Their Own

Economists have developed their own lingo. The terminology includes concepts created by prominent theorists during the evolving discipline of economics. Some of the terms have their origins in mathematics. Although this book does not expect you to know advanced math, such as calculus, realizing that a word is grounded in math can provide some context. Only the most commonly used expressions are provided in this brief overview. Other vocabulary will be defined in the relevant chapters.

Here are some terms you will often come across in studying economics.

Aggregate: A common term meaning *sum* or a *collection of particulars,* in macroeconomics aggregate is famously associated with *aggregate demand* and *aggregate supply.* They are listed here because of their significance to macroeconomics and their use in economic policy. *Aggregate demand (AD)* is the sum of all individual demand curves and the total demand for final goods and services in the economy at a given time and price level. It is composed of consumption (C), investment (I), government spending (G), and net exports (NX) to form the equation C + I + G + NX = AD. *Aggregate supply* is the sum of the total supply of goods and services that firms in a national economy plan to sell during a specific time period. Aggregate demand and supply are discussed in detail in Chapter 18.

Curve: A curve is a line on a graph that shows the relationship between two variables. The line can be nonlinear or straight. This chapter will describe in detail how to calculate a curve.

Marginal: Based on a math concept in calculus, *marginal* means incremental, or one additional unit. *Marginal analysis* is the method of comparing the incremental cost or benefit of doing a little bit more of something when deciding if an activity is worth undertaking. A rational decision is made at the margins based on the marginal effect of each incremental decision rather than considering the total costs and benefits of all decisions.

The *marginal cost* (MC) is the cost of doing one more unit of an activity. The *marginal benefit* (MB) is the additional benefit of doing one more unit of an activity. You will come across *marginal* when evaluating other matters including *marginal rate of substitution* (MRS), *marginal revenue* (MR), *marginal tax rate, marginal utility, marginal propensity to consume* (MPC), and more. In all cases you are considering the incremental increase or decrease. Examples are detailed throughout this book along with instructions on how to use marginal analysis.

Maximize: M*aximize* is another case of a term based in calculus, but it can also be understood in its common sense. *Maximize* is usually used in conjunction with *optimal*, as in maximizing profits by finding the price and quantity levels that return the greatest, or optimal, profit.

Schedule: A *schedule* is a table containing variables that are used to create a curve, such as in a supply curve or a demand curve.

Shift: A *shift* in the demand curve or the supply curve represents a change in demand (or supply) caused by an external, or outside, event. For example, there usually will be an increase in demand for a good if there is an increase in income. The curve will be shifted to the right at all price points. Alternatively, there will be a shift of the demand curve for tea to the left if the price of coffee goes down. This is explained in greater detail in Chapter 7.

Shock: A shock is an unexpected or unpredictable event that affects an economy, either positively or negatively. Central banks and governments use monetary and fiscal policy to stabilize economies after a negative shock.

Models and Graphing

You are probably familiar with graphs and charts from reading the newspaper or other courses you've taken in school. Graphs are a depiction of how two or more variables relate to each other; that is, when we want to know how one factor affects another factor at different values, we can find out by plotting the values of each factor, or variable, on a grid and connecting the dots. We will be able to see whether a stock goes up over time, whether pressure goes up or down with added heat, whether wages go up or down according to the age of the worker, whether your electric bill goes up or down in the summer or the winter, or whether price goes up or down with added supply.

Let's take a look at how a graph is constructed.

How to Construct a Graph

For example, to see how the outside temperature affects the number of ice cream cones sold, we will put the outside temperature readings in degrees Fahrenheit, the **x** *variable*, on the **x** axis and the number of ice cream cones, the y variable, on the y axis. The outside temperature is called the *independent variable* because it affects the number of ice cream cones sold, the *dependent variable*.

 **DEFINITION**

A **variable** is a symbol in mathematics that can change in value within a problem set. The **independent variable** in a causal relationship is a mathematical variable that is independent of the other variables. The value of the independent variable determines one or more of the values of the dependent variable.

To begin, we construct a table with three columns—a column for the temperature readings, a column for the number of ice cream cones, and the letter of the point where the data intersect.

Table of Variables and Plot Points for Graph

Outside Temperature x (Independent) Variable	Number of Ice Cream Cones Sold y (Dependent) Variable	Point
50°F	10	A
60°F	20	B
70°F	40	C
80°F	60	D
90°F	80	E

We draw the y and x axes and a grid to plot the numbers where the data points intersect. Then we take the data points from the table and put a point where they intersect on the grid. We can then connect the points to make a line, also called a curve.

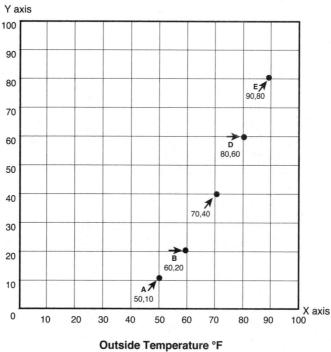

Number of Ice Cream Cones Sold at a Given Temperature

Outside Temperature °F

What Graphs Tell Us

As you can see from the above graph, as the outside temperature rises, more ice cream cones are sold. We might have guessed that, but by plotting the values of the variables, we are able to see the precise relationship between specific outside temperatures and how they affect the number of ice cream cones sold just by looking at the graph.

Graphs are used by economists to illustrate the concepts they would like to convey. The line connecting the points on a graph, whether the line is linear or curved, shows the relationship between two or more variables representing a value that is part of an economic model. For example, if you are told that a business will produce more of a product if the prices are rising, you might not understand or believe it. If you were to take actual price points and plot it against real quantities supplied, you would be able to see for yourself whether it is true.

We can get more information by examining the shapes of the curves that the data provide. A linear relationship will yield a straight line on a graph. For example, for every 10-degrees increase in outside temperature, 10 additional ice cream cones are sold. An example of an equation that has a linear relationship is y = 2x + 3.

Graph of a Straight Line

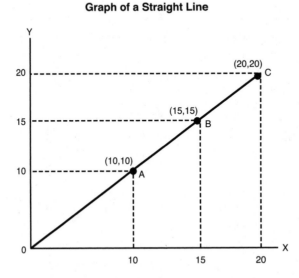

When the points on the graph are connected and result in a curve that is not a straight line, the variables have a *nonlinear relationship*. An example of an equation that has a nonlinear relationship is y = 2x² + 3. Any equation of a degree higher than one is nonlinear.

Graph of a Nonlinear Curve

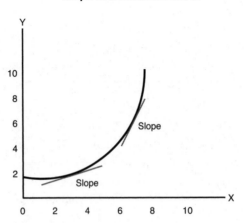

Math Concepts Depicted in Graphs

A few techniques you might have learned in algebra will come in handy when studying economics. First, we'll briefly review calculating the *slope* of linear and nonlinear curves and how they appear on graphs. In general …

- If the line is headed upward toward the right, it is increasing, and the slope is positive.

- If the line is headed downward toward the right, the line is decreasing, and the slope is negative.

- If the line is horizontal, the slope is zero and is said to have a constant function.

- If the line is vertical, the slope is undefined.

DEFINITION

A **slope** is the measure of the direction and steepness of a curve. It is calculated by dividing the change in the y-variable, also called the *rise*, by the change in the x-variable, also called the *run*.

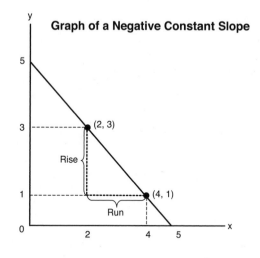

Graph of a Positive Constant Slope

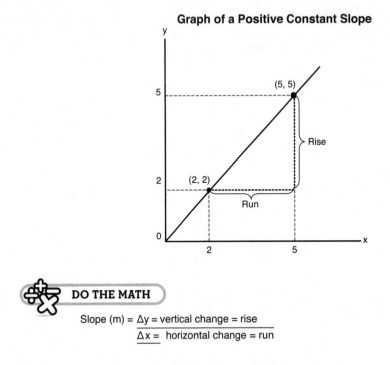

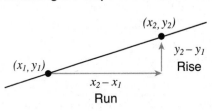

DO THE MATH

Slope (m) = $\frac{\Delta y}{\Delta x} = \frac{\text{vertical change} = \text{rise}}{\text{horizontal change} = \text{run}}$

When calculating the slope of a linear curve, divide the change in the y-variable, also called the *rise*, by the change in the x-variable, also called the *run*.

Calculating the Slope of a Linear Curve

One way to calculate the slope of a nonlinear curve is the point method. This method calculates the slope at only one point on the curve by drawing a straight line, the *tangent line*, which touches the point. The same mathematical formula is used to calculate the slope:

$$\frac{\Delta y = \text{vertical change} = y_2 - y_1 = \text{rise}}{\Delta x = \text{horizontal change} = x_2 - x_1 = \text{run}}$$

**Calculating the Slope of a Nonlinear Curve
with the Point Method**

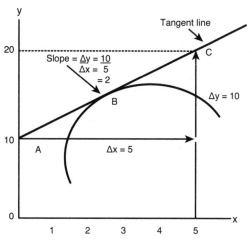

A graph of the slope at the maximum and minimum points of curves is an example of how an image can clarify a difficult concept. Remember, as mentioned in the list of terms above, the word *maximum* is important when optimizing price, profit, or other variables. For example, economists could calculate a minimum point when showing how a producer's costs might change with an increase in output.

As you can see on the graphs, the point where the slope changes from positive to negative is at its maximum point; the point where the slope changes from negative to positive is the minimum point.

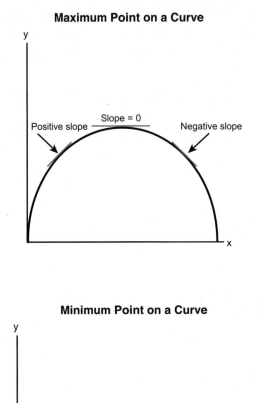

Why Use Models?

Why do economists use models, and what is a model anyway? A model is a simplified, idealized version of a complex concept, often represented in the form of a graph. The model can be used to attempt to predict future situations using available data. Economists use models to make a concept more understandable. The many interacting factors in an economic process make evaluation very difficult without extracting the important variables and their relationships and then illustrating them with models.

Some of the considerations a model might examine include individual or group behavior, limitations of resources, government regulations, or legal requirements, to give a few examples. The economist must decide which of these variables to include in the model in order for it to function as a measuring or predictive tool.

Economists use models to make policy suggestions, forecast economic activity, help businesses plan how much to produce, or advise individuals how much they should spend and save. Quantitative models use mathematics and statistics for evaluation. Less often, models can be qualitative, as when using a decision tree.

DEFINITION

A **model** is a simplified version of a complex idea that can be used to predict outcomes in theory or in the real world. In economics, models are often illustrated in graph form.

Let's take a well-known model as an example: the supply and demand curves at equilibrium. (More details on supply and demand curves are in Chapter 7.) Below is a graph of a nonspecific supply and demand curve at equilibrium. The concept, in brief, is that supply and demand reach equilibrium at the point where the curves for each intersect.

Supply and Demand Curve at Equilibrium

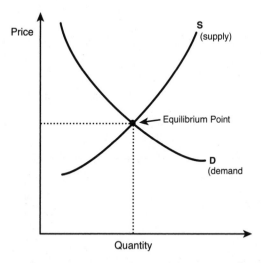

Example of an economic model: equilibrium price is found where the supply and demand curves intersect

As you work your way through this and other economics books, you will come across many models of how economists believe the markets function. These include how the consumer makes choices, what causes a market to become inefficient, how taxes affect demand, why a necessary item like insulin makes the price inflexible or inelastic, how costs affect output of production, and much more. The models are generally based on an overall theory of how markets and the economy work. They are usually based on mathematical relationships. Since models are tools for analyzing the economy, the economist must decide which model fits a given situation. If existing models cannot explain the problem in question, perhaps a new model is required.

Not all economists agree on one model. Economic theories have developed over the course of history, but the most coherent and impactful models were conceived during the advance of capitalism. The classical and neo-classical models presented in traditional microeconomic theory—how individuals and firms behave—begin with Adam Smith's ideas and Jeremy Bentham's philosophy of the "principle of utility" presented in 1780, which claims that people act in their self-interest and that added together, the sum of the individual interests is the interest of the community. Using this concept, most economists believe that the market economy will be propelled in a direction to maximize efficiency and yield the greatest benefit to society.

Some economists, though, disagree with this premise, pointing out that individuals are not alike and therefore cannot have the same preferences. They believe, among other differences, that the demand curve of one individual is not necessarily the same as that of other individuals. Therefore, individual demand curves cannot be added together to make one demand curve for all the components of society.

Models have been constructed to describe how the macro economy—the overall economy as opposed to individuals and firms—behaves. The most well-known theorist of macroeconomics is John Maynard Keynes. More on macroeconomic theories is covered in Part 4. New schools of thought have evolved and branched out in the field of macroeconomics since its inception.

Since the time of Adam Smith, at the inception of the market economy, reality has tested each dominant model of how the economy works. Population growth and technological advancement has transformed the landscape from budding capitalism to globalization and companies international in scope. During this evolution, stresses and shocks to the economy inspired some economists to re-evaluate their beliefs and respond to events by advancing new theories with their accompanying models. Economists are therefore divided into schools of thought that also influence economic policy. As one school or another gains influence, their model can be assessed in a real-time experiment. Those economists open to accepting the results of the experiment might develop a new model for the economy. And so the development of economic thought goes on.

While you should be aware that there are differences of opinion in the academic world, the models presented here will reflect the most common views. Keep in mind that these models make assumptions in order to be true, and the assumptions will be presented along with the models. Economic schools of thought that differ from the mainstream schools are called heterodox schools of economic thought. This information will be presented more fully throughout this book.

The Least You Need to Know

- Be acquainted with some of the useful economic terms to ease your understanding of economics.
- Economists and mathematicians use graphs to show the relationship between two or more variables.
- Models help explain complex economic processes in a simplified form.
- Economic theory has evolved since the rise of capitalism in the eighteenth century. This book presents the dominant views and their models.

Microeconomics: Business and the Consumer

The interaction of supply and demand is the heart of the market economy. Part 2 describes in detail how the mechanism of supply and demand results in your getting the best price for your purchase. It is price that is almost always the final determination for your purchase, is it not?

The market would not exist if it were not for two key players: the consumer and the firm. Each wants to get the best deal. You might have had the experience of shopping at an open market. Lively bargaining continues until a price and quantity are reached on which both you and the seller agree. Each agent acts in his or her own best interest.

To get the most satisfaction from the purchase, the consumer wants just the right amount of his or her preferred product at the best price within his or her budget. The firm wants to maximize its profit.

How both players go about getting what they want, and the underlying market forces that enable the exchange, is described in Part 2.

Supply and Demand

Supply and demand is a concept that most people understand intuitively because they have a lot of experience buying products they need and want. When your supermarket has a large supply of your favorite crackers, they will mark down the price to sell their inventory. When the store has difficulty getting a supply of your popular cracker brand, the store will raise the price.

Economists use the supply and demand model to explain how a market works. The model works best in a competitive market, where there are many buyers and sellers of the same good or service. Markets that are not competitive will be described in Part 2.

As with all models, the supply and demand model is a simplification of reality to facilitate analysis. Sometimes, a model can be oversimplified, and errors can be made in specific instances. We focus on the model used by most economists because, as you will soon see, the model can tell us a good deal about how the marketplace works.

In This Chapter

- Understanding the supply and demand model
- Steps to construct a demand curve and a supply curve
- Identifying the equilibrium point of supply and demand
- The effect of external factors on the supply and demand curves
- Calculating the elasticity of demand and supply

If you recall from Chapter 6, we explained how to compare two variables by constructing a curve. The first step was to put the data for each variable on a schedule, or table. We were able to plot those points on a graph and connect the coordinates of the points to derive a curve. To create the complete supply and demand model, we will first construct the demand curve. Later we will construct the supply curve. The final step is to plot the demand curve and the supply curve on a graph. The market is in equilibrium where the two curves cross.

The Demand Curve

Demand is the quantity demanded of a good or service at any given price. Later on, we will cover demand as affected by other factors. The *law of demand* states that, all else being equal (*ceteris paribus*), the quantity demanded is related to the price—as price increases, quantity decreases.

> **DEFINITION**
>
> The **law of demand** states that the quantity demanded is related to the price, such that as price increases, quantity decreases, all else being equal. **Ceteris paribus** is Latin for "holding other things constant." In economics this refers to evaluating the effect of one variable against the other while the effect of other variables are held constant.

Constructing a Demand Schedule and a Demand Curve

The first step to constructing the supply and demand model is to create a *demand schedule*, which simply lists the data points we will use to create the *demand curve* in table format.

> **DEFINITION**
>
> A **demand schedule** is a table of data that shows how much of a good or service a consumer wants to buy at different prices. A **demand curve** is a graphical representation of the demand schedule showing the quantity demanded by a consumer at any given price.

Let's construct a demand schedule for bags of chocolate bars. (We might as well have pleasant thoughts while working through the supply and demand model.) The two variables are defined in the law of demand: price and quantity demanded.

Demand Schedule for a Bag of Chocolate Bars

Price	Quantity of a Bag of Chocolate Bars Demanded
$5.00	2
4.00	3
3.00	4
2.00	5
1.00	6

The next step is to use this information to construct a demand curve. Realize that while there are specific prices and quantities listed on the schedule, the demand curve takes all prices and quantities demanded into account, so it forms a smooth curve.

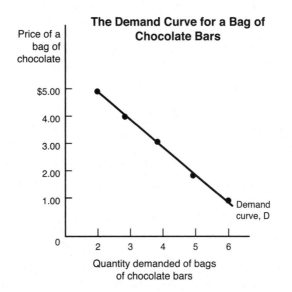

The demand schedule for a bag of chocolate bars is plotted to form the demand curve, which shows how many bags of chocolate bars consumers want at any given price. Note that the demand curve slopes downward.

What you notice from the demand curve in the accompanying figure is that it slopes downward. This is a characteristic of demand curves because as the price decreases, the quantity demanded increases.

Shifts in the Demand Curve

Recall that the law of demand states that, all else being equal (*ceteris paribus*), the quantity demanded is related to the price—as price increases, quantity decreases. Now we will focus on *ceteris paribus*—holding everything else constant. What happens when the other factors are no longer held constant?

External factors can cause a change in demand. Let's see how the demand curve is affected by a change in one of these factors. Demand is represented by the demand curve. When the *demand* changes (not *quantity demanded* at a given price), the entire curve *shifts* to the right or left. A shift in the demand curve represents a change in the quantity demanded at any given price. Why would this happen?

Let's take an example using bags of chocolate. What if you and all the other chocoholics in the world woke up one morning to find that there was a shortage of cocoa beans. Initially, there would be an increase in demand for chocolate bars as chocoholics of the world rushed to buy the remaining chocolate bars before they got too expensive or were no longer available.

The demand for chocolate bars would go up, and in our model of the demand curve, the curve would shift to the right. The external effect that caused the shift to the right was the *expectation* that the price was going to rise as chocolate bars became scarce.

On the other hand, if chocolate bars became too expensive, chocoholics might take a break from chocolate and go for something that was less expensive but still satisfied their sweet tooth. While we chocoholics know that nothing can ever take the place of chocolate, we will imagine that a hazelnut bar covered in carob would do. The hazelnut bar is a *substitute* for the chocolate bar. Since there is a less expensive substitute, the demand for chocolate bars would decrease. *This shifts the entire demand curve to the left.* When the demand goes down for chocolate bars, the quantity demanded goes down at any given price.

Remember not to confuse a movement *up or down along the demand curve*, where the quantity demanded changes as the price goes up or down, with a *shift in the demand curve*, where the entire demand curve reacts to a *change in demand* by shifting to the right or left.

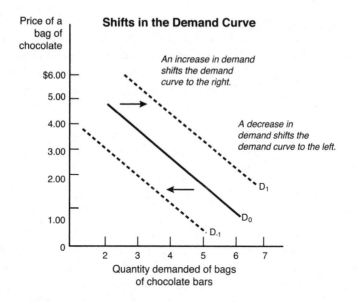

An increase in demand shifts the demand curve to the right as the quantity demanded increases at every given price. A decrease in demand shifts the demand curve to the left as the quantity demanded goes down at every given price.

Factors That Change Demand

A few of the common factors that can cause a change in demand are:

- Price expectations

- Substitutes and complements

- Changes in income

- Changes in tastes

Examples of *price expectation* and *substitutes* were mentioned in our chocolate bar example. A substitute is considered a related good. Two goods are substitutes if a rise in the price of one of the goods makes consumers more willing to buy the other good.

A *complement* is also a related good. Examples of complements are hot dogs and hot dog rolls, a Kindle and an e-book, or gasoline and a car. Two goods are complements if a fall in the price of one good makes people more willing to buy the other good. A fall in the price of a Kindle will make you more likely to buy e-books. Likewise, a rise in the price of one good makes people less willing to buy the other good.

> **DEFINITION**
>
> Two goods are **substitutes** if a fall (or rise) in the price of one of the goods makes con-sumers less (or more) willing to buy the other good. Two goods are complements if a fall (or rise) in the price of one good makes people more (or less) willing to buy the other good.

A *change in income* will shift the demand curve to the right or left. An increase in income will typically increase your demand for a good, and a decrease in income will typically decrease your demand for a good. An increase in demand with an increase in income does not apply to some goods. Those that have a positive correlation are called *normal goods*. When income rises, people tend to purchase higher-quality goods or services. If you can afford it, you might buy a car instead of using public transportation. Goods whose quantity demanded do not have a positive correlation with income are called *inferior goods.*

> **DEFINITION**
>
> A **normal good** is a good that experiences an increase in demand when income rises. An **inferior good** is one that experiences a decrease in demand when income rises.

A *change in taste or preference* can cause a shift in the demand curve for a product. When the iPhone was introduced to the marketplace by Steve Jobs, eager buyers lined up starting early in the morning at the Apple stores. There was a big demand for the iPhone, and it could command a hefty price. When other cell phone manufacturers came out with appealing smartphones and an operating system made by Google that could be used on multiple smartphone brands at a lower price, Apple, Inc. started to lose market share.

Now that you know how the demand curve is constructed and shifts with an increase or decrease in demand, we can use the same methods for analyzing the supply curve.

The Supply Curve

Producers who create the supply of goods or services are more likely to increase production if they can get a higher price. *The law of supply* states that as the price of a good or service increases, the quantity of goods or services offered by suppliers increases, all else being equal (*ceteris paribus*). The opposite is true when the price of a good decreases.

> **DEFINITION**
>
> **The law of supply** states that as the price of a good or service increases, the quantity of goods or services offered by suppliers increases.

When we complete the construction of the supply curve, you will see that it has an upward slope, as the higher the price, the more quantity the producer is willing to supply.

Constructing a Supply Schedule and a Supply Curve

The same steps used to construct the demand curve are followed to construct the supply curve. The first step is to create a supply schedule.

Supply Schedule for a Bag of Chocolate Bars

Price	Quantity of a Bag of Chocolate Bars Supplied
$5.00	6
4.00	5
3.00	4
2.00	3
1.00	2

Just looking at the numbers on the supply schedule tells you that the bags the producer is willing to supply increases with an increase in price, but let's see what it looks like on a graph of the two variables, price and quantity supplied.

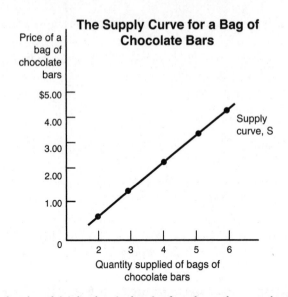

The supply schedule for a bag of chocolate bars is plotted to form the supply curve, showing how many bags of chocolate bars producers are willing to supply at any given price. Note that the supply curve slopes upward.

Just as there can be an increase or decrease in demand, there can also be an increase or decrease in supply. Let's see how this works.

Shifts in the Supply Curve

A change in an external factor will shift the supply curve at any given price. This shift is not to be confused with a movement *along the supply curve*, reflecting the relationship between a rise in price and the quantity producers are willing to supply.

An increase in supply will shift the supply curve to the right. A decrease in supply will shift the supply curve to the left.

Factors That Change Supply

Economists identify three main reasons for a shift in the supply curve:

- Changes in input prices
- Changes in technology
- Changes in expectations

An *input* is a good that is used to produce another good. A change in the cost of inputs will shift the supply curve. An increase in the cost of an input will shift the supply curve to the left. A producer cannot make as much profit on his product if the cost to produce it cuts into his profit margin, so he will decrease production. A decrease in the cost of an input will shift the supply curve to the right because the profits will increase when the inputs are less expensive.

Technological improvements can contribute to an increase in supply. If new machinery is able to improve production capabilities in a plant at a lower cost, it is more profitable for the producer. She is willing to increase the supply of her good.

A producer's expectations of future prices can also shift the supply curve. A very dry summer that parched the corn crop would increase the price of corn for the baker, and he would plan to decrease the supply of cornbread. The supply curve would shift to the left. If he learned that Brazil had had a bumper crop, the baker's expectations would change, and he would increase the supply, which would shift the supply curve to the right.

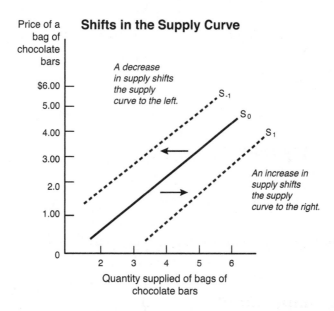

An increase in supply shifts the supply curve to the right as the quantity supplied increases at every given price. A decrease in supply shifts the supply curve to the left as the quantity supplied goes down at every given price.

Finding the Equilibrium in Supply and Demand

Our ultimate goal is to find the point at which price and quantity demanded and supplied come together at an equilibrium point on the graphic model. This is the point where all buyers and sellers agree on a price—the price *clears*. The equilibrium price is also called the *market clearing price*. The supply and demand graphic model can now be completed.

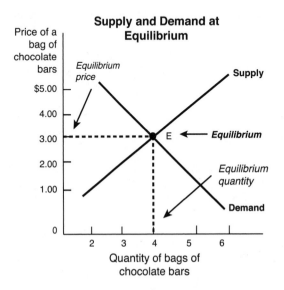

The equilibrium is at the point where the demand curve and the supply curve intersect, point E. The equilibrium price is $3.00, and the equilibrium quantity is 4 bags of chocolate bars. This is the point where quantity demanded equals quantity supplied.

Now that we have the basic concept of supply and demand reaching equilibrium, we can use the model to understand what happens under different circumstances in a market, such as when there is a surplus or shortage of a good.

Surplus and Shortage

Markets will eventually work their way to equilibrium. When price and quantity are higher or lower than the equilibrium point, some adjustments will have to be made for the market to clear.

Without relying on a graphic model—you might try your hand at drawing one—you can imagine what a shortage in a good would look like using the supply and demand model. A *shortage* is when the market price is below the equilibrium price. Why would this cause a shortage?

Recall that suppliers offer more supply when the price is higher. In this case, the equilibrium price is higher than the market price, so in order for the market to clear, the price has to move up to the equilibrium point.

Let's take apples as an example. At a low price, the supplier is not willing to grow many apples, but because of the low price, there is a large quantity demanded. Consumers bid up the price of apples, but there isn't enough supply. Producers decide that at the higher price, it's worth growing more apples. As price rises, there is more supply, but there is still a shortage of apples. As consumers bid up the price, the producer supplies more apples. This continues until a price is reached where the quantity of apples supplied equals the quantity of apples demanded—the equilibrium price. The market for apples has reached its equilibrium, market clearing price, and there is no longer a shortage.

A *surplus* is just the opposite. The market price is above the equilibrium price—the good is too expensive for buyers. The price must go down for the goods to sell. As long as the price is above the equilibrium point, the producer can't sell many apples. As the price drops, there is more demand for the apples. The producer is happy to be selling more apples even though the price is lower. Eventually a price is reached where the quantity supplied equals the quantity demanded, the equilibrium or market-clearing price. There is no longer a surplus.

 **DEFINITION**

A **shortage** occurs when the market price is *below* the equilibrium price. A **surplus** occurs when the market price is *above* the equilibrium price.

How an Increase in Demand or Supply Affects the Equilibrium

Here is a brain teaser. What happens to the equilibrium when there is an increase in demand? (Hint: Remember that the entire demand curve shifts to the right with an increase in demand.) Try your hand at drawing the supply and demand curves with the equilibrium point located where the curves cross. Draw the price on the Y axis and the quantity demanded on the X axis. What happens to the price and quantity supplied when there is an increase in demand? The answer is that the demand curve shifts to the right along the supply curve, resulting in a higher equilibrium price and higher equilibrium quantity.

What happens when there is an increase in supply? Try to figure this out using the supply and demand model starting at equilibrium. The answer is that an increase in supply shifts the supply curve to the right along the demand curve to a new equilibrium point at a lower equilibrium price and a higher equilibrium quantity.

Here is one last scenario. What happens when both the supply curve and the demand curve shift? Try to work this out before reading on. Work on the shift of the demand curve first and then the shift of the supply curve. Notice whether the price goes up or down and whether quantity goes up or down for each curve.

Here is the answer. When the demand curve and the supply curve shift in *opposite directions*, the change in *price is predictable*, but the change in *quantity is not*. When they shift in the *same direction*, the change in *quantity is predictable*, but the change in *price is not*. Read the following sidebar to see what each scenario looks like when both the supply and demand curves shift.

DO THE MATH

D = Demand; S = Supply; Q = Quantity; P = Price

When the demand curve and the supply curve shift in *opposite directions*, the change in *price is predictable*, but the change in *quantity is not*.

When D↑ and S↓ then Q? and P↑

When D↓ and S↑ then Q? and P↓

When the demand curve and the supply curve shift in the *same direction*, the change in *quantity is predictable*, but the change in *price is not*.

When D↑ and S↑ then Q↑ and P?

When D↓ and S↓ then Q↓ and P?

We have just scratched the surface of our study of supply and demand. Economists also want to know how a change in price impacts the quantity demanded or supplied. Said another way, we want to measure the *responsiveness* of the quantity demanded to price. This is called the *elasticity of demand* or the *elasticity of supply*.

Price Elasticity and Inelasticity of Demand

What do we mean by *elasticity of demand*? To understand elasticity, think about a rubber band. A new rubber band can be easily stretched. It is very elastic. An old rubber band is hard and will break when it is pulled. The old rubber band is inelastic. The responsiveness of the rubber band is its elasticity.

Elasticity of demand is the ratio of the percent change in the quantity demanded to the percent change in the price.

Producers are interested in knowing the elasticity of demand for their product. They want to know how sensitive their product is to a rise or fall in price. Initiating a new product at a price that is too high could ruin a product launch. Alternatively, a price that is too low could reduce potential profits. If not a new product, it is still important to know how much prices could be raised or lowered so as not to have a big effect on quantity demanded. You don't want to scare away buyers with a price that is higher than consumers are willing to pay, and you don't want to lose potential profits by reducing the price too much. Like Goldilocks, you want the price to be just right.

The elasticity of demand is defined as the ratio of the percent change in the quantity demanded to the percent change in the price. A product is very *elastic* when a given percentage change in *price* results in a *large percentage change in quantity demanded*. A product is very *inelastic,* when a given percentage change in *price* results in a very *small percentage change in quantity demanded*.

The restaurant market has *elastic* demand because there are many competitors, and consumers do not have to go out to eat. The quantity demanded of any restaurant is sensitive to a change in price.

As an example of *inelastic demand*, think about a person who needs insulin all his or her life because of diabetes. This person has no choice—he or she must buy insulin. The producer can charge any price within reason without changing the quantity demanded. Since insulin is essential for life, the price is *inelastic*—the quantity demanded will not decrease with a change in price.

Measuring Elasticity of Demand

Economists and producers want to know how much a change in price affects the quantity demanded. Let's use the apple example again. A hypothetical move up the demand curve for a pound of apples goes from point A at $2.00 and a quantity demanded of 10 to point B at $2.10 per pound at a quantity of 9.9. Let's do the math.

DO THE MATH

The demand curve for apples shows that at a price of $2.00 the quantity demanded is 10 pounds. At a price of $2.10 the quantity demanded is 9.9 pounds. The change in the quantity demanded is 0.1 pounds.

Percent change in quantity demanded = 0.1 pounds/10 pounds × 100 = 1%

The initial price is $2.00 and the change in price is $0.10, the percent change in price is:

% change in price = $0.10/$2 × 100 = 5%.

Price elasticity of demand = % change in quantity demanded/% change in price so 1%/5% = 0.2.

Since the demand curve slopes downward, 0.2 would be a negative number. By convention, economists use the absolute value (the number without the minus and plus signs) and call it 0.2.

Midpoint or averaging method of calculation:

The price elasticity of demand can also be calculated using the average of the starting and final values. The general equation for this method using two points on a demand curve is:

$$\frac{\dfrac{Q_2 - Q_1}{(Q_1 + Q_2)/2}}{\dfrac{P_2 - P_1}{(P_1 + P_2)/2}}$$

Again, use the absolute value.

A Quick Read on the Degree of Elasticity

Here is a rule of thumb to know if the price elasticity of demand is elastic or inelastic. When the price elasticity of demand is *greater than 1*, the demand is *elastic*. When the price elasticity of demand is *less than 1*, the demand is *inelastic*.

When the price elasticity of demand *equals 1*, the demand is *unit-elastic*. A unit-elastic demand is interesting because the demand curve is a smooth one-to-one relationship between the percentage increase or decrease in price and the percentage decrease or increase in quantity demanded. Try drawing this demand curve using price on the Y axis and quantity demanded on the X axis. Use the example of a 10% increase in the price generating a 10% decrease in the quantity demanded.

A *perfectly elastic demand* occurs when the price elasticity of demand is infinity. This occurs when even an infinitesimally small change in price results in an infinitely large change in quantity demanded.

Let's go back to our bag of chocolate example. Suppose there were two vendors next door to each other that sold Lindt chocolate bars. The first store sells a bag of chocolate bars for $15.00. The second store sells the same bag of chocolate bars for $14.95. Since everyone likes a bargain, we'll assume that all consumers choose to buy their chocolate bars from the second store. The quantity demanded is very, very sensitive to price. This is an example of perfectly elastic demand. The demand curve for a good that has *perfectly elastic demand is a horizontal line at a particular price.*

A *perfectly inelastic demand* is when the price elasticity of demand is zero. In our insulin example, a diabetic needs a certain amount of insulin per week. No matter what the price is, within reason, the quantity demanded will be the same. This is an example of perfectly inelastic demand. A *perfectly inelastic demand curve is a vertical line* because no matter what the price is, the quantity demanded will always be the same.

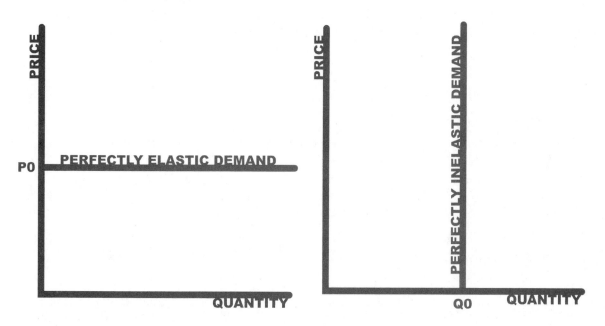

Total Revenue and Price Elasticity of Demand

Price elasticity of demand is very important to producers because they will be able to calculate how a change in price will affect their *total revenue.* Total revenue is equal to price multiplied by the quantity.

Imagine you are selling a pair of Nike sneakers, and you want to know whether your total revenue would increase or decrease if you lower the price. You think, "If I lower the price, I'll make less per pair of sneakers, but maybe I'll sell more. On the other hand, if I raise the price, even if I sell less, maybe my total revenue will increase. I don't know what to do."

By knowing the price elasticity of demand, you can calculate the prices that will increase or decrease your total revenue:

- If demand is elastic (the price elasticity of demand is more than 1), total revenue falls when the price increases and rises when the price decreases.

- If demand is inelastic (the price elasticity of demand is less than 1), total revenue rises when the price increases and falls when the price decreases.

- If the price elasticity of demand is equal to 1, it is unit elastic and the total revenue does not change.

As you might imagine, the price elasticity of demand also depends on whether close substitutes for your sneakers are available. The price elasticity of demand is also affected by whether consumers consider the good a necessity or a luxury.

Cross-Price Elasticity of Demand and Income Elasticity of Demand

Elasticity is also used to calculate the effect of change in one good's price on the quantity demanded of the other good. This is called the *cross-price elasticity of demand*. The cross-price elasticity of demand between, for example, apples and pears, is % change in quantity of apples/% change in price of pears. These are *substitutes*. If apples are too expensive, consumers can replace them by eating pears. *The cross-price elasticity of demand is positive for substitutes*. Close substitutes have a larger number for cross-price elasticity of demand than substitutes that are not close. Using this information can tell economists how well one good substitutes for another.

The cross-price elasticity of demand for *complements*, like fuel and cars, is *negative*. A rise in the price of fuel causes consumers to buy fewer cars. The demand curve shifts to the left for cars. What the cross-price elasticity of demand between two complements tells us is whether they are weak complements (slightly below zero) or strong complements (very negative cross-price elasticity of demand). When calculating the cross-elasticity of demand for substitutes and complements, economists don't use the absolute number, since knowing the negative or positive sign determines whether the goods are substitutes or complements.

When we want to know how much a consumer's income changes the demand for a good, economists calculate the *income elasticity of demand*. The income elasticity of demand is % change in quantity demanded/%change in income.

The positive or negative sign of the income elasticity of demand tells us whether the goods are normal goods (consumption rises with income increase) or inferior goods (consumption falls with income increase). If it is *positive*, the good is a *normal* good. If it is *negative*, it is an *inferior* good.

Price Elasticity of Supply

The price elasticity of supply is % change in quantity supplied/% change in price. We use the data points along the supply curve to give us the information we need. For example, you decide to start a business selling chocolate chip cookies. When you opened up your store, you sold the cookies for a price of $1.00 per bag, and you supplied 10 bags of cookies. The following week you sold the cookies at a price of $2.00 per bag, and you supplied 16 bags of cookies.

1. The *percent change in quantity supplied* is 16 minus 10 = 6. The midpoint between 16 and 10 is 13. Divide 6 by 13 = *46%*.

2. To find the *percent change in price,* first calculate the average or midpoint between $1.00 and $2.00, and $1.50. Then divide 1 by 1.5 to get about *67%*.

3. The *elasticity of supply*—which is % change in quantity supplied/% change in price equals 46%/67% = 0.46/0.67 = 0.69.

If the quantity does not change, the elasticity of supply is *perfectly inelastic,* and the supply curve is vertical. The elasticity of supplied is *perfectly elastic* if an infinitesimal price change, whether up or down, causes a dramatic change in the quantity supplied.

As you can see, using the supply and demand model provides important information about the marketplace. The next chapter explains what else the supply and demand model reveals.

The Least You Need to Know

- Demand is the quantity demanded of a good or service at any given price. The demand curve slopes downward. Supply is the quantity supplied of a good or service at any given price. The supply curve slopes upward.

- External factors can cause a shift to the right or left of the demand curve and the supply curve.

- The equilibrium point on the supply and demand model is where the demand curve and the supply curve cross—where supply equals demand.
- External factors can cause a shift in the demand curve along the supply curve to a new equilibrium point.
- External factors can cause a shift in the supply curve along the demand curve to a new equilibrium point. Both curves can shift to a new equilibrium point.
- Price elasticity of demand or supply measures the responsiveness of quantity demanded or supplied to a change in price: % change in quantity demanded (supplied)/% change in price.

CHAPTER 8

Consumer and Producer Surplus

Imagine a new game show called *Name Your Price*. The show's host stands between two tables at which contestants are seated. On one side are three buyers; on the other side are three sellers. The host shows a picture of a beautiful red convertible Mustang. The buyers are told to type into their computer what price they are willing to pay for the Mustang. The sellers are told to type in the price at which they are willing to sell the Mustang. In this game, the buyers and sellers can win the difference between the market price of the Mustang and the price they were willing to pay for it, in the case of the buyers, or the price they were willing to accept, in the case of the sellers.

Only the show's host knows the real market price of the Mustang. The host gives chips, worth money, to the buyers. The buyers are told that if the market price is less than the price they are willing to pay, they can keep the difference and cash in the chips. The sellers are told that if the market price is higher than their acceptable sales price, they will get the difference in chips, which they can cash in.

In This Chapter

- Consumer surplus: the benefits of being in the market
- Deriving the demand curve using consumer surplus
- Producer surplus and the gains from trade
- Deriving the supply curve using producer surplus
- How price controls, sales taxes, and deadweight loss reduce society's welfare

Buyer #1 types in $30,000. Buyer #2 types in $25,000. Buyer #3 types in $23,000.

Seller #1 types in $13,000. Seller #2 types in $15,000. Seller #3 types in $17,000.

The host announces, "The market price is $20,000!" All the buyers are happy because the price they were willing to pay for the Mustang was higher than the market price. The difference in the price each buyer is willing to pay and the market price is the buyer's *individual consumer surplus*.

The sellers were also happy because they were willing to sell it for a lower price than the market price. The difference in the price at which each seller is willing to sell the Mustang and the market price is the seller's *individual producer surplus*. Everyone is happy; but in this show, nobody gets the Mustang!

Consumer Surplus

The opening story gives you an idea of *consumer surplus*. When the consumer is willing to pay more for a good than the market price, the difference between the two prices is the *consumer surplus*. Each consumer has his or own preferences, so the consumer surplus will be different for every consumer. A stair-step demand curve of price and quantity can be constructed for individual consumers. In a large market, a smooth demand curve can be derived.

Consumer Surplus and the Demand Curve

Let's move away from the game show example to a market of slightly damaged peaches. Damaged peaches are a far cry from a red Mustang convertible, but consumer surplus is an important concept for all markets. Economists can measure the benefits to consumers and producers of any market using the consumer surplus and producer surplus model.

> **DEFINITION**
>
> A **consumer surplus** occurs when the consumer is willing to pay more for a given product than the current market price. It is calculated by the area above the market price and below the demand curve.

We want to understand the market for slightly damaged peaches, so we construct a demand curve using the price each consumer is willing to pay for a pound of slightly damaged peaches. First, we need a demand schedule of the price and quantity at that price for a pound of these peaches.

Demand Schedule for a Pound of Slightly Damaged Peaches

Price	Quantity of a Pound of Slightly Damaged Peaches
$5.00	1
4.00	2
3.00	3
2.00	4
1.00	5

Next, we plot the coordinates on a graph using price on the Y axis and quantity on the X axis. The price represents the maximum price at which a particular consumer will buy a pound of slightly damaged peaches. It has a stair-step appearance because we are going to look at the individual consumer surplus for now.

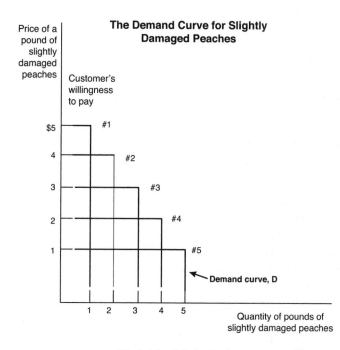

Each step represents one consumer. The height of the box is the consumer's willingness to pay. The width of the box is the quantity.

The green grocer has a sale on slightly damaged peaches. The market price for a pound of slightly damaged peaches is $2.50 per pound. We can now measure the consumer surplus for each consumer because we know what he or she is willing to pay and the market price. *Consumer surplus* is the difference between the highest price the consumer is willing to pay and the market price.

Customer	Willingness to Pay	Price Paid	Consumer Surplus
#1	$5	$2.50	$2.50
#2	4	2.50	1.50
#3	3	2.50	0.50
#4	2	—	—
#5	1	—	—
Total consumer surplus: $4.50			

Each customer who is willing to pay the market price or more than the market price has an individual consumer surplus equal to the difference between the highest price the consumer is willingness to pay and the market price. Customers who were not willing to pay the market price or more than the market price were not buyers. The total consumer surplus is the sum of the individuals' consumer surpluses below the demand curve and above the market price.

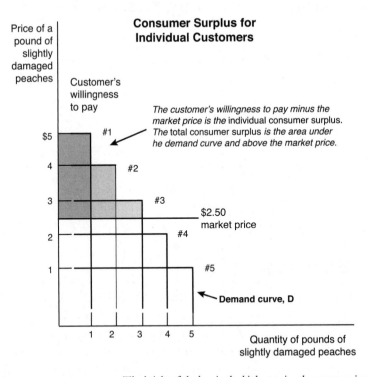

Each step represents one customer. The height of the box is the highest price the customer is willing to pay; the width of the box is the quantity. The customer's individual consumer surplus is the highest price the customer is willing to pay less the market price. The total consumer surplus is the area under the demand curve and above the market price.

In a large market, the demand curve is smooth. In this case, the total consumer surplus would look like a triangle, with sides that are the price, the quantity, and the demand curve. To calculate the area of the triangle, multiply one-half times base times height: $\frac{1}{2}(b \times h)$. In the accompanying figure, consumer surplus can be calculated as $\frac{1}{2}(\$1,000 \times 100) = \$50,000$.

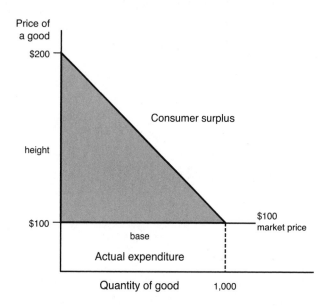

The consumer surplus in a large market with many individuals can be calculated as the area of a triangle, $\frac{1}{2}$ (base × height), with the base = quantity, the height = maximum willingness to pay at q=0 minus market price, and the diagonal = the demand curve. In this case, to find the total consumer surplus, represented by the shaded triangle—the area under the demand curve and above the market price—calculate $\frac{1}{2}$ of ($1,000 × 100) = $50,000.

A rise in the price of a good reduces consumer surplus, and a fall in the price increases consumer surplus.

Producer Surplus

The *producer surplus* is the difference between the market price, or price received, and the minimum price the producer is willing to receive for the good. The supply curve can be derived by finding the minimum price a producer would want to receive in order for him or her to produce a certain quantity of the good. A producer might think about the options he or she has in terms of allocating his resources. Producing one good means he or she gives up the opportunity to produce a different good with the same resources—*the opportunity cost.*

> **DEFINITION**
>
> The **producer surplus** is the difference between the market price, or price received, and the minimum price the producer is willing to receive for the good. The difference is the benefit the producer gets by selling the good in the market.

Producer Surplus and the Supply Curve

The individual producer surplus is the net gain to a seller from selling a good. Recall that it is the difference between the price received and the minimum price the producer is willing to receive for the good. Another way to think of the minimum price the producer is willing to receive for the good is his opportunity cost for not doing something else with his resources. The supply curve for the individual producer has the same stair-step pattern as the individual consumer demand curve because producers have different opportunity costs or minimum prices at which they are willing to sell their product. We will not show the producer's individual supply curve here. Try your hand at drawing one.

Calculating the Producer Surplus

Let's say, hypothetically, that farmers in Punjab, India, can plant two crops on their land: wheat and cotton. They customarily plant wheat on two thirds of the land and cotton on one third. The farmers choose to sell more wheat than cotton so long as they stand to gain more from the sale of wheat than from the sale of cotton. As long as the producer surplus is more for wheat than for cotton, they will continue to plant more wheat.

The farmers keep track of the price and quantity that they can sell the wheat, measured in metric tons, and what they would have to give up to produce the next metric ton. A supply schedule can be created to record the price and quantity at which they would be willing to sell the wheat. The next step is to derive the supply curve for the data. The supply curve can be considered an *opportunity cost* curve because the land used to plant wheat is land not being used to plant cotton or something else.

With this information we can draw the producers' supply curve in terms of the minimum price farmers want to produce a given quantity of wheat. Stated another way, what is the opportunity cost to arrive at an acceptable price? The data on our supply schedule for wheat shows a one-to-one correlation between price and quantity, so we will draw that on the graph. A demand curve is drawn so you can see how we arrive at the market price, the equilibrium point.

Supply Schedule for a Metric Ton of Wheat

Price in Thousands	Quantity of 1 Metric Ton of Wheat
$5.00	5
4.00	4
3.00	3
2.00	2
1.00	1

From the farmers' point of view, they would have to sell their wheat at $1,000 (really 1,000 rupees in our India example) to produce 1 metric ton of wheat. If they do not receive $1,000 for the metric ton, they are giving up the opportunity cost of using the land for something else, perhaps cotton or renting the land. The opportunity cost at each price and quantity is represented on the graph by the dotted rectangles along the quantity axis.

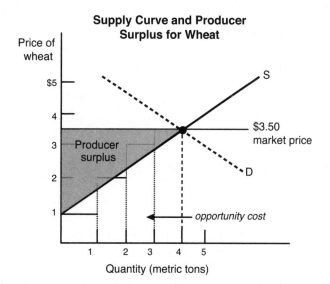

The graph shows the hypothetical supply curve for wheat in units of metric tons and price in the thousands. The demand curve is added to show the market price at equilibrium. The shaded triangle is the producer's surplus—the area above the supply curve and below the market price.

The producer surplus is the area of the triangle: ½ (base × height). In this case, with price calculated in the thousands, the total is ½ [($3,500 − $1,000 = $2,500) × 4] metric tons. The total producer surplus is $5,000.

What happens when there is a rise in the price? If you do a thought experiment, you can imagine that a rise in price will increase the producer surplus, since it is an amount further above the market price, when price and quantity are at equilibrium. Producer surplus increases further if the quantity produced is also increased beyond the equilibrium quantity to the quantity on the supply curve corresponding to the higher price.

 **DO THE MATH**

A rise in price from market equilibrium price from $3,500 to $5,000 at a quantity of 4 metric tons ...

$5,000 – $3,500 = 1,500 × 4 = $6,000

... would add an additional $6,000 in producer surplus.

An increase of 1 metric ton beyond the market equilibrium quantity of 4 metric tons for a total of 5 metric tons would add ...

The area ½ base × height = ½ × 1 × 1,500 = 750

... $750 of additional producer surplus.

Remember: base = quantity; height = price.

We use the area of a triangle because the area above the supply curve and the new price of $5,000 is:

½ base (5 – 4 = 1 metric ton) × height ($5,000 – $3,500 = $1,500) = ½ × 1 × $1,500 = $750.

The increase in producer surplus included in the rise in price where the quantity remains at the equilibrium is attributed to the original sellers. The producer surplus that is gained by the increase in price *and* quantity above the market equilibrium is from the new sellers that came into the market because the price at which they could sell their wheat was attractive.

When there is a fall in price, the reverse takes place. There is a fall in the producer surplus.

Total Surplus and Market Efficiency

The *total surplus* in a market is the sum of the consumer and the producer surplus. We can also think of the total surplus as the *total net gain* to consumers and producers from *trading* in the market. Consumer surplus and producer surplus facilitates trade because they are trading the benefit of paying less than they had planned to pay or selling for more than they had planned to sell. Yet another perspective is that it is the *total benefit to society* from the production and consumption of a good.

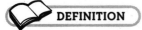 **DEFINITION**

Total surplus is the sum of the consumer surplus and the producer surplus.

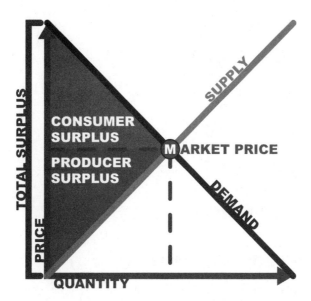

The most efficient market is one where the total surplus is greatest. This occurs when the market is at equilibrium. We can use what we know about consumer and producer surplus to understand how price ceilings and floors reduce market efficiency. Let's see how this happens.

Price Controls, Sales Taxes, and the Deadweight Loss

Society gets the most benefit from efficient markets. Buyers and sellers get the quantity of a good at the best price, which is also where total surplus is the greatest—at the market equilibrium. The imposition of price controls and taxes can reduce the efficiency of the market by reducing consumer surplus and/or producer surplus, reducing total surplus, and decreasing the benefits of trade, which is a *deadweight loss* to society.

 **DEFINITION**

A **deadweight loss** is the cost to society of inefficiency created by price controls and taxes, among other things.

Rent Control and Deadweight Loss

In some cities, local governments have laws that cap the rent of an apartment at a certain price for some number of years before the landlord can raise the rent. The purpose of the control on rents is to prevent the rental price from becoming unaffordable. The consumer surplus and producer surplus model challenges the notion that society benefits from this kind of control, which is effectively a price ceiling. The model shows that rent control causes society to lose some benefit and redistributes the consumer surplus and producer surplus that existed before the rent control was imposed.

For this example, we can call the supply curve the marginal cost (opportunity cost) curve, and the demand curve the marginal benefit curve. Recall that *marginal* means each incremental unit. We are substituting these names because we will be evaluating the loss of benefit to society resulting from rent controls.

The accompanying figure shows the consumer surplus that is gained when the consumer is able to rent the apartment at a price above the market price and below the marginal benefit curve. The producer surplus (landlord or developer) is gained when the apartment can be rented anywhere above the marginal cost curve and below the market price. The consumer surplus is the area of the triangle labeled "consumer surplus," and producer surplus is the area of the triangle labeled "producer surplus." The total surplus is the sum of the consumer surplus and the producer surplus.

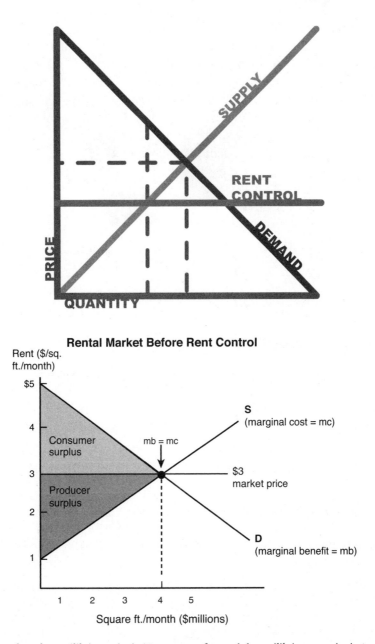

Rental Market Before Rent Control

Rent ($/sq. ft./month)

$5

4

Consumer surplus

mb = mc

S (marginal cost = mc)

3    $3 market price

Producer surplus

2

1

D (marginal benefit = mb)

1   2   3   4   5

Square ft./month ($millions)

The rental market equilibrium price is $3 per square foot, and the equilibrium quantity is 4 million square feet. At this point, the maximum total surplus is achieved. The consumer surplus and producer surplus are evenly distributed in this example: marginal benefit equals marginal cost (mb = mc).

When the government decides rents are too high and initiates rent control, the producer surplus decreases, and the consumer surplus increases. The accompanying figure shows why this is so. If the rent control is $2 per square foot per month rather than the $3 the landlord would have gotten at the market price, there is a decrease in producer surplus. The consumer picks up some of that benefit, but since the landlord has no incentive to rent out the apartment for less than his marginal cost curve, the consumer surplus is limited by the 2 million square feet supplied.

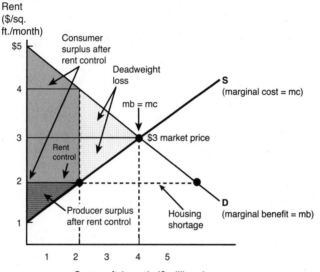

When a rent control is imposed of $2 per square foot, the producer surplus is decreased, and the consumer surplus is increased to the extent that the consumer benefits from a reduction in price from $3 per square foot to $2 per square foot. Both the consumer and the producer lose some benefit because the producer, the landlord, is unwilling to rent out or build additional housing beyond the marginal cost curve. The total surplus is reduced by the area above the marginal cost curve, below the marginal benefit curve, and between the quantity built or rented of 2 million square feet and the equilibrium quantity. Since the producer is not willing to rent or build until there is some benefit, there is also a housing shortage.

The consumer surplus after rent control is imposed is the area bounded by the net rent ($5 − $2/square foot), the $2 rent control, the 2 million square feet supplied, and the marginal benefit curve. This can be calculated by dividing the consumer surplus into a rectangle and a triangle, taking the area of each and summing them.

The producer surplus after rent control can be calculated by the area of the triangle with the height equal to the rent capped at $2 per square foot and starting at $1 per square foot; the base is at the 2 million square feet supplied.

After calculating the consumer surplus and producer surplus after rent control, we can find the total surplus after rent control, which is consumer surplus plus producer surplus. We can then find the difference between the total surplus before rent control and after rent control. This difference is the *deadweight loss* to society.

Let's do the math.

DO THE MATH

Producer surplus before rent control:

$\frac{1}{2}$ base × height = $\frac{1}{2}$ [4 × (3 – 1 = 2)] = **4 (in $millions)**

Consumer surplus before rent control:

$\frac{1}{2}$ base × height = $\frac{1}{2}$ [4 × (5 – 3 = 2)] = **4 (in $millions)**

Total surplus before rent control:

= 4 + 4 = 8 **(in $millions)**

With a rent control of $2/square foot/month, the producer surplus is re-calculated.

Producer surplus after rent control:

$\frac{1}{2}$ base × height = $\frac{1}{2}$ [2 × (2 – 1 = 1)] = 1 **(in $millions)**

To calculate the consumer surplus after rent control, sum the area bounded by the net rent ($5 - $2/square foot), the $2 rent control, the 2 million square feet supplied, and the marginal benefit curve. The area above the producer surplus after rent control is divided into a rectangle and a triangle. The sum of the two areas is the consumer surplus after rent control.

Consumer surplus after rent control:

The triangle = $\frac{1}{2}$ base × height = $\frac{1}{2}$ [2 × (5 − 4 = 1)] = 1

The rectangle = (base = 2) × [height = (4 – 2 = 2)] = 4

Triangle + rectangle = 1 + 4 = **5**

Consumer surplus before rent control = **$4 million**

Consumer surplus after rent control = **$5 million**

Producer surplus before rent control = **$4 million**

Producer surplus after rent control = **$1 million**

Total surplus before rent control = **$8 million**

Total surplus after rent control = 5 + 1 = **$6 million**

Deadweight loss =

Total surplus before rent control – total surplus after rent control = $8 million – $6 million = $2 million

The example of rent control shows how imposing a binding price ceiling reduces the total surplus. It also shows how rent control redistributes consumer surplus and producer surplus, with the consumer surplus increasing for those who still find housing and the producer surplus decreasing.

Another downside to rent control is the loss of incentive for producers to supply additional units of rental space. The marginal benefit, or demand curve, of the consumer is below equilibrium price and above equilibrium quantity: there is demand for more housing at a lower price. At the same time, suppliers will only supply housing at a lower price at their marginal cost curve of 2 million square feet, creating a housing shortage. The housing shortage is the difference between the quantity demanded and the quantity supplied at the rent controlled price. This can be seen on the accompanying figure.

How Price Ceilings and Floors Create a Deadweight Loss

Rent control is a form of *price ceiling*. The same mechanism is in play with the imposition of a *price floor*. A *minimum wage* is an example of a price floor. A minimum wage is the lowest wage an employer may offer to a worker. The government sometimes enacts a minimum wage to protect workers' ability to earn enough money to get by. Without a minimum wage, it is possible that employers will pay such a meager wage that the worker resorts to supplementing his or her income with a second or third job or with a government supplement.

> **DEFINITION**
>
> A **price ceiling** is a maximum price imposed by law, and a **price floor** is a minimum price imposed by law.

The supply and demand model demonstrates how a minimum wage creates a deadweight loss for society as employers pay more than the equilibrium price. If you flip over the rent control chart, you can imagine a minimum wage or price floor chart. The supply curve represents the supply of labor. The demand curve represents the demand for the employers of labor. If the equilibrium price is at $3.50 per hour, and the minimum wage is $7.00 per hour, the employer pays $3.50 per hour more than the market price. The worker gets paid $3.50 per hour more than at market price. The quantity of labor supplied at $7.00 per hour is much higher than the quantity of labor demanded at that wage, causing an oversupply of labor. Calculating the consumer (employer) surplus and producer (labor) surplus before and after the imposition of a minimum wage confirms a transfer of surplus from the consumer (employer) to the producer (worker). So the worker with a job does benefit from the minimum wage, which is the goal of the minimum wage; but, if you add up the total consumer surplus and producer surplus before and after the minimum wage is enacted, there is less total surplus after a minimum wage is imposed. The difference is the deadweight loss. The oversupply of labor, it can be argued, causes a small increase in unemployment.

The net benefit of enacting a minimum wage remains controversial. For example, a recent comparison of U.S. contiguous states shows there is no reduction in employment as a result of imposing a minimum wage.

INTERESTING FACT

Black markets pop up when there is a shortage, sometimes caused by a price ceiling. Shortages result from binding price ceilings because there is more demand than supply, as we saw from the rent control example. Black markets satisfy a portion of the lack of supply, but usually not at market price.

Price ceilings can cause other market inefficiencies. The shortages created by a price ceiling forces consumers to waste time trying to find what they need, whether it is an apartment or gasoline during a gas shortage. Another negative of price ceilings is that suppliers have no incentive to spend money for a quality product when they can't get at least the market price.

Price ceilings and floors are usually put in place to be of benefit to the disadvantaged. Sometimes they are enacted to support an industry that is vital to society, such as agriculture. Since farmers can lose crops because of the whims of nature, yet society needs food, governments sometimes support the agriculture industry with a price floor. As we have seen, this can create inefficiencies in the market, but governments have to weigh all the costs and benefits beyond market efficiency when they develop policies.

The Effect of a Sales Tax on the Market

A sales tax is imposed by the government to generate revenue. We can use the supply and demand model to learn how a sales tax affects consumer surplus and producer surplus.

A fixed sales tax, or *excise tax*, added to the purchase of a product shifts the supply curve to the left at every given price by the amount of the tax. The market equilibrium moves up along the demand curve from E_1 to E_2, resulting in a new equilibrium at a higher price and a lower quantity. Both the consumer surplus and the producer surplus are reduced. Part of the reduction goes to the government in the form of taxes. In addition, a deadweight loss is created, where no party receives a benefit.

A percentage tax has the same effect as a fixed tax, but when calculating S_2, the price rises more with a percentage tax as the quantity increases.

Effect of a Fixed Sales Tax on the Market

A fixed sales tax raises the price for consumers and reduces the income of producers. The supply curve shifts to the left and the market equilibrium shifts up along the demand curve from E_1 to E_2. Both consumer surplus and producer surplus decrease, and a deadweight loss is created.

In theory, the market is most efficient when the forces of supply and demand can operate freely. Price controls—whether price ceilings or floors—and sales taxes can create inefficiencies in the market, resulting in a loss of the benefits of trade. Government policymakers must weigh all factors when enacting laws that affect the natural movement of the market towards equilibrium, including the loss of these benefits.

The Least You Need to Know

- The consumer surplus is the benefit the consumer receives by buying a good below the price they are willing to pay. It is calculated by the area above the market price and below the demand curve.
- The producer benefits from selling his or her product when the market price, or price received, is above the minimum price the producer is willing to receive for the good. The difference is the producer surplus. It is calculated by the area below the market price and above the supply curve.
- Gains from trade are greatest at the market equilibrium price and quantity.
- The total surplus is the sum of the consumer surplus and the producer surplus. It is decreased when the market is inefficient, such as when the government imposes price controls or a sales tax.

CHAPTER 9

How Consumers Make Choices

Consumers are a vital part of the economy. Consumer spending accounts for well over 50 percent of GDP in most countries. Understanding consumer behavior is therefore of deep interest to economists and businesses.

Most economists believe that consumers are rational and therefore always do what is in their best interests. Whether at a restaurant, a supermarket, or buying from an online mega-store like Amazon, consumers will choose products that give them the most satisfaction. What's more, they have a limited budget, so they will only spend as much as they can afford. The choices consumers make form the basis of the demand curve.

This chapter describes how consumers make choices, why they choose products and services that give them the most satisfaction, how to measure the mixture of a bundle of goods and services that makes them happiest, the basis of the demand curve, and how income and substitution effects play a role in consumer choice.

In This Chapter

- Measuring consumer satisfaction
- Getting what you want within your budget
- Maximizing consumer utility
- Utility and the demand curve

Consumers Aim for Maximum Happiness

Understanding what makes a consumer tick is less quantifiable than analyzing a firm. Although in the United States corporations are treated as people under the law, businesses don't make choices because of a preference or to be maximally satisfied. Yet economists studying consumer behavior need a way to understand how consumers do make their choices.

Economists use the concept of *utility* to describe the satisfaction a consumer gets from a good or service. The theory is that the rational consumer tries to maximize his or her utility, or happiness. Starting with this assumption, economists constructed a model to understand individual and collective consumer behavior.

> **INTERESTING FACT**
>
> In 1789, Jeremy Bentham published a book titled *An Introduction to the Principles of Morals and Legislation*, which popularized the concept of utility. In it, he writes, "By utility is meant that property in any object, whereby it tends to produce benefit, advantage, pleasure, good, or happiness, ... if a particular individual, then the happiness of that individual ...." Bentham became known as the founder of Utilitarianism. The idea was also put forth by Thomas Bayes—the mathematician/statistician famous for "Bayes' Theorem" in probability theory—and Daniel Bernoulli, another brilliant mathematician. Utilitarianism is a broad theory and takes many forms. Consumer theory incorporates a narrow form of utilitarianism.

The first step in analyzing how a consumer makes choices is to identify the individual's *consumption bundle*—the assortment of goods and services consumed. The next step is to measure the amount of utility, or satisfaction, the consumer gets from the consumption bundle. The relationship between the two—the consumption bundle and the amount of utility it generates—is the *utility function*.

> **DEFINITION**
>
> **Utility** is a measure of the satisfaction the consumer derives from the consumption of goods and services. A **consumption bundle** is the set of all goods and services consumed by an individual. The **utility function** is the total utility generated by any given consumption bundle.

A consumer's utility is measured in units of utils. The util is an imaginary unit, since it is measuring a feeling—satisfaction or happiness. Real or not, it is used to quantify a consumer's utility and is fundamental to our understanding of how consumers make choices.

Total and Marginal Utility

How does all of this relate to the real world?

Imagine it's a hot day, and you have a craving for a strawberry ice cream cone. You go to the nearest Ben and Jerry's or Häagen-Dazs store and buy a strawberry ice cream cone with chocolate sprinkles. You take a walk around the block as you finish the ice cream and think to yourself, "Boy, was that good!" You can still taste the strawberry ice cream as a little voice inside tries to convince you to buy another.

Straining to tame the urge to have another cone and weighing calories versus pleasure, you give in to your dark side and head back to the ice cream store. After finishing a second ice cream cone, the little voice re-emerges, tugging at your better instincts. You cave in again and go back to the ice cream store for another strawberry cone with chocolate sprinkles. You continue your stroll while finishing the cone. Then you wonder if you should have just one more. This time, having another ice cream cone is not as appealing because your craving is satisfied. You have just experienced *diminishing marginal utility*. We can plot this.

The *total utility* is the aggregate amount of satisfaction, also called utility, gotten from a good or service. When the total utility is plotted against the quantity of the good or service, the total utility rises at first until it reaches a peak, the maximum total utility, and then diminishes as the good or service generates less satisfaction. The *marginal utility* is the incremental change in total utility as more is consumed. The marginal utility curve shows the relationship between marginal utility per good or service and the quantity of the good or service. The *principle of diminishing marginal utility* describes the incremental decrease in total utility received by consuming one more of the good or service. The more consecutive ice cream cones you eat, the less satisfaction you get from each additional cone. The principle of diminishing marginal utility has some exceptions, but it is true in most cases.

📖 **DEFINITION**

> **Total utility** is the aggregate amount of satisfaction received from a good or service. **Marginal utility** is the change in utility generated by consuming one additional unit of the good or service. The **principle of diminishing marginal utility** states that each successive unit of a good or service consumed adds less to total utility than the previous unit.

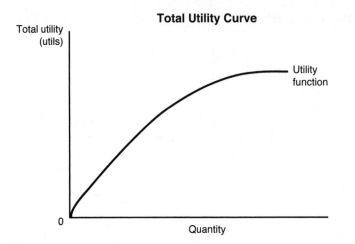

The total utility of a good or service is measured against the quantity consumed. The total utility peaks
to a maximum utility level and then begins to diminish as more of the good or service is consumed.

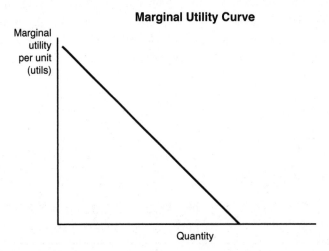

The marginal utility curve slopes downward, since the consumer receives
diminishing utility with each additional good or service consumed.

Budget Constraints

Even with a credit card, most consumers spend within their budget. Given all the goods and services a consumer needs or wants, he or she will choose which good or service is more important
than another. The consumer ranks which goods and services generate the most satisfaction but
also lie within his or her *budget constraint.* Income and the price of goods and services limit what

the consumer can spend. Economists call the set of all *affordable* consumption bundles his or her *consumption possibilities*.

How does this work? Let's go to the deli to find out. The Main Street Deli sells two of your favorite foods—chicken tidbits and baked beans. Your income per day is $30. You have already spent $14 of your daily income on breakfast and lunch, leaving you with $16 to spend on tidbits and baked beans for dinner. So you have to decide how much of each you want, assuming you will spend the entire $16. If you want more tidbits, you will have to forego some baked beans. The opportunity cost of buying more chicken tidbits is giving up some baked beans.

DEFINITION

> **Budget constraint** refers to combinations of goods and services that a consumer may purchase given current prices with all of his or her given income. **Consumption possibilities** are the set of all affordable consumption bundles.

The first step is to determine your *budget line*. The budget line depicts all the possible combinations of quantities of chicken tidbits and baked beans you can make if you spend all of your income. To see what this looks like on a graph, we need to know the price per pound of the tidbits and baked beans. We already know that you have $16 to spend. Chicken tidbits cost $2.00 per pound, and baked beans are $1.00 per pound. We can create a table of a few possible consumption bundles that are on your budget line. The budget line is the boundary between what is affordable or not given your budget.

In order to find out what some combinations of chicken tidbits and baked beans would equal your available income, use this equation: **(quantity of tidbits × price of tidbits) + (quantity of baked beans × price of baked beans) = $16.00.**

Consumption Possibilities Given Price of Tidbits = $2.00, Price of Baked Beans = $1.00, and Available Income = $16.00

Consumption Bundle	Quantity of Tidbits	Quantity of Baked Beans
A	8	0
B	6	4
C	4	8
D	2	12
E	0	16

With this information, you can draw the budget line.

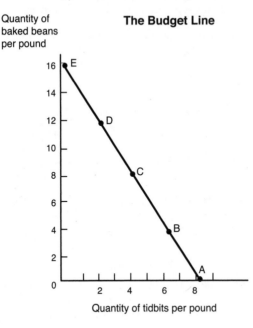

The budget line in this example is the set of combinations of chicken tidbits and baked beans that equals your expendable income of $16.00.

The budget line in this example is the set of combinations of goods and services that equals income. The possible combinations are on the budget line. They represent trade-offs, or the opportunity cost of choosing more of one good at the expense of the other. Any combination of goods or services outside the budget line is unaffordable. Any consumption bundle below the budget line is affordable but does not maximize utility for that consumption bundle because some money is saved.

The slope of the budget line tells us the opportunity cost of each good in terms of the other. This trade-off of goods and services is necessary because of the consumer's budget constraint. The relationship between the amounts of each good that must be foregone to have more of the other is the *relative price* of one good in terms of the other. The relative price of the good on the X axis in terms of the good on the Y axis is minus the slope of the budget line.

When income increases or decreases, the entire budget line shifts outward or inward. As income increases, more of each good and service can be consumed; with less income, less of each good or service is consumed.

Optimizing Consumption Choice

So far, we know that we can choose combinations of our favorite goods and services as long as we keep within our budget. We would also like to know how to make the *best* choice—the optimum choice. To find out, we have to measure your satisfaction using the unit called utils. Since this is a subjective measure, only you can assign these numbers. You can fill in your own table and follow the logic of optimal consumption with a budget restriction by adding a column to the accompanying table for the amount of utils you might get from chicken tidbits, representing how much utility you get, and another column for the amount of utils you might get from baked beans. We will add util quantities as well.

Consumption Bundle	Quantity of Tidbits	Utility from Tidbits (utils)	Quantity of Baked Beans	Utility from Baked Beans (utils)	Total Utility (utils)
A	8	31	0	0	31
B	6	28	4	16	44
C	4	21	8	28	49
D	2	12	12	32	44
E	0	0	16	34	34

You can see that consumption bundle C gives you the maximum utility, with a total utility of 49 utils. The *optimal consumption bundle* is the consumption bundle that maximizes a consumer's total utility given his or her budget line. All the consumption bundles must also be on the budget line.

✏️ **TAKE-AWAY MESSAGE**

Since a consumer is restricted by a budget, the consumption bundles must lie on the budget line. In the example of chicken tidbits and baked beans, you are choosing some of each. If you want more chicken tidbits, you have to give up some baked beans. If you want more baked beans, you must give up some chicken tidbits. Out of all the combinations of choices that make up your consumption bundles, your goal is to choose the bundle that gives you the greatest satisfaction, or utility.

Using a util as the unit of satisfaction, you want to know *the consumption bundle that gives you the greatest total utility given your budget constraint*. In the example shown in the accompanying table, you would choose consumption bundle C, where the total utility is 49.

We can get a more precise measurement of how much utility can be obtained from a consumption bundle by using marginal analysis. Using marginal analysis, we will be able to find out how much of your dollar (or other currency) you would like to spend on either chicken tidbits or baked beans.

Marginal Utility per Dollar (or Other Currency)

To see if your favorite consumption bundle gives you the most benefit, we will have to do a bit of math. We want to know how much additional satisfaction you get from spending more on tidbits versus baked beans—the *marginal utility per dollar* is the additional utility from spending one more dollar on that good or service. Knowing how much additional satisfaction you get per dollar quantifies the utility you get as it relates to price and allows you to compare marginal utility per price across consumption bundles.

Marginal utility per dollar is calculated by dividing the marginal utility of one unit of the good by the price of one unit of the good: MU_{good}/P_{good}. Applying this relationship to each consumption bundle in our example of chicken tidbits and baked beans gives an accurate picture of satisfaction per dollar spent.

Using information from the table that includes utility, we'll add columns for marginal utility per dollar for chicken tidbits and baked beans.

Quantity of Tidbits (pounds)	Utility from Tidbits (utils)	Marginal Utility per Pound of Tidbits (utils)	Marginal Utility per Dollar (utils) Of Tidbits	Quantity of Baked Beans	Utility from Baked Beans (utils)	Marginal Utility per Pound of Baked Beans (utils)	Marginal Utility per Dollar (utils) of Baked Beans
8	31			0	0	—	—
		1.5	$.75			4	$4
6	28			4	16		
		3.5	$1.75			3	$3
4	21			8	28		
		4.5	$2.25			1	$1
2	12			12	32		
		6	$3			.5	$.5
0	0	—	—	16	34		

Using the information on the table above, we will find the marginal utility per dollar of each consumption bundle. We want to see if the marginal utility for each food and each consumption bundle changes when we factor in price.

The *optimal consumption rule* or the *equal marginal principal* states that the marginal utility per **dollar** spent on each good or service in a consumption bundle is the same when a consumer maximizes utility: $MU_{good1}/P_{good1} = MU_{good2}/P_{good2}$. A consumer can choose the combination of goods that is closest to maximizing his or her utility by spending $1.00 more on the good that has the **higher** marginal utility and $1.00 less on the other good.

 DO THE MATH

The marginal utility is the change in utility generated by consuming one additional unit of the good or service. Recall that from the ice cream cone example, we found that the marginal utility decreases the more a good is consumed.

- Marginal utility (MU) = change in total utility = ΔTU

    Change in quantity = ΔQ

- To find the marginal utility per dollar:

    1. Find the marginal utility (MU) of each good, as listed in the accompanying table.

    2. Find the price per pound. Here the price for chicken tidbits is $2.00/pound and for baked beans $1.00/pound.

    3. Divide the marginal utility per pound by the price using marginal analysis: $MU_{tidbits}/P_{tidbits}$ and $MU_{baked\ beans}/P_{baked\ beans}$.

- To find the bundle that maximizes utility with a budget constraint, follow the optimal consumption rule:

    $$MU_{tidbits}/P_{tidbits} = MU_{baked\ beans}/P_{baked\ beans}$$

The only consumption bundle where both goods have an equal marginal utility per dollar is C. Therefore, C is the optimal consumption bundle, where the marginal utility per dollar is 2 for both goods.

Consumer Utility and the Demand Curve

The demand curve we've been using in the supply and demand model is familiar to us. Price on the Y axis is related to quantity demanded on the X axis by the law of demand: as the price of a good decreases, the quantity demanded of that good increases. Marginal utility can offer additional insight into why the demand curve has a downward slope.

The optimal consumption rule is one reason the demand curve has a downward slope. To review, it tells us that all goods have the same marginal utility per dollar. If the marginal utility for one good in a consumption bundle declines, an individual can maximize his or her utility by choosing another good in the bundle with a higher marginal utility *per dollar*. Since the combination of goods chosen by the consumer will be the bundle that maximizes his or her utility, the curve representing the consumer bundles will be downward sloping: a lower price will result in a higher quantity of goods demanded and vice versa.

Another way to look at the demand curve is to think about the opportunity costs, as we did with producer surplus. The consumer is choosing a particular consumption bundle and in doing so foregoes spending his or her dollar on another good. The consumer substitutes a less expensive good for the more expensive good, thereby increasing the quantity demanded for the less expensive good. This is known as the *substitution effect*.

The *income effect* describes how a change in the price of a good, such as a person's house, affects the demand curve. Since buying a house uses up a large portion of an individual's expendable income, the purchase will influence how much the consumer is willing to spend on other goods. If it is a *normal good*—where demand rises with an increase in income but falls with a decrease in income—purchasing a house can result in the consumer's purchasing less expensive goods. Demand for an inferior good will decrease with a rise in income and increase with a fall in income.

The Least You Need to Know

- Consumers choose a basket of goods and services by weighing which combination offers the greatest amount of satisfaction, which economists call utility.
- The total utility, or satisfaction, a consumer receives by consuming a good reaches a peak and then diminishes as the consumer gets less satisfaction with each additional unit of the good or service, known as diminishing marginal utility.
- Consumers make choices that are restricted by their budget, known as their budget line.

- When choosing a consumer bundle that maximizes his or her utility under a budget constraint, consuming more of one good means foregoing more of the other good.

- The most accurate way to determine the optimal basket of goods and services is to calculate the marginal utility per dollar or other currency.

- The demand curve is related to the choices a consumer makes to maximize his or her utility. It is downward sloping as the consumer chooses higher quantities of goods and services at lower prices.

CHAPTER 10

The Firm: Maximizing Profit

An entrepreneur who starts a company is enthusiastic about an idea and hopes to launch a profitable business. That's a worthwhile plan because being creative, building something from nothing, and also being able to make a living doing what you love is the best of all worlds. Every successful business was started by someone with an idea.

This chapter describes what all businesses need to know: how much to produce in order to maximize profits. Each industry has its own characteristics, but all businesses in a competitive market—where many firms compete for the favor of the consumer—face similar market realities: they have revenue and expenses. Gaining more revenue than costs is the name of the game.

In This Chapter

- What is a profit?
- The cost structure of a firm
- Maximizing profits
- When a firm should call it quits
- Short-run and long-run decisions of a firm

How to Make a Profit

Having a good idea and selling it to others is the first step in building a business. Whether Susan wants to establish an organic food store in her neighborhood or whether Mark envisions a network of college students posting their thoughts, activities, and pictures on the internet, doing research on potential competitors is a worthwhile next step. If the idea is viable, the other necessities are capital (whether from the business owner himself or herself, a bank loan, or venture capital), materials needed for production, and labor. Other costs include rent for the office and/or warehouse, marketing, and professional advisors—an accountant and a business lawyer. Established businesses have the same considerations, but on a larger scale.

Once the business is up and running, it's time to take a hard look at how to increase revenue and produce just the right amount at a minimum cost so that revenue exceeds expenses. The business is then profitable, at least from an accounting point of view. In a perfectly competitive market, the sales price will be the market price. Is it as profitable as it could be? We'll dig down into the numbers to see how they add up.

Computing the Profit: Accounting Profit vs. Economic Profit

In a competitive market, profit is made when total revenue (TR) is greater than total costs (TC). The difference is the profit: **TR − TC = Profit.**

Total revenue is the price multiplied by the quantity sold: **TR = PXQ.**

We're assuming the market is competitive, with enough competition so that the firm has to take the market price as its own. So if the market price for a widget is $5.00, the business will have to sell widgets for no more than $5.00. If it charges more, there will be no buyers. Each additional unit of widgets will sell for $5.00, which is also called its *marginal revenue (MR)*.

The costs are either *explicit* or *implicit.* Explicit costs are the expenses of a business that are paid outright with money. Implicit costs are the opportunity costs representing the value, in dollar terms or other currency, of benefits lost by not doing something else.

There are two kinds of profit: the *accounting profit* and the *economic profit.* The accounting profit is calculated for the purpose of taxes and public reporting. The explicit costs and depreciation are deducted from the revenue to find the profit.

> **DEFINITION**
>
> **Accounting profit** is the revenue of a business minus the explicit costs and depreciation. **Economic profit** is the revenue of a business minus the explicit and implicit costs and depreciation—the reduction in value for use over time.

The opportunity costs are important because businesses make better decisions when they can compare the gains or losses they incur by not using their resources in other ways. The implicit cost of capital—foregone salary, other potential uses of money, equipment, and property—is sometimes less than the accounting costs.

Opportunity costs also provide a more informed basis for individuals to make career choices. Calculating the opportunity cost of leaving a job to go to school is a worthwhile step to take before making a final decision. A salary received now might or might not be as valuable as going back to school to learn new skills. These decisions can best be made after comparing the potential benefits of being in business against the value of a more desirable or satisfying career. Likewise, the choice of leaving a good-paying job to start a business should take into account the opportunity costs of the salary not earned. That doesn't mean starting a business wouldn't be the right decision, but knowing the opportunity cost results in a selection backed by the numbers.

The implicit costs can be listed on a balance sheet in the same way as the explicit costs. Let's compare a balance sheet for a one-year-old business using the accounting profit and the economic profit. Let's say revenue is $200,000, and accounting costs—including food, labor, rent, and equipment rental—total $150,000. Using the accounting profit method, the pre-tax profit is $50,000.

The economic profit method includes the opportunity cost of the salary not earned resulting from the decision to open a business instead. We'll assume that the new business owner had a salary of $75,000 before opening the business. The opportunity cost of starting the business is therefore $75,000. This would show as a loss of $25,000 because the $75,000 salary is an implicit cost listed under expenses. Since this is only the first year for this business, it is still possible to make an economic profit in the future if revenue grows more than the explicit and implicit costs.

Accounting Profit vs. Economic Profit

Accounting Profit Year 1	Economic Profit Year 1
Revenue: $200,000	Revenue: $200,000
Expenses:	Expenses:
	Explicit
Food: $15,000	Food: $15,000
Labor: $60,000	Labor: $60,000
Rent: $40,000	Rent: $40,000
Equipment rental $35,000	Equipment rental: $35,000
Total Expenses: $150,000	*Implicit (opportunity costs)*
Pre-tax accounting profit: **$50,000**	Wages foregone: $75,000
	Total Expenses: $225,000
	Economic profit (loss): **($25,000)**

You may realize by now how important the concept of opportunity cost is in order to understand the economy of consumers and firms. Opportunity costs play a role in producer surplus, in the marginal benefit curve, in generating a demand curve, and here in figuring economic profit.

Analyzing a Firm's Cost Structure

The costs a business incurs come in two flavors: *fixed costs* and *variable costs*. Fixed costs are those that have to be paid whether or not the firm is producing anything. Examples are the rent on office and warehouse space and land, utilities, and loan payments and other recurring costs. Variable costs relate to production, and so change with the amount of production or the kind of products the business creates. Variable costs include salaries and employee perks, materials, marketing, shipping costs, and all other expenses of production. Both fixed costs and variable costs include opportunity costs. The opportunity cost for the fixed cost might be the money spent on capital equipment in another business that could have been spent for more labor, for example. The opportunity cost for variable costs might be not having produced a different product.

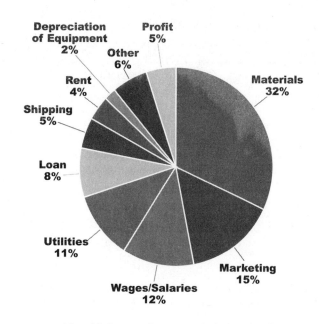

Businesses analyze costs to identify how to improve their bottom line. Let's see what's involved.

Fixed and Variable Costs

Now that you know what fixed and variable costs represent, we turn to the *cost structure* of a business. The cost structure is the various types of expenses a firm takes into account when analyzing the business operations. It involves the relationship between input and output, fixed and variable costs, and when producing one more unit would become unprofitable. These calculations help businesses streamline their operations so they can maximize their profits.

Let's start by identifying the relationships between the costs.

- *Total costs* of a business are simply the sum of the fixed costs (FC) and variable costs (VC): **TC = FC + VC**.

- *Fixed costs* (FC) are costs that have to be paid whether or not the firm is producing anything.

- *Variable costs* (VC) are business expenses that depend on production output. Output is units produced by a business (Q).

- *Averaged fixed costs* (AFC) are fixed costs (FC) divided by *output* (Q): **FC/Q = AFC**.

- *Average variable costs* (AVC) are variable costs divided by output (Q): **VC/Q = AVC**.

- Average total costs are total costs (TC) divided by output (Q): **TC/Q = ATC**.

- Marginal Costs (MC) are the change in total costs divided by the change in output (Q): **MC = ΔTC/ΔQ**.

These relationships are better understood by seeing the data in a table or visualizing them in a chart. You can get a better sense of how the costs relate to each other by looking carefully at the accompanying table of the cost structure for Widget, Inc., a company that produces the famous widget. Notice patterns of increasing and decreasing numbers as they relate to the number of workers or output.

Worker Productivity

Comparing the number of workers added with the output produced, you will see that at first, output increases as workers are added. When there is one worker, 1,000 widgets are produced. Two workers produce 3,000 widgets; three workers produce 6,000 widgets, a difference of 3,000 widgets. Four workers produce 7,000 widgets, a difference of just 1,000 widgets from adding another worker. At this point in production, division of labor and specialization has increased output at a fast pace.

As workers are added, the quantity of output per worker diminishes. Each incremental, or marginal, worker produces less and less output. This is called the *law of diminishing returns to an input,* in this case labor. The reason output diminishes varies depending on the industry. Production may have a bottleneck at some point. Employees may have to work together on a project and may sometimes get in each other's way, or they may have to spend time coordinating with each other, whereas they might have gotten more done when working alone. Whatever the reason, the *productivity* of workers decreases as workers are added. The law of diminishing returns to an input also applies to the materials used in production, such as when too much fertilizer added to a field harms the crop. Labor and fertilizer are both *inputs* to production.

DEFINITION

The **law of diminishing marginal returns to an input** describes the decline in the marginal product of that input when the quantity of the input increases, if levels of all other inputs are fixed. **Productivity** is the measure of the amount of output per unit of input.

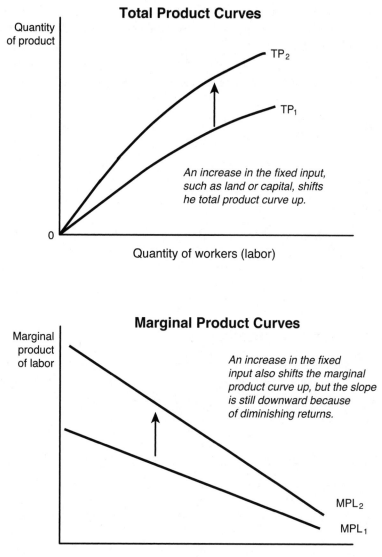

The *production function* is the relationship between the quantity of inputs a firm uses and the quantity of output it produces for a given *fixed input,* such as capital, which includes buildings and equipment. The total product curve shows how the quantity of output depends on the quantity of the *variable input* for a given quantity of the fixed input. Again, labor is a variable input as are resources. The additional quantity of output that is produced using one more unit of labor or other variable input is the *marginal product of labor* or other variable input. The marginal product of labor is equal to the slope of the total product curve—rise over run. It is calculated by the change in quantity of output divided by the change in quantity of labor: $\mathbf{MPL = \Delta Q/\Delta L}$.

In the short run, firms can add or subtract the amount of variable inputs to increase productivity.

 **DEFINITION**

A **fixed input** is an input whose quantity cannot be varied in the time period considered, usually the short run. Capital is a fixed input. A **variable input** is an input whose quantity can vary. Labor is a variable input. The **marginal product of labor** is the additional quantity of output that is produced using one more unit of labor.

Total, Average, and Marginal Costs

Returning to the table of the cost structure of Widgets, Inc., the column labeled **fixed costs** shows how the costs do not vary either with the number of workers or with the quantity of output. These costs must be paid whether 100,000 widgets are manufactured or zero widgets are manufactured, so fixed costs can be a headache if business is slow.

Variable costs increase with the number of workers added. Although variable costs only include the cost of labor in this table, in reality variable costs also include other expenses.

The **total costs** are the fixed costs and the variable costs combined. The total costs increase as more workers are added and output grows. The curve steepens with additional workers because of diminishing returns.

The **marginal cost**, which we will come back to, is the change in total costs divided by the change in the quantity of output: $\mathbf{MC = \Delta TC/\Delta Q}$. The slope of MC—the rise over run of the total cost curve—increases with an increase in output because of diminishing worker productivity.

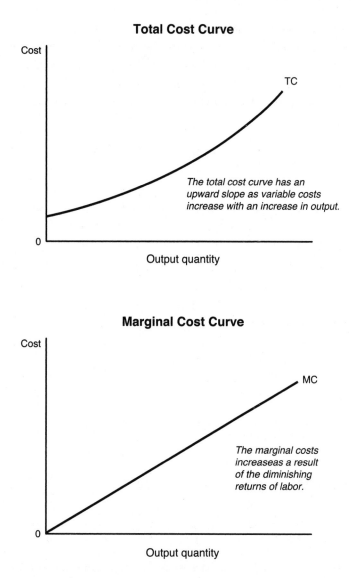

Total Cost Curve

Cost

TC

The total cost curve has an upward slope as variable costs increase with an increase in output.

0

Output quantity

Marginal Cost Curve

Cost

MC

The marginal costs increaseas a result of the diminishing returns of labor.

0

Output quantity

The next column for the cost structure of Widgets, Inc. is the **average fixed costs**. Taking an average of the fixed costs spreads them evenly over the quantity of output. These numbers descend as the output quantity increases, but since the output gradually decreases after it peaks, the average fixed costs begin to rise slightly.

Notice the **average variable cost** column—the average variable costs increase with more output. The bulk of the variable costs are labor costs, and when more labor is added, the variable costs rise. As long as the output continues to increase, the profits generated by the additional revenue will justify the addition of another worker. Once worker productivity begins to slow, the business owner will have to consider his or her next move.

The **average total costs** increase with a growth in output, since the variable costs rise as workers are added and become a greater portion of total costs.

What the business owner wants to know is will adding more workers increase profits or not? Will producing one more widget result in greater profits, or would it be better to keep production of widgets at its point of maximum profitability and produce something else instead? These questions can best be answered using marginal analysis. The column labeled **marginal costs (average)** provides important information to help the business owner decide what to do. The marginal costs are the costs to produce one more widget.

Notice that the marginal cost (MC) numbers do not ascend in a straight line. Instead, they peak at 100 and then descend. The data for other firms will yield different results, but the general relationship holds. (See the figures that include the marginal cost curves.) The increase in output slows down while the cost of labor goes up at the same pace. Marginal costs become negative because a tipping point is reached as the productivity of workers decreases, and additional workers can actually hamper the production process.

A typical graph of the marginal cost curve, which is idealized, does not usually reflect this drop. The idealized version looks like the Nike logo.

The Cost Structure of Widget, Inc.

Workers	Output	Fixed Costs	Variable Costs	Total Costs	Average Fixed Costs	Average Variable Costs	Average Total Costs	Marginal Costs (Average)
1	1,000	5,000	10,000	15,000	5.0	10.0	15.0	—
2	3,000	5,000	20,000	25,000	1.67	6.67	8.33	5
3	6,000	5,000	30,000	35,000	0.83	5.0	5.83	3
4	7,000	5,000	40,000	45,000	0.71	5.71	6.43	10
5	7,500	5,000	50,000	55,000	0.67	6.67	7.33	20
6	7,600	5,000	60,000	65,000	0.66	7.89	8.56	100
7	7,100	5,000	70,000	75,000	0.70	9.86	10.56	(20)

Let's review and summarize the relationship of the average total costs (ATC), the average fixed costs (AFC), and the average variable costs (AVC). The average total costs first decrease and then increase. This occurs because the total cost is a combination of the average fixed cost and the average variable cost. The average fixed costs are spread evenly over the total output. The fixed cost divided by the quantity of output is the fixed cost per unit of output, or the average fixed cost. As more units are produced, the average fixed cost goes down. The average variable cost is also divided by the quantity of output, so it is called the variable cost per unit of output:

TC = FC + VC

AFC = FC/Q

AVC = VC/Q

The average fixed cost moves in the opposite direction from the average variable cost: the average fixed cost decreases as the output increases because the fixed cost is spread out over more output. The average variable cost increases as the output increases because although each additional unit of labor costs the same amount, output per worker is decreasing.

At the start of production, average fixed costs have a greater impact on the average total cost because the fixed costs are spread over a few workers. This results in the average total cost curve and the marginal cost curve sloping downward. As more workers are added and output increases, the curves reverse because even as output increases, labor is less productive. At the same time, fixed costs are spread over more workers.

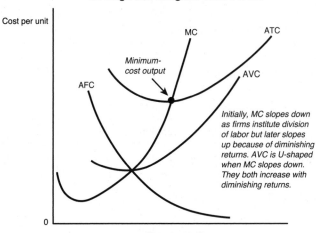

Average and Marginal Cost Curves

Initially, MC slopes downward as firms institute division of labor and specialization but later slopes upward because of diminishing returns. AVC is U-shaped when MC slopes down. They both increase with diminishing returns. The minimum-cost output occurs when the average total cost is equal to the marginal cost (ATC = MC).

The figure depicting the average cost curve and the marginal cost curve shows that the marginal cost curve crosses the average total cost curve at the *minimum average total cost:* ATC = MC. This is called the *minimum-cost output.* If the marginal cost is above the minimum-cost output, the average total cost is rising. If the marginal cost is below the minimum-cost output, the average total cost is falling.

> **DEFINITION**
>
> The **minimum-cost output** is the quantity of output at which average total cost is the lowest—when marginal cost equals the average total cost: **MC = ATC.**

Now that we've explored how to get the minimum-cost output, we turn to finding the quantity to produce that will maximize profit.

Maximizing Profit

The goal of every business is to achieve the maximum profit possible. This involves producing just the right amount of output so that every unit produced will be profitable. Let's see how that can happen.

Producing in a Perfectly Competitive Market

In a perfectly competitive market, there are many firms that sell the same product. Each firm represents a small share of the industry. The firm is therefore a *price taker* because it has to take the price that the market offers. Raising its price even a little bit would result in no sales.

It is also true that all consumers are price takers in a competitive market because the market is so large that the consumer cannot influence the price.

In a perfectly competitive market, the assumption is that the product under discussion is standardized—consumers view a particular good from one producer to be equivalent to the same good from any producer.

Another characteristic of a perfectly competitive market is that producers have free entry and exit into and out of the industry. The perfectly competitive market is covered in more detail in Part 4.

The assumption that the firm is part of a perfectly competitive market is the basis for the way it goes about calculating the optimal output required to maximize profit as well as the marginal revenue.

Producing the Optimal Quantity to Maximize Profit

To capture the maximum profit, the optimal quantity of output to produce occurs when the *marginal revenue* equals the marginal costs: **MR = MC**. This called the *profit maximization rule.*

Since the producer is a price taker, the marginal revenue is the market price, which is a horizontal line on a graph.

The marginal revenue is the change in total revenue generated by an additional unit of output. It is calculated by dividing the change in total revenue by the change in output: **MR = ΔTR/ΔQ.**

In the short run, producing as many units as possible spreads the fixed costs over more units. However, the quantity produced is limited by the marginal revenue.

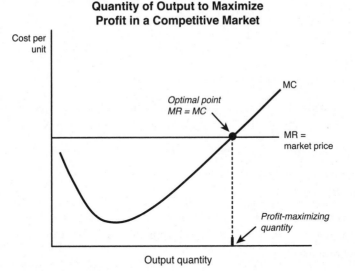

The quantity of output that maximizes profit is where the marginal cost curve crosses the marginal revenue curve, which is the market price in a perfectly competitive market: MR = MC.

A profit isn't always possible even if a firm is producing at its optimum output level, when MR = MC. It does mean that, given the firm's cost structure and the market price, when MR = MC the optimal quantity possible is produced so that either a small profit can be eked out or any loss is minimized.

Recall that a business is profitable when total revenue (TR) exceeds total cost (TC). Whether or not a profit is made depends on the following relationships:

- If TR is greater than TC, there is a profit.

- If TR equals TC, the business breaks even.

- If TR is less than TC, the business loses money.

Now the business owner wants to know what **market price per unit of the product** would guarantee a profit. At a minimum, he or she wants to know the break-even price and the price where the business loses money.

The first step is to find the per-unit profit. We can divide the equation Profit = TR − TC by output quantity: **Profit/Q = TR/Q − TC/Q.**

Since revenue is based on the market price in a perfectly competitive market, **TR/Q = ATR = market price (P).**

The **average total cost is TC/Q = ATC.**

As long as the market price is higher than the **average total cost (ATC)** of the quantity produced, the firm makes a profit. If the market price is less than the ATC, the firm loses money:

- If P (price) is greater than the ATC, the firm is profitable.

- If P is equal to ATC, the firm breaks even.

- If P is less than ATC, the firm loses money.

The three figures, *Market Price and Profitability,* show what factors cause the producer to break even, make a profit, or suffer a loss. As you study these figures, notice that the average total cost curve (ATC) begins at a high per-unit price and low output quantity. At the beginning of production, the fixed cost per unit produced is spread out over a small quantity, so the fixed cost is a greater portion of the ATC. As more units are produced, the fixed cost per unit decreases, and the variable costs become a larger component of the ATC.

The marginal cost (MC) rises for each additional unit produced, as the law of diminishing returns of the variable cost becomes a more important factor of the ATC than the fixed cost component. The goal is to produce the maximum output where MR = MC. In a competitive market, MR is the market price. If more units are produced than when MR = MC, each additional unit produced will be a loss to the producer, since cost is more than revenue. To find the optimal quantity to produce on the graph, locate the point at which MR = MC and find the corresponding output quantity. That is the *profit-maximizing point.*

The **total revenue (TR)** is the area of the rectangle with the market price as the height multiplied by the quantity of units produced as the width when MR = MC. The **total cost (TC)** is the area of a second rectangle with the ATC as the height and the quantity of units produced as the width.

The **profit** is the area of the rectangle with the height as the difference between the MC and ATC and the quantity of units produced as the width.

TR = P × Q

Profit = (MC – ATC) × Q

🖉 TAKE-AWAY MESSAGE

The goal is to produce the number of units (Q) when MR = MC, the profit-maximizing point.

Total revenue (TR) = P × Q; P = MR = market price in a competitive market.

Total cost (TC) = Price at ATC × Q

Profit = (MC – ATC) × Q; since MC = MR, the MR can be used instead of MC in this equation.

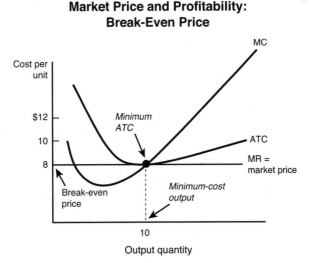

**Market Price and Profitability:
Break-Even Price**

The break-even price occurs when the market price of $8 is at the minimum-cost output of 10 units. The minimum-cost output occurs at the lowest point of the average total cost (ATC) curve. This is also the profit-maximizing quantity of output, which occurs when market price (MR) equals the marginal cost (MC).

The firm breaks even when the market price equals the average total cost, depicted in the figure *Market Price and Profitability: Break-Even Price.* In this figure, the market price is $8, and the minimum-cost output, which is at the lowest point of the ATC curve, is 10 units. The marginal cost (MC) crosses the ATC at this point, which is also the profit-maximizing quantity of output—when market price equals the marginal cost (also MR = MC).

Market Price and Profitability: Profit

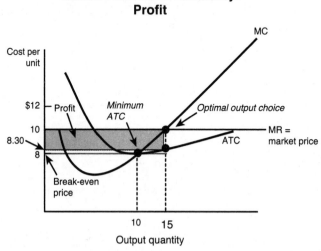

The firm is profitable when the market price is greater than the average total cost (ATC). Here the market price is $10 and the break-even price is $8, the minimum point on the ATC curve. The optimal output choice is the point where MC = MR (market price) at 15 units. The profit is the rectangle with (MC − ATC) × Q = ($10 − $8.30 = $1.70) × 15 = $25.50.

In the figure *Market Price and Profitability: Profit*, the market price, which is also the MR, is $10. The minimum-cost output is the lowest point of the ATC curve, in this case 10 units. We know that the break-even price is $8.00, where the MC curve crosses the ATC curve. The optimal output choice is where MC = MR, which is at $10. The profit is calculated by multiplying the optimal output choice, here at 15, by the difference between the MC (or MR) and the ATC ($8.30): ($10 − $8.30 = $1.70) × 15 = $25.50.

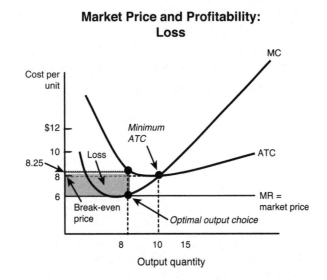

**Market Price and Profitability:
Loss**

*The market price is below the minimum ATC, which is at 10 units. The optimal output choice is
where MR = MC, here 8 units. At 8 units, the price at the ATC curve is $8.25. The loss to the firm
is ($8.25 − $6.00) × 8 units = ($18.00).*

A loss occurs when the market price is below the ATC. In the figure *Market Price and Profitability:
Loss*, the market price is $6.00, and the price at the ATC is $8.25 because the market price equals
the MC at the optimal output choice of 8 units. The loss is represented by the area of the rectangle ($8.25 − 6.00) × 8 units = ($18.00).

Losing Money: When to Call It Quits

Let's examine the decisions a producer must make when a product is not profitable or is losing
money. The only costs that the producer can control are the variable costs because as long as
the business stays in the industry—a long-run decision—the producer must continue to pay the
fixed costs. The fixed costs are considered a *sunk cost*, a cost that cannot be recovered. Here, we
are considering production in the short run.

We are addressing a production choice, not whether to go out of business. The goal is to maximize profits or minimize losses. Assuming that the fixed costs are sunk costs, the key option is
to monitor the variable costs to make sure they are covered by the revenues. This can be accomplished by comparing the relationship between the minimum average total cost and the market
price.

Determining the Short-Run Shutdown Price

The bottom line for the producer concerning when to stop producing in the short run is whether or not the market price is *below the minimum average variable cost*. Since the variable costs continue as long as units are produced, there is not enough total revenue to recoup the variable costs because no quantity of output sold at the market price exceeds the average variable cost. This fact outweighs any benefit that might be gained by offsetting some of the fixed costs if production continues. The minimum average variable cost is therefore the *shutdown price*—the price at which the firm must stop producing in the short run.

If, on the other hand, the market price is higher than the minimum average variable cost, the firm can continue production in the short run, since the cost is covered by the revenue.

Another scenario is that the market price is between the shutdown price and the break-even price. In this case revenue pays for the per-unit variable cost and some of the per-unit fixed cost. If the firm shuts down, it will be responsible for most of the fixed costs, even though the variable costs would be covered. So it is more profitable in this situation to keep producing in the short run.

If the market price remains above the shutdown price, or the minimum average variable cost point, the firm will continue to produce where MR = MC, which is also the marginal cost curve. The individual supply curve in the short run is therefore the same curve as the marginal cost curve above the minimum average variable costs. Below the minimum average variable cost, the firm would shut down or produce zero output.

When considering whether or not to stop production, the firm should compare the projected profits of producing with the profits or losses generated if production is discontinued. The decision would be the choice that yields the greatest profit or the smallest loss.

We will continue our discussion of the characteristics of perfect competition in Chapter 11. We will also explore profit maximization in the long run and how this incentive generates the long-run industry supply curve.

The Least You Need to Know

- Accounting profit or loss considers the total revenue and total explicit cost. Economic profit includes the opportunity cost as an implicit cost.
- Total cost is composed of fixed costs and variable costs. Average fixed costs decrease with increased output. Average variable costs increase with increased output.

- The optimal output quantity to maximize profit is when the marginal revenue of the last unit produced equals the marginal cost. The marginal revenue is the market price in a perfectly competitive market, with a horizontal curve at the market price.

- A firm is profitable if total revenue is equal to or greater than total cost. It is also profitable when the market price is higher than the break-even price at the minimum average total cost. If the market price is less than the break-even price, it suffers a loss.

- The firm's shutdown price is when the market price is below the minimum average variable cost. When the market price is higher than the shutdown price, the output quantity is where MR = MC.

- Fixed cost is not important in the short run when the firm considers when to shut down. In the long run fixed cost determines whether a firm will exit the market if the market price remains below the minimum ATC.

PART 3

Microeconomics: Market Structure

When firms are competing for your business, you have the advantage. The more firms, the better. With many firms producing a similar product, you get the best price. The competitive market is a healthy market.

Sometimes a firm will buy out its competitors or owns the bulk of a natural resource and is the sole supplier of goods to the market. As a result, it has complete control of the industry. This type of firm is a monopoly. Monopolies disadvantage the consumer because you, as a consumer, will have to accept the price set by the company. There is no choice. You may have a visceral dislike of monopolies, but here you will discover the economic reasons behind your emotional response.

The oligopoly and monopolistic competition are market structures that are less competitive than a market with perfect competition but more competitive than a monopoly. You might be surprised to learn which familiar companies belong in these categories.

After reading Part 3, you will likely conclude that, as a consumer, competition is your best friend.

Perfect Competition

The economic models that are used to describe how the consumer and producer achieve their goals assume that the market structure is one of perfect competition. Perfect competition is considered the most advantageous market condition in which to conduct business or, for the consumer, to buy his or her favorite products at the best price. Supply and demand function as they should in theory. Predictions of market behavior when there is a change in conditions are assumed to be reliable.

In this chapter we will explore the perfectly competitive market in greater detail.

In This Chapter

- The perfectly competitive market: many consumers and producers are price takers
- Free entry and exit into the market and the long-run supply curve
- Consumers and producers have perfect information on price, utility, and production
- Factor mobility, no transaction costs, and efficiency

Conditions for Perfect Competition

Certain conditions must exist for a market to be considered perfectly competitive. The hallmark of a perfect competition is a market with many sellers that all make the same or very similar products—they are standardized—so that a consumer can easily choose the best price and quantity available. Likewise, there must be many buyers to maintain a liquid demand. This condition lays the foundation for the other characteristics of the perfectly competitive market structure.

In a perfectly competitive market no existing firm has an advantage. Any new firm can enter the market and try to gain market share.

Producers and Consumers Are Price Takers

As we discussed in Chapter 10, in a perfectly competitive market, firms produce where marginal cost equals marginal revenue (MR = MC) to maximize profits. This is also the demand curve, which appears as a horizontal line at the market price on a diagram. (Do not confuse the demand curve of the firm with the demand curve for the entire market, which is downward sloping.)

The demand curve is *perfectly elastic*. Price elasticity of demand is the relationship of a change in the quantity demanded of a good and a change in its price. The more elastic the price, the more sensitive it is to a change in price by the firm above or below the market price. This means that if the producer raises the price even a little bit, there will be no sale because the consumer can get the product elsewhere at the market price.

For example, if you went to a bazaar in your favorite destination, you might see the same T-shirt with a picture of the city's major point of interest in many shops. The price is the same wherever you go. The shop that has a higher price is the one vendor that will not sell any T-shirts. He or she does not realize it's a perfectly competitive market!

DEFINITION

Perfect elasticity of demand is an elasticity in which infinitesimally small changes in price cause infinitely large changes in quantity.

The formula to calculate elasticity of demand is percent change in quantity divided by the percent change in price:

Elasticity of demand = $\%\Delta Q / \%\Delta P$

In a perfectly competitive market, MR = market price (P). Since there is no change in price at any quantity, the denominator, percent change in price, is zero, so it is undefined. Any price increase will result in a "no sale." At the same time, no matter the quantity produced, the market price will remain the same.

Price is also equal to the average revenue (AR), since the average revenue is just the revenue per unit (example: price per pound). We now have the equalities:

$$P = MR = MC = AR$$

The equalities P, AR, and MR only exist in a perfectly competitive market structure. The next few chapters examine the kind of market structures where these equivalences are *not* true.

These relationships explain why buyers and sellers are considered price takers in a perfectly competitive market. Since each firm has a very small share of the market, no individual seller can influence the market price; and since there are so many consumers, no buyer can influence the market price. Both sellers and buyers must take the price the market gives them.

> ✏ **TAKE-AWAY MESSAGE**
>
> In a market with perfect competition, since there are many buyers and sellers, they are price takers. This means they must buy or sell at the market price (P). The market price is also the marginal revenue (MR) and the average revenue (AR). On a diagram, it is a horizontal line at the given market price. A change in quantity does not change the price, which is also the marginal cost (MC), since the producer maximizes profit when MR = MC.
>
> The demand curve of the firm is also the market price, the same horizontal line, and it is perfectly elastic. Do not confuse the demand curve of the firm with the demand curve for the entire market, which is downward sloping.

In a very large market, such as the market for milk, the consumer is not in a position to bargain for a lower price. Since there are many other consumers that want to buy milk, the consumer has no choice but to buy at the market price. The milk producer is in the same position. With many competitors selling a homogeneous, interchangeable product, milk has to be sold at the market price.

The accompanying figure shows that the market price of $2.00 on a graph of the milk market is a horizontal line. A horizontal line indicates that quantity does not affect price. In a perfectly competitive market, no matter how many gallons of milk are bought or sold, the price of $2.00 remains the same. The market price is also the demand curve (D) for the milk-producing firm as well as the MR curve. At a quantity of 2 gallons of milk at point A, MC = MR. This is not the profit-maximizing output, though. The profit-maximizing output is 5 gallons of milk, at point B, where the MC curve cuts the MR curve from below.

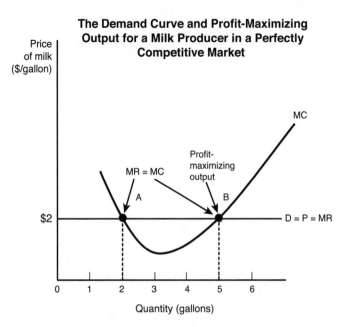

The demand curve (D) of the milk producer is a horizontal line at the market price of $2.00. The market price is also the marginal revenue (MR) price. The marginal cost (MC) curve intersects the MR curve at a quantity of 2 gallons at point A, where MR = MC. The profit-maximizing output is at a quantity of 5 gallons at point B, where the MC curve cuts the MR curve from below.

The market price can change for the milk industry with a change in demand or supply on the industry's supply and demand diagram (See Chapter 7). If there is an increase in demand because of news that milk is actually healthier than anyone thought, for example, the demand curve for milk would shift to the right, and the market price and quantity would be higher. Alternatively, if the news reported that milk was contaminated by radioactive traces, the demand would go down along with the market price and quantity, as the demand curve shifts to the left.

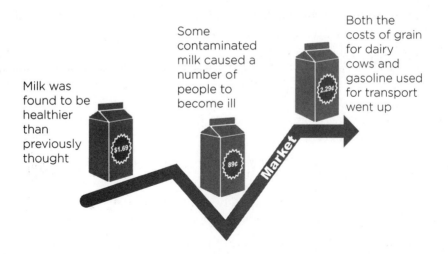

Milk was found to be healthier than previously thought

$1.69

Some contaminated milk caused a number of people to become ill

89¢

Both the costs of grain for dairy cows and gasoline used for transport went up

2.29¢

Market

The same would occur with a shift in the supply curve. Too much supply results in a decrease in market price and quantity, and too little supply results in an increase in market price and quantity.

The effect of too many or too few suppliers brings us to the next important characteristic of a perfectly competitive market: free entry and exit of firms.

Free Entry and Exit of Firms

In a perfectly competitive market, producers can decide whether or not it makes sense to produce in the short run or shut down production or remain in the industry in the long run by reviewing their individual cost-benefit analysis to determine what price and quantity gives them an economic profit. While there are many producers in a market or industry, each producer has a unique cost structure that determines whether the market price is high enough to generate the revenue they need to make an economic profit. The individual firm can continue producing or shut down in the short run, decide the quantity to produce if indeed the firm does not stop production, and choose to enter or leave the industry in the long run.

Entry and exit into and out of an industry depends on the time frame. In the previous chapter, we discussed the decision a producer faces when a product is unprofitable. The choices are:

- When the market price (P) is **greater than** the minimum **average variable cost (AVC)**, the producer should produce in the short run. If P is **less than** the minimum **average total cost (ATC)**, the variable costs will be covered as well as some of the fixed costs. If P is **greater than** the minimum ATC, the firm will be able to cover both the variable and the fixed costs.

- If P is **equal to** the minimum AVC, the producer can choose to produce product or not. Only the variable cost will be covered.

- If P is **less than** the minimum AVC, the firm must shut down production in the short run because the variable costs cannot be covered.

Now let's consider how the short-run production decisions relate to the idea of free entry and exit into and out of a market or industry.

In the short run, there are a fixed number of suppliers: firms do not enter or exit the industry. To review, firms can make an economic profit with a market price above the break-even price, or they can shut down production of a good if the market price is below the average variable cost (AVC). Under this condition the firm cannot earn enough revenue to cover its variable cost.

The firm continues to produce in the short run if the market price is greater than the minimum AVC. If the market price equals the minimum AVC, the firm can either produce or not, since the variable costs are covered. The firm must stop producing if the market price is below the minimum AVC.

Now let's consider the long run. Given enough time, firms can enter and leave the market or industry freely in a perfectly competitive market. They will be encouraged to enter the industry if the industry makes an economic profit—which includes the opportunity cost, when market price is above the minimum average total cost (ATC), and exit if it is unprofitable, when market price is below the minimum ATC. If the firm breaks even, there is no entry or exit. In the long run, firms make no economic profit because there is no incentive for firms to enter or leave the market. The equilibrium price where there is no economic profit forms the long-run supply curve.

Producers have choices. In the agriculture industry, a farmer who plants corn or wheat can decide to remain in the industry but switch from planting corn to planting wheat if the market price of corn reduces his or her economic profit.

The accompanying figure *The Long-Run Supply Curve: Supply and Demand and Zero Economic Profit,* continues our discussion of the short-run supply and demand curve from Chapter 10. You will see how a change in market equilibrium price and quantity in the short run causes firms to make production decisions. In contrast, the long-run industry supply curve is horizontal at zero economic profit, or nearly so, because firms freely enter and exit the industry depending on whether or not the firm can make an economic profit, but ultimately the equilibrium always returns to the price and quantity where there is no economic profit.

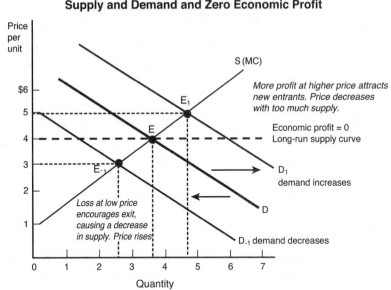

**The Long-Run Supply Curve:
Supply and Demand and Zero Economic Profit**

In the short run, producers buy and sell at equilibrium point E. At this point there is zero economic profit. A decrease in demand shifts the demand curve to the left to point E-₁ at a price below the initial equilibrium price and quantity. When some firms lose money, they shut down production. This decreases supply, which increases price back to point E. An increase in demand shifts the demand curve to the right to a new equilibrium price and quantity E₁. The industry is now very profitable, and firms enter the market. This results in too much supply, which lowers the price back to equilibrium point E at zero economic profit. At zero economic profit, there is no reason to enter or leave the market. This becomes the long-run supply curve.

Let's first look at a supply and demand curve in the short run for a product that has an equilibrium price of $4.00 and a quantity of 3.65. At the equilibrium price, point E, the economic profit is zero. The fact that the economic profit is zero does not mean the firm is not making an accounting profit. At zero economic profit the firm is neutral as to whether or not to continue producing. An economic profit of zero is also called the *normal profit*. Normal profit is the minimum amount of profit needed for the firm to be competitive in the market.

📖 **DEFINITION**

Normal profit occurs when economic profit is zero. It is the minimum amount of profit needed for the firm to be competitive in the market

If the market price is above the equilibrium price, the business owners will want to continue producing. If the market price is below the equilibrium price, the business owners will shut production down and do something else. As described above, a shift in the demand or supply curve will change the market price and form a new equilibrium price and quantity below or above the original equilibrium, where, in the long run, zero economic profit is earned and the producers are neutral as to whether or not to stay in the market or industry.

While a market may be viable in the long run, in the short run, as we've shown, an individual firm will be unable to profit at a market price below its variable costs. Other companies in the same industry may have a different cost structure and can be profitable during the same time period. There may also be aspiring business owners who are eager to be in a market but not at the current market price. Producers who are unable to survive over longer time frames go out of business, leaving fewer suppliers in the industry. Since the perfectly competitive market allows easy entry and exit into and out of an industry, the individual firm can make a decision based on its own numbers. Likewise, an industry that is profitable encourages firms to enter.

The accompanying figure *The Long-Run Supply Curve: Supply and Demand and Zero Economic Profit,* shows what happens when there is a decrease in demand in the short run. The demand curve shifts to the left. Price and quantity both decrease, and the equilibrium price and quantity move *below* the price and quantity where economic profit is zero to E_{-1} at a market price of $3.00 and quantity of 2.5. Now the producer must decide whether or not to shut down. It is still worthwhile to produce in the short run to pay off some of the fixed costs, but as time goes on and contracts expire, there is no reason for the firm to renew the contracts or buy new equipment if it continues to lose money. For this reason, in the long run the fixed costs are no longer a factor.

When firms stop production in the short run or go out of business in the long run because the current market price at point E_{-1} is below the equilibrium price with zero economic profit, point E, there is less supply in this market, causing the price to rise until it gets back to the original equilibrium price of $4.00 and quantity of 3.65 at point E.

An increase in demand shifts the demand curve to the right. Price and quantity increase, converging at a new equilibrium price and quantity with a higher price and quantity at point E_1. At this equilibrium, the market price is $5.00—greater than it was at point E, when the economic profit was zero. The new equilibrium quantity is 4.75, greater than the original equilibrium quantity. A higher price will attract new businesses into this market. Then as the number of producers increases, there is greater supply, and price and quantity will decline until they reach the former equilibrium price and quantity at point E with zero economic profit.

In the long run, the equilibrium price and quantity at zero economic profit is the long-run supply curve. Firms are neither encouraged by high prices to enter the market, nor discouraged because they can't make enough profit, causing them to leave the market.

In sum, in the long run producers can choose to leave an economically unprofitable industry and enter an economically profitable industry in a perfectly competitive market with free entry and exit into a market.

Perfect Information

Good information on price, utility, and production methods should be available to all consumers and producers. When consumers know what each business is charging for a product, they can comparison shop to get the best offer. A seller has the same information and can price a product to his or her advantage.

When all producers are aware of consumers' tastes and preferences, they can tailor their products and marketing campaigns to win over buyers. Or, if an entrepreneur is extraordinarily imaginative and ingenious, he or she can create a product that consumers don't know they need, as did Steve Jobs with the Apple product line or Mark Zuckerberg with Facebook. Once the Apple products became a necessity, the information was freely available to all other producers. After some years, Apple faces strong competition.

A revolution in production methods began in Japan in the 1970s when the just-in-time (JIT) system of production was introduced at the Toyota automobile manufacturing plants. The JIT production method replaced the "just-in-case" inventories that had been a mainstay of manufacturing. The idea was to only carry enough inventories for the very short term. JIT was used at every stage of production, resulting in enormous savings. The Toyota plant workers had greater control of their immediate inventory needs. The assembly lines were able to work on more than one model at a time, rather than completing one model and then having to retool the line for the next model. By not warehousing large quantities of inventories, there was a reduction in waste and cost to the manufacturer.

> **INTERESTING FACT**
>
> The just-in-time production method may predate the Toyota experience, according to a June 6, 2009, article in *The Economist*. In the 1950s, Japanese shipbuilders made good use of a glut in the steel industry by ordering steel whenever they needed it. They were able to cut their inventories from a 30-day supply to a 3-day supply.

The JIT approach was picked up by manufacturers globally because of perfect information. In the United States, manufacturers applying the JIT method were able to cut their inventories by 70 percent, their labor costs by 50 percent, and their space requirements by 80 percent on average over a 5-year period.

No Transaction Costs

A perfectly competitive market has no transaction costs. Transaction costs are the costs to be in a market. These include …

- The cost of researching the product to find the best price or other information needed to make a buying decision.

- The cost of drawing up and signing a contract to purchase a product or service.

- The cost to enforce the agreement.

If you are buying a house, there are many transaction costs. There are the many hours spent researching and looking at houses, whether on the internet or with a real estate agent. If you find a house you like, you and the seller enter protracted negotiations on the price, what is included and excluded in the sale, the closing and move-in dates, and so on. A mortgage is usually necessary to buy a house, and shopping around for a good rate also takes time. You then must be approved for the mortgage. A lawyer is involved in drawing up the closing agreement on the house, and all parties meet to sign the contracts—an expensive part of the process. Finally, if the seller reneges on the agreement, your lawyer has to resolve the situation. All of these are transaction costs.

Perfect Factor Mobility

Factor mobility is the degree to which a factor of production, such as labor, capital, or land, is able to move among industries or countries or be put to a different use in response to a change in market conditions. In the long run, this flexibility helps to eliminate the factor price differences. For example, if there is a change in conditions in the garment industry, where manufacturing is less expensive in suburban areas rather than near major cities, garment workers are able to move to the new location.

Factor mobility has been found to be a more effective use of resources in the economy. An experiment on trade policy and factor mobilization in the Philippines, described by Zohre Salehezadeh and Shida Henneberry of Oklahoma State University, found that "For a given trade policy, a higher degree of factor mobility results in a higher economic growth rate and an improvement in overall economic welfare." (http://agecon.okstate.edu/faculty/publications/659.pdf)

Labor Mobility

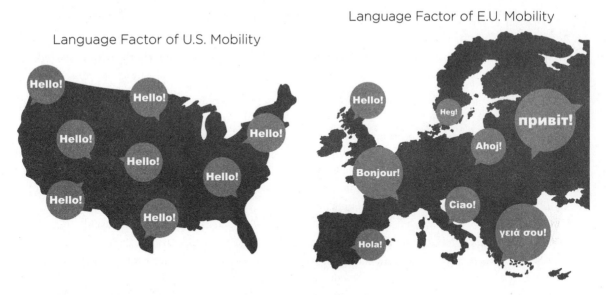

Language Factor of E.U. Mobility

Language Factor of U.S. Mobility

Perfect Competition Creates Efficiency

In the long run firms are extremely efficient in perfectly competitive markets. Perfect competition drives firms to make the best use of their resources. Inefficient firms have higher costs, which could force them to leave the industry. A firm is producing efficiently when output is at the minimum average total cost (ATC). On a diagram for a firm the equilibrium is at the minimum point of the ATC curve.

Economic efficiency extends the idea of efficiency to the entire society. Efficiency is the optimal use of society's scarce resources. Perfect competition provides an environment for both *productive efficiency* and *allocative efficiency*.

📖 **DEFINITION**

Productive efficiency is the ability to produce a good using the fewest resources possible. For a firm, productive efficiency is when the equilibrium price and quantity are at the minimum point of the ATC curve. **Allocative efficiency** is a characteristic of an efficient market in which capital is allocated in a way that benefits all participants.

Allocative efficiency in a society occurs when firms produce according to the needs of all participants. Here, firms produce the products that are in high demand and that society needs. On a diagram, allocative efficiency occurs when market price equals marginal cost: $P = MC$, which is the same as when marginal benefits (MB) equal marginal costs: $MB = MC$. At this point, consumers and society get the most benefit from the combination of products that can be produced for a society at the least cost. Investment flows to the projects in the public and private sectors that will be the most profitable, which should promote growth.

In sum, perfect competition provides the environment for consumers to buy what they prefer at the best price, for producers to create the quantity of products that maximizes their economic profits most efficiently, and for society to benefit from the optimal allocation of its resources.

The Least You Need to Know

- A perfectly competitive market has many producers, each having a very small market share, and many consumers.
- Producers and consumers are price takers in a perfectly competitive market. Neither can influence the market price.
- Free entry and exit is a characteristic of perfectly competitive markets in the long run.
- Other characteristics of perfectly competitive markets are that goods are standardized; consumers and producers have perfect information about prices, utility, and production methods; there are no transaction costs; and the market is highly efficient in the long run.

CHAPTER 12

Monopoly

The monopoly is a market structure that is the antithesis of perfect competition. Where there are many firms in a perfectly competitive market, a monopoly controls the entire industry. The differences in the two market structures are stark.

The models with which we are familiar that assume perfect competition, where no firms can influence the market price, demonstrate what happens when one firm has market power—the ability to raise prices by reducing the output quantity.

This chapter outlines the mechanism by which a firm that has complete control of supply makes a profit, how a monopoly reduces social welfare, and how the characteristics of a monopoly compare to the perfectly competitive market.

In This Chapter

- How the monopoly differs from a perfect competition
- How a monopolist maximizes profits
- The effect of the monopolist on society and the response from public policy
- The monopolist and price discrimination

Characteristics of a Monopoly

When a firm is the only producer of a good that has no close substitutes, it is a *monopolist*. The industry it controls is a *monopoly*.

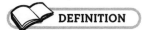 **DEFINITION**

> A **monopoly** is an industry that controls the entire source for a good. A **monopolist** is a firm that is the sole producer of a good with no substitutes.

Standard Oil was such a firm. By 1904, Standard Oil controlled 91 percent of production in refined oil in the United States before being broken up in 1911 under the Sherman Anti-Trust Act. The De Beers diamond company dominates the diamond industry globally. In more modern times, Microsoft had been accused of being a monopolist in Europe, since all software manufacturers and consumers had no choice but to use its operating system, which was installed in most computers. In recent years competitors have begun to eat away at Microsoft's domination.

Companies emerging whole or growing substantially from the breakup of Standard Oil in 1911

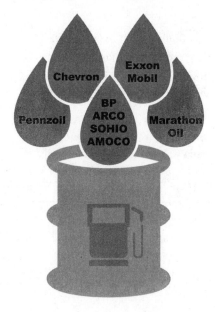

Let's look at the distinguishing features of a monopoly.

A Monopoly Is the Single Source of a Product

By definition, a monopoly controls nearly all of a market. It gains control because there are no close substitutes for its product. Competitors are prevented from entering the industry because they face barriers. Barriers to entry include:

Scarce resources: Resources such as oil and precious metals for which the monopolist controls the market. Unless new sources of resources are discovered, it is not possible for a firm to break into this market.

Economies of scale: Industries that require the building of infrastructure—such as cable television, telephone, natural gas, and electricity—are able to profit, as the average total cost of the initial capital investment falls with an increase in output.

 **DEFINITION**

Economies of scale refers to the cost advantage that arises with increased output of a product as fixed costs are spread over additional units of output.

Technological superiority: Although technology is subject to innovation, an industry that has the first-mover advantage in a technology can behave as a monopolist as long as it stays ahead of its competition. Microsoft, Intel (the chip maker), and Google are examples of companies that have been able to keep competitors at bay or to a minimum.

Legal barriers: Patents and copyrights are given by the government to inventors of new technologies, pharmaceuticals, and creative products that prevent other firms from entering a market. These exclusive rights can last for decades, preventing other firms from entering the industry.

The Monopolist Is a Price Maker

In Chapter 11, we described the demand curve for a firm in a perfectly competitive market as perfectly elastic. When a market is perfectly elastic, it is very sensitive to a change in price. A consumer will not buy any product if the sales price is higher than the market price. No matter how much quantity is produced, the market price will not change in a perfectly competitive market. The demand curve appears as a horizontal line at the market price on a diagram. (Don't confuse the demand curve of a firm with the demand curve for the market, which is downward sloping.) The marginal revenue is the market price. The optimal output quantity that maximizes profit is the point where MR = MC.

Now let's turn to the monopolist's demand curve. The demand curve of a monopolist is *downward sloping*. This is a key difference from the demand curve of a firm in a perfectly competitive market. Why might this be true? Remember that in a perfectly competitive market, the demand curve for the *market* is downward sloping. Since a monopolist *is* the market, its demand curve is also downward sloping.

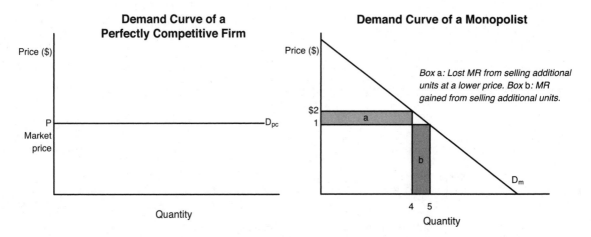

The demand curve for a perfectly competitive firm, D_{pc}, is a horizontal line at the market price (P). The demand curve for a monopolist, D_m, is a downward-sloping curve. The demand curve for a perfectly competitive market is also downward sloping. The monopolist essentially is the market. The monopolist must trade off gaining MR from selling more units (Box b) with the loss in MR from selling more at a decreasing price (Box a) in order to earn the most MR. MR = Box A + Box B.

Since the monopolist is the sole supplier of the good, it can set its own price—it is a *price maker*. That is its advantage over the firm in a perfectly competitive market, which is a price taker because it must sell at the price the market offers.

The monopolist can only keep the price high if it reduces the quantity produced, which it can do because it has *market power*. If it sells more, it must reduce the price of the product. The firm in a perfectly competitive market has no market power. It must sell at the given market price.

The monopolist can control the price at which its profits are maximized by controlling its output quantity. If it increases the output, the price falls. If it decreases output, the price rises. The monopolist calculates a trade-off in order to earn the most marginal revenue (MR): it gains MR from selling more units, but it loses MR from selling more at a decreasing price.

In the accompanying figures, *Demand Curve of a Perfectly Competitive Firm* and *Demand Curve of a Monopolist, Box a* represents the lost revenue from a decrease in price on every additional unit. *Box b* represents the revenue gained from selling an additional unit. When *Box a* is greater than *Box b*, the monopolist loses MR. When *Box b* is greater than *Box a*, the monopolist gains MR.

MR = Box A + Box B

Under what condition does the monopolist maximize its profits? We need a few more pieces of the puzzle to find out how this happens.

The Monopolist Maximizes Profits

Let's review the implications of a downward-sloping demand curve. As the output increases, the price decreases. Each additional unit of output corresponds to a lower price, which means that total revenue (P × Q) is also declining. The *marginal revenue* (MR) curve is therefore below the demand curve, since MR = the change in TR divided by the change in quantity demanded. The monopolist cannot maximize profits when the MR curve is negative.

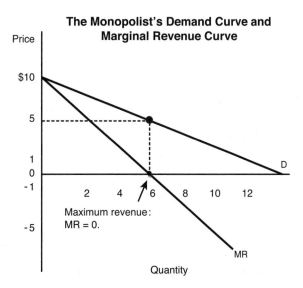

The downward-sloping demand curve (D) implies that as output quantity increases, price decreases. The marginal revenue (MR) curve is always below the demand curve. Each incremental unit of output lowers MR as price decreases. Total revenue is maximized when MR = 0. Marginal revenue eventually becomes negative.

The monopolist's *total revenue* (TR) curve is hill-shaped: total revenue, which is price multiplied by quantity, climbs the hill when the quantity is low. During the ascent, the low quantity dominates the effect of a rising price. Total revenue peaks at the quantity and price where marginal revenue (MR) equals zero. The TR curve then begins to descend, as the monopolist sells a higher quantity of units at increasingly lower prices.

The Monopolist's Total Revenue Curve

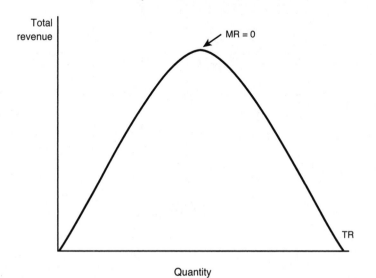

The total revenue (TR) curve shows that when the quantity produced is low, the price increases up to the point where the marginal revenue (MR) equals zero. As the monopolist sells more units at lower prices, total revenue declines.

After the peak in revenue, as TR decreases, MR goes below zero: each additional unit sold is losing marginal revenue.

The monopolist maximizes its profits by comparing its marginal revenue (MR) with its marginal cost (MC). Unlike the firm in the perfectly competitive market, the monopolist can decide to increase its profits by producing more when MR is greater than MC. If MR is less than MC, the monopolist can decrease its loss by reducing its output. Once MR is above MC, it will again be profitable.

So here's the twist: a firm operating in a perfectly competitive market maximizes its profit when MR = MC. The marginal revenue (MR) is equal to the market price (P), which is also equal to the marginal cost (MC). The monopolist maximizes profit using the optimal output rule, MR = MC, but at the price on the demand curve at the monopolist's profit-maximizing quantity of output.

Maximum Profit for a Monopolist

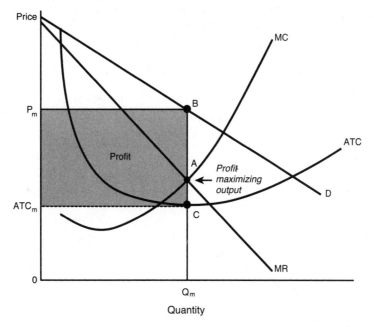

The monopolist maximizes profit when MR = MC, the profit-maximizing output Q_m at point A. The monopolist's price is the point on the demand curve that is directly above point A at point B. The monopolist's profit is the area of the shaded rectangle formed by point ATC_M, point C, point B, and P_M.

In the figure *Maximum Profit for a Monopolist*, the monopolist maximizes profit when the MR and MC curves cross—point A—which is the profit-maximizing output. To find the monopolist's price, look straight up above point A to point B on the demand curve. The total revenue (TR) is the area of the rectangle $P_M \times Q_M$. The total cost (TC) is the area of the rectangle $ATC_M \times Q_M$. Remembering that Profit = TR – TC, we can find the profit by subtracting the product of the average total cost (ATC_M), at point C, and the profit-maximizing quantity (Q_M) from the product of the price (P_M) on the demand curve at Q_M, point B:

Profit = TR – TC

= ($P_M \times Q_M$)–($ATC_M \times Q_M$)

Using a little algebra (factoring out Q_M), this equation becomes **(P_M – ATC_M) × Q_M = Profit.**

The shaded area of the rectangle, where the height is P_m – ATC_m, and where the width is Q_m is the monopolist's profit (area = height × width).

Price Elasticity of Demand and Total Revenue

The price elasticity of demand plays a role in how much profit the monopolist makes. The percentage change in quantity is related to the percentage change in price by elasticity. The percentage change in total revenue can be calculated by knowing the elasticity and the percentage change in price. So the elasticity of demand of a good or service is a factor in the monopolist's choice of price.

The greater the elasticity of demand of a good, that is, the sensitivity of the quantity demanded of the good to a change in its price, the greater the profit as price declines down the monopolist's demand curve to MR = 0. At MR = 0, TR is maximized, elasticity of demand is unit-elastic, and price has no effect on TR. As output increases past the point where MR = 0, demand becomes less elastic. Once the price elasticity of demand is less than one, MR will be negative. Total revenue will decrease.

> **DEFINITION**
>
> The **price elasticity of demand** is a measure of the relationship between a change in the quantity demanded of a particular good and a change in its price. It is calculated by the %change in quantity demanded/%change in price.
>
> Demand is …
>
> **Elastic** if the price elasticity of demand is **greater than 1.**
>
> **Inelastic** if the price elasticity of demand is **less than 1.**
>
> **Unit-elastic** if the price elasticity of demand is **equal to 1**. (See Chapter 7.)

The accompanying figure *Price Elasticity of Demand and the Monopolist,* shows how the elasticity of demand decreases as the quantity produced increases with the monopolist's downward-sloping demand curve. The total revenue (TR) curve is also shown. The symbol for elasticity of demand is η. When $\eta > 1$, the demand is relatively elastic as the total revenue (TR) is increasing. Even as TR increases in the relatively elastic zone, MR is still decreasing, as each additional unit gains less revenue than the previous unit.

The peak of the TR curve is also where MR = 0 and $\eta = 1$: demand is unit-elastic (a change in price will not affect TR). When $\eta < 1$, demand is relatively inelastic, TR decreases as price decreases, and MR becomes negative. Monopolists are not likely to produce in the inelastic zone, when the price elasticity of demand is negative and the MR is negative (the lower portion of the demand curve). The monopolist is only able to maximize profit by producing a quantity of output that falls in the elastic range of the demand curve.

To sum up the relationship between marginal revenue and elasticity:

- If the demand is elastic, MR is positive.

- If the demand is inelastic, MR is negative.

- If the demand is unit-elastic, MR is zero.

The monopolist cannot maximize profit when MR is negative because it must create output at the profit-maximizing output level, MR = MC. If MR is negative, however, MC would also have to be negative, which is not possible. You can't have a negative cost.

DO THE MATH

It's easy to calculate the marginal revenue (MR) if you know the price and the point price elasticity of demand*. Just plug in the numbers. The formula is:

MR = P(1 + 1/η)

*If you are not given the point price elasticity of demand, you will not be able to use this formula unless you know differential calculus.

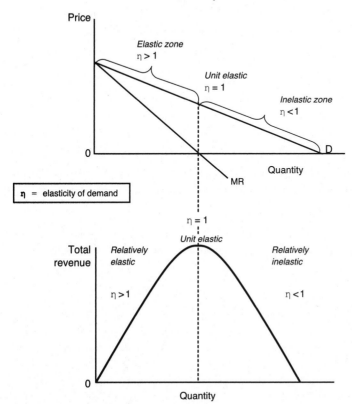

Price Elasticity of Demand and the Monopolist

The monopolist's demand curve, marginal revenue (MR) curve, and total revenue (TR) curves are shown. In the upper part of the demand curve, the price elasticity of demand (η) is positive (elastic zone), when MR is positive. The corresponding TR diagram shows that the elasticity of demand is relatively elastic (η > 1) as TR rises. Total revenue (TR) peaks when MR = 0, and elasticity is unit-elastic (η = 1). As TR begins to decrease and elasticity decreases, the MR curve becomes negative in the inelastic zone (η < 1).

Let's compare how the monopolist and the producer in a perfectly competitive market go about maximizing profits.

Comparing Characteristics of the Monopolist and the PC Producer

Monopolist	PC Producer
Price maker	Price taker
P > MR = MC at the monopolist's profit-maximizing quantity of output	P = MC at the PC firm's profit-maximizing quantity of output
Produces a smaller, monopolist-chosen output	Produces a market-determined output
No supply curve	Market-determined supply curve
Profits in the short run and the long run	Can profit in the short run but no economic profit in the long run
Barriers to entry	Free entry and exit in the long run

We said at the beginning of this chapter that there were stark differences between the monopolist and the producer in a perfectly competitive market. The table makes clear that both the consumer and society benefit from a perfectly competitive market. The producer in a perfectly competitive market is probably envious of the monopolist, which has no competitors and can choose the quantity and price at which to produce and sell.

Now we'll explore how a monopoly affects the welfare of society.

> **INTERESTING FACT**
>
> What about the supply curve? Monopolists do not have a supply curve. The monopolist doesn't need a supply curve, which—in a perfectly competitive market—shows the quantity that firms are willing to supply at a given market price. The monopolist has **market power** and can choose the production quantity that will maximize its profits.

The Monopolist, Society, and Public Policy

The characteristics of a monopoly, outlined above, paint a picture of inefficiency. To maximize its profits, a monopolist has to produce less and sell at a higher price than a producer in a perfectly competitive market. This harms the consumer, who would benefit from a price and quantity determined by the equilibrium of supply and demand. Since the monopolist is the sole producer in the industry, there is no supply curve. The consumer has to take the price the monopolist gives, rather than the price the market offers, if the consumer wants the product or service.

The negative impact of a monopolist's maximizing profits goes beyond the consumer to the welfare of society as a whole. The consumer's loss is not equal to or less than the monopolist's gain; it is *greater* than the monopolist's gain. The economy loses because a monopoly is an inefficient market structure.

Monopoly Inefficiency

The inefficiency of the monopoly can best be understood by comparing the consumer surplus, producer surplus, and total surplus generated by a transaction in a perfectly competitive market with the consumer surplus, producer surplus, and total surplus generated by a monopoly. (See Chapter 8 for more on consumer and producer surplus.)

The Inefficiency of a Monopoly

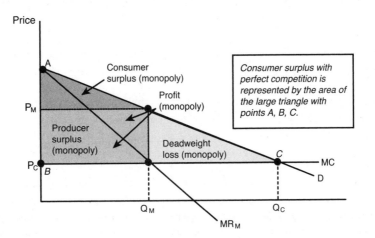

Consumer surplus in a perfectly competitive market is also total surplus. It is represented by the area of the large triangle with points A, B, and C. The MC is the price (P$_C$) and the profit-maximizing output, Q$_C$, is also MC. There is no producer surplus when MC = P. In a monopoly, to maximize profit, the monopolist lowers output to Q$_M$ and chooses price P$_M$ on the demand curve. The monopolist has a profit, taken from consumer surplus. There is now a producer surplus, which is also profit, because P$_M$ is higher than MC. Total surplus is reduced, and there is a deadweight loss where no mutually beneficial transactions occur.

In a market with perfect competition, MR = MC = P. The *consumer surplus* and the *producer surplus* are maximized. Since the monopoly sells at a price that is greater than marginal cost, P > MC, the consumer surplus and producer surplus cannot be maximized.

In the figure *The Inefficiency of a Monopoly*, consumer surplus is represented by the area of the large triangle with points A, B, and C. In a perfectly competitive market when MC = P, it is also the total surplus. The MC is the price (Pc), and the profit-maximizing output, Qc is also MC and Pc. There is no producer surplus when MC = P. In a monopoly, to maximize profit, the monopolist lowers output to Qм and chooses price Pм, on the demand curve. The monopolist has a profit, taken from consumer surplus. There is also profit from the producer surplus, which exists because Pм is higher than MC. Total surplus is reduced because the monopolist's price is too high for some consumers. The area of the triangle where no mutually beneficial transactions occur because of monopolist pricing is a deadweight loss. This is a loss for the economy.

> **DEFINITION**
>
> **Consumer surplus** is the additional benefit to consumers beyond the price paid for a good or service. **Producer surplus** is the benefit the producer receives beyond the price of sale gained by selling the good in the market.

Public Policy Measures

When a single company has control of the source of supply of an industry and exploits that position to produce a smaller quantity at a higher price, the public cries "foul!" Since government represents the public, it is tasked with finding a way to offer protection. What are the ways a government can handle monopolies?

One solution is to break up a monopolist. In the United States, the Sherman Anti-Trust Act was passed in 1890 to do just that. Senator John Sherman, the lead author of the law, said its purpose was "To protect the consumers by preventing arrangements designed, or which tend, to advance the cost of goods to the consumer." In practice, the law has been used to protect competition in the marketplace. The Clayton Antitrust Act of 1914 further refined which practices should not be allowed.

Competition law is practiced globally. The European Union is less tolerant of monopoly practices than the United States. Its market dominance law aims to prevent market dominance by a single firm that has as little as 38 percent market share. In the United States, 60 percent control by one company is required before the government can intervene.

Governments generally try to rein in such practices as limiting supply, predatory pricing, price discrimination, refusal to deal, exclusive dealing, and product bundling, among others.

Certain monopolies are not as harmful as others, and in the case of a *natural monopoly*, it could be the best alternative for delivering a product or service. A natural monopoly, such as a natural gas company, has a lower average total cost (ATC) than individual suppliers because of the need to build infrastructure. Even with a lower ATC, the natural monopoly is in a position to charge higher prices than would a firm in a perfectly competitive market. The natural monopoly makes an economic profit because its marginal cost is lower than the price it charges.

Some countries have chosen to nationalize natural monopolies, either by supplying the good itself or by owning a firm that supplies the good. In the United States, the railroad system Amtrak is an example, as is the U.S. Postal Service.

The United Kingdom had owned British Telecom and British Airways, but they both were privatized during the great wave of privatizations in the 1980s under Prime Minister Margaret Thatcher. Russia privatized natural monopolies in the 1990s. These include Gazprom, LUKOIL, Mechel, MMC Norilsk Nickel, Novolipetsk Steel, Surgutneftegas, and Yukos. So it seems that economics, in many cases, follows political philosophy when it comes to natural monopolies.

Another strategy for curbing any anticonsumer behavior by a monopolist is through *regulation*. Price regulation limits the price a monopolist can charge. Local electric companies in the United States have to submit requests to increase prices to a government agency before being allowed to increase prices. Although price ceilings in a market with perfect competition cause inefficiencies, a monopolist would charge a price that is higher than marginal cost to make a profit or break even.

The reason price regulation can work for a natural monopoly, such as electricity or natural gas, is that the ATC curve is downward sloping as output increase. That is because the fixed cost—which is substantial for infrastructure—is spread out over more units. The monopolist is willing to produce more at a lower price. The ideal price and quantity are when the ATC curve crosses the demand curve. If the price is lowered further, the monopoly will begin to sustain a loss, and will not produce additional quantities. Lowering the price to the optimal combination of price and average total costs helps consumers and increases consumer surplus while not harming the natural monopoly, so the needs of both the consumer and monopoly are satisfied.

Measures to deal with the tendency by monopolies to gain at the consumer's expense fluctuate historically. A combination of politics and differences in opinion among economists shows no clear direction in public policy, although there is agreement on how to resolve the most extreme cases.

Price Discrimination

We have been examining the monopolist that charges a single price to all consumers. Without regulation, the monopolist reduces consumer surplus, taking some as profits, and any producer surplus gained by charging a price higher than the marginal cost is also profit. Monopolists can do even better by engaging in price discrimination.

Price Discrimination and Consumer Surplus

Unlike the producer in a market with perfect competition, the monopolist can extract more consumer surplus by knowing what the consumer is willing to pay and charging that amount. Recall that in a perfectly competitive market, consumer surplus is the difference between what a consumer is willing to pay and the market price. With a monopolist, there is no market price … there is the monopolist's price. The price is usually more than the monopolist's marginal cost, resulting in a profit.

A monopolist can use *price discrimination* to charge customers what they are willing to pay—their *reservation price*. The monopolist's challenge is to understand the customer and to find out what the customer is willing to pay. The more information the monopolist has about the customer, the closer it will get to being able to identify their reservation price.

 **DEFINITION**

> **Price discrimination** is a pricing strategy by a monopolist that aims to get the most consumer surplus possible by charging different prices to different customers depending on the consumer's willingness to pay. **Reservation price** is the maximum price that a customer is willing to pay for a good.

One way to segment the marketplace is by degree of wealth. For example, a monopolist that sells internationally will sell its product at a high price to consumers in wealthy countries and a low price to consumers in poorer countries.

The pharmaceutical industry charges U.S. citizens over 100 percent more for the same medicine in many other countries. A particular brand-name drug costs $160 for a 30-day supply in the United States, but in Canada the price for the same drug at the same quantity is $18.80 Canadian—about $17 U.S. The state of Maine is advancing legislation at this writing to allow Maine residents to buy drugs from Canada or other countries with much lower prices. Another example is that some publishers of textbooks charge much more to customers in wealthier countries than in poorer countries.

There would be *perfect price discrimination* if the monopolist were able to charge each individual customer their reservation price. In this way, there is zero consumer surplus. Although total surplus is maximized, the surplus goes entirely to the producer. With perfect price discrimination, there is no marginal revenue curve. The incremental revenue from each unit sold is what is actually paid and is therefore the same as the consumer's demand curve. There are no inefficiencies with perfect price discrimination.

DEFINITION

> **Perfect price discrimination** is the ideal form of price discrimination whereby every consumer pays the monopolist the price he or she is willing to pay.

Forms of Price Discrimination

There are three forms of price discrimination:

1. First degree price discrimination, where the monopolist charges the consumer the price he or she is willing to pay.

2. Second degree price discrimination, where the monopolist gives discounts for purchasing in greater quantities.

3. Third degree price discrimination, where the monopolist segments groups of customers by their price elasticity of demand and charges accordingly.

Third degree price discrimination treats each group as if it is a separate market and tries to maximize profits for each group by charging the group a price that matches its ability to pay.

Examples are common: Senior citizens get many discounts because they often have less income, and their time is flexible. They can, for example, go to a movie or a show when others are at work. Some expensive hard liquors are sold at high prices for the firm's best label, but the same liquors are poured into bottles with a different label and sold at a much lower price.

Airlines group customers into weekend or weekday travelers and travelers who buy tickets well in advance and those that must travel right away. These groups usually fall into the categories of business and leisure. Airlines can get as much revenue as possible at the business price as well as from the leisure group, which would be priced out at the business price.

Each group, or market segment, has its own demand curve, marginal revenue (MR) curve, marginal cost curve (MC), and price elasticity of demand. The optimal price and quantity for each group is where MR = MC. The higher price is charged to the group with lower price elasticity of demand. These are the airline customers who are less flexible with time, for example, and must be at a business meeting the next day. With less flexibility, customers are willing to pay more.

Some companies use discount coupons to appeal to customers who are willing to take the time to clip coupons and bring them to the store. These consumers have a high elasticity of demand because they are more sensitive to a change in price. The firm is able to sell more to these consumers at a discount, who might otherwise not have bought the product.

The monopoly is the first of a few market structures that deviate from perfect competition, where supply and demand meet at an equilibrium of price and quantity. The next chapter examines another inefficient market structure, the oligopoly.

The Least You Need to Know

- A monopoly is the single source of a product enforced by barriers to entry. As a result, it has market power.
- The monopolist has a downward-sloping demand curve and no supply curve.
- The monopolist maximizes profits where marginal revenue equals marginal cost at a price on its demand curve at the profit-maximizing output quantity.
- The monopolist benefits when there is less output quantity and a higher price.
- The monopolist profits in the short run and the long run.
- Society is harmed by the monopoly market structure via inefficiencies that reduce total surplus and anticompetitive practices. Anticompetition laws attempt to prevent monopolistic practices by breaking up monopolies and through regulation.
- Monopolists practice price discrimination to extract the most consumer surplus possible in order to earn greater profits.

CHAPTER 13

Oligopolies

On the spectrum of market structures, perfect competition, with many producers taking the market price as given, would be on one end, and the monopoly, with one firm dominating supply and making its own price, would be on the other end. Between these two extremes lie two prevalent market structures: oligopoly and monopolistic competition. This chapter describes the oligopoly.

The oligopoly, with a few firms dominating an industry, must find ways to profit in a landscape where they are price makers, but with limited competition. They have some information on their competitors' output and pricing, but not enough to make an informed decision for their company. The oligopolists can be associated with collusion, cartels, or simply try their best to differentiate their product from the competition. This chapter will explore the characteristics of this unique market structure.

In This Chapter

- When a few firms compete
- The oligopoly: when a market is dominated by a few firms
- The unique interdependence and behavior of oligopolists
- Collusion and cartels in the oligopoly
- When the oligopolist declines to engage in collusion

Examples of Oligopolies

The word oligopoly is derived from two Greek words, *oligoi* (few) and *polein* (sellers). The oligopoly is an industry that is dominated by a few firms that supply and control a good or service to the market. This market form is quite common in our economy. If you think about it, you can probably list many industries that fall into this category. Some well-known examples are …

- The soft drink industry (Coca-Cola and Pepsi-Cola).

- The airline industry—with certain routes dominated by only one or two airline companies.

- The cell phone industry in the United States (Verizon, AT&T, Sprint, and T-Mobile).

- The computer operating system industry (Microsoft, Apple).

- The smartphone operating system industry (Google Android, Apple iOS).

- The U.S. pharmaceutical industry (Pfizer, Merck, Novartis).

- The U.S. beer industry (Anheuser-Busch, MillerCoors).

- The U.K. banking industry (Barclays, Halifax, HSBC, Lloyds TSB, NatWest).

- The U.K. grocery market (Tesco, Sainsbury's, Asda, Morrisons).

- The Australia media outlets (News Corp, TimeWarner, Fairfax Media).

- The Australia grocery retail industry (Coles, Woolworths).

- The Canadian internet service provider industry (Rogers, Bell, TELUS, Shaw).

- The worldwide airliner market (Boeing, Airbus).

- The worldwide candy industry (Nestlé, The Hershey Company, Mars, Inc.)

There are many more examples both within countries and worldwide. The concentration ratio of firms in an oligopoly makes up well over 50 percent of the industry, putting them in a position to control prices and output. The oligopoly is therefore an imperfect form of competition. Under some conditions, as we'll see later, the oligopoly can behave as a monopoly.

Characteristics of the Oligopoly

By now you are familiar with the characteristics economists use to compare the various market structures. Let's examine the features of the oligopoly that are similar to and dissimilar from other market forms and those that are unique to the oligopoly.

Barriers to Entry Are High

As with the monopoly, barriers to enter the industry the oligopoly dominates are high.

Exclusive control of a *resource*, such as the oil industry, is one of the main barriers to entry. While this is also true of a monopoly, a few firms were able to enter and control a resource in certain areas to form an oligopoly.

Economies of scale strengthen the position of existing firms, since they have the advantage of being able to spread fixed costs over a large quantity of output. This prevents upstart companies from entering unless they are able to obtain significant financial backing. New entrants are faced with heavy investment in capital if new factories have to be built and new equipment purchased. The marketing campaigns of new firms to generate initial sales lag payment of the short-run costs.

Production techniques may be exclusive to one or two firms, and a new entrant could be challenged with developing its own.

Government-granted *patents* and other intellectual property give exclusive rights to the patent owner to produce a good for a certain period of time. The World Trade Organization allows a minimum of 20 years or more of patent protection for the member nations.

Existing firms in the oligopoly will sometimes use *tactics that discourage* new entrants. Dividing territories between firms in an oligopoly is one such practice. Here, the firms agree to not compete in the other firm's territory to reduce competition. Emerging firms are sometimes bought out by firms in an oligopoly to reduce competition or to enhance their own business.

The smartphone operating systems industry controlled by the firms Google and Apple is challenging to enter. Google and Apple have the talent and capital to invest in equipment, labor, and marketing, which makes it very difficult (but not impossible with a better idea) for an aspiring operating system entrepreneur to get a foothold in this industry. Firms like Apple and Google commonly buy small, innovative firms. A firm that is in a related industry, such as Samsung in the smartphone manufacturing industry, that has access to capital and talent, might be a good candidate to break into the smartphone operating systems industry.

The capital and expertise necessary to enter the airliner market, dominated by Boeing and Airbus, is formidable. There are only two firms in this industry worldwide.

Scanning the list of oligopolies above, you can appreciate the obstacles facing an aspiring new business in any of these industries.

As a result of the high barriers to entry, oligopolistic firms can make profits in the short run and in the long run.

Concentration Ratio

The *concentration ratio* is the percentage of the total output of an industry the oligopoly controls. Economists judge the concentration ratio by the proportion of the output or revenues of the largest firms in the industry. For example, in the United Kingdom, five firms in the sugar industry control 99 percent of output. In the tobacco products industry, five firms control 99 percent of output.

Product Differentiation

The firms in an oligopoly can offer products that are either *homogeneous*, where there are few distinguishing attributes, or they can be *differentiated*. Firms that differentiate their products can compete by highlighting their advantages over competitors within the industry to gain market share. Some economic researchers have found that product differentiation benefits a firm by reducing the impact of lower prices caused by competition in an industry.

Homogeneous products tend to be in the raw materials industry, such as steel, oil, and aluminum. The supermarket industry might also be considered homogeneous. If you were blindfolded and taken into a supermarket, you would be hard pressed to know in which supermarket you were when the blindfold was removed. On the other hand, the automobile manufacturing industry and other consumer products industries offer a wide variety. Consumers will often favor one brand over another. Firms can compete within the industry to win over customers from another brand.

Perfect or Imperfect Information?

Recall that one of the characteristics of perfect competition is that firms and consumers have perfect information about prices, utility, quality, and production methods. How does the oligopoly compare? The answer is mixed. As we'll see later on, the individual firms in the oligopoly do not have enough information to correctly price their goods or decide on the output quantity to maximize profits. The firm only knows its own costs and has an adequate estimate of demand for its products. The consumer has only partial information on the product quality and prices.

Interdependence and Behavior of Oligopoly Firms

A distinguishing feature of the oligopoly is the *interdependence* among firms in the industry. With only a few firms providing supply, the demand for one firm's product depends on the price and output decisions of its competitors. Likewise, the output and price decision of one of the firms affects the price and output decisions of the other firms. Each firm must take into account how its actions will affect its rivals, and how it expects its rivals to react. Imperfect information on pricing and output of rival firms leads to a variety of situations and outcomes for price, output, and profit maximization. Since the oligopoly is unlike the monopoly or the firm in perfect competition in this regard, economists developed models describing the behavior of firms in an oligopoly.

> **DEFINITION**
>
> **Interdependence** occurs when the few firms in an oligopoly are mutually dependent on one another to make pricing and output decisions.

Equilibrium in an Oligopolistic Market

In a market with perfect competition, the equilibrium price occurs when quantity supplied equals quantity demanded. We saw that in a monopoly, the equilibrium price occurs where marginal revenue equals marginal cost. Competitors could be ignored, as firms were able to take price or market demand as given. Unlike those market forms, firms in an oligopoly must consider the behavior of their competitors when making output and pricing decisions.

A market in equilibrium has three properties:

1. The behavior of firms is consistent.

2. No agent has an incentive to change its behavior.

3. Equilibrium is the outcome of a dynamic process and is stable. This property gets attention when a market is *not* in equilibrium. Ultimately, a market will rebalance and revert to its equilibrium, such as when there is a surplus in supply or demand.

What might be the equilibrium when firms must take their rivals' behaviors into account? In economics, the *Nash equilibrium* incorporates the actions of the firm's competitors into its calculations. The Nash equilibrium is a set of strategies or actions in which each firm in an oligopoly does the best it can, given its competitors' actions. No firm can improve its outcome by choosing a different strategy. The strategies primarily relate to pricing and output. This equilibrium was invented by mathematician John Nash and is used in *game theory*, the study of strategic decision making. The Nash equilibrium is used to model production and pricing strategies for the interdependent firms in an oligopoly.

DEFINITION

Nash equilibrium is an equilibrium in which no firm has an incentive to deviate from its chosen strategy after considering its competitor's decision. **Game theory** is the study of strategic decision making.

When only a few firms control most of an industry, each must be vigilant to the decisions of the other firms in order to succeed. The problem is that the firm doesn't *know* the decisions of the other firms until it's too late. Such uncertainty motivates firms to either *collude*, by forming a *cartel* to maximize profits, or to compete. If a firm in an oligopoly chooses to collude, the oligopolists will reduce output and raise prices. If a firm in an oligopoly chooses to compete, it will try to undercut the price of its competitors to gain market share, differentiate its product line, or increase advertising.

DEFINITION

Collusion is an agreement by two or more firms in an oligopoly, usually illegal and secret, to limit open competition in order to raise profits for their mutual benefit. In an oligopoly, a **cartel** is an agreement among competing firms to fix prices, set output quotas, allocate territories, and other methods of limiting competition.

Collusion and Cartels

The goal of all firms in every market structure is to maximize profits. How is it possible to maximize profits when the price and output quantity are neither determined by the market nor by a monopoly's known profit-maximizing output and price on the demand curve? To make things more confusing, the price and quantity of a firm's competitors in an oligopoly are also unknown.

Since every firm in an oligopoly is in the same boat, one solution is for all firms to decide on a sales price and an output quantity. They agree not to compete with each other. Doing so will eliminate the worry that competitors will challenge their prices. The firms maximize their collective profits by acting as a cartel.

Assuming all firms have identical costs and are of equal size, as an example, the cartel behaves as a monopoly. As with a monopoly, the demand curve is downward sloping, and the marginal revenue curve is beneath the demand curve at all times. The monopoly/cartel price is on the demand curve at the profit-maximizing output quantity. As with a monopoly, MR = MC, but at a lower quantity and a higher price than the competitive firm, which has a market price and quantity. This assumes that there is no cheating.

Of course, this behavior is illegal. The only industry that can get away with setting output quantity and price is the Organization of the Petroleum Exporting Countries (OPEC). OPEC can openly set price and quantity for production because members are sovereign states.

Since collusion is illegal in most countries, how are oligopolists protected if they don't have sovereign state legal status? "I won't tell if you won't tell," is one possibility (also known as *omerta*—silence—in some circles). Agreements among oligopolists are not usually written down.

Collusion goes under the radar with a verbal "gentlemen's agreement." These compacts can involve any of the strategies that enhance profits by agreeing to set a high price, reduce output, divide territories, and other tactics to keep out competitors.

Once firms agree to work together, the colluding oligopolists or cartel must decide how to divide the profits and choose an output quota for each firm.

The output quota is significant. Each firm in the cartel has an incentive to produce more than its quota in order to take advantage of the high price set by the cartel. Production will also occur at a lower average total cost (ATC) because it is able to spread its fixed costs over more units. The more the firm produces, the greater the profit.

If the cartel is like a monopoly, why doesn't increasing output lower total revenue? The answer is that although an output increase by a single member *does* decrease revenue, the amount is smaller than under a monopoly structure because one firm produces only a portion of the industry output.

Let's return to OPEC as an example of a cartel and see how it functions. Each member of OPEC is given a production quota and a price at its conference, usually held in September and March. Each member has one vote, and the decision must be unanimous. With all of this formality, you would think the members would play by the rules. The danger in any cartel is that one or more rogue members will cheat. OPEC is no exception. Once a member's representative returns home, there is no guarantee that the country will adhere to the agreement signed at the conference. There is nothing OPEC can do to punish these cheaters.

Cartels are inherently unstable because the temptation to cheat can be overwhelming for some firms, or countries, in the case of OPEC. This is a problem for any oligopoly that colludes to maximize profits. With an artificially high price, one or more members will inevitably produce beyond its quota, thus generating output at a lower average total cost than the other members and increasing its profits.

It is obvious that, while collusion is more profitable than competition, it is not a stable situation. The firm is not respecting the cartel's agreement. When each firm acts in its own self-interest, it is considered noncooperative behavior.

> **INTERESTING FACT**
>
> OPEC's stated mission is "to coordinate and unify the petroleum policies of its Member Countries and ensure the stabilization of oil markets in order to secure an efficient, economic and regular supply of petroleum to consumers, a steady income to producers and a fair return on capital for those investing in the petroleum industry."

Oligopolies can set prices rather than output quotas to increase profits. Once again, cheating is a risk. Oligopolists have to stay on their toes, or "watch their backs." A firm in the colluding group may undercut the prices of the other members to gain market share.

Cheating comes in forms other than violating a quota or undercutting prices. Firms can cheat on their cartel agreement by preferential treatment for favored customers, such as special discounts, priority delivery dates, velvet-glove sales service, and other perks.

Noncollusive Approach

Collusion is the most successful way to maximize profits for oligopolists. If this option is too distasteful for some firms, noncollusive options are available for oligopolistic firms to advance their interests. Oligopolies design strategies for maximizing their profits in an interdependent market. Here are some of the strategies.

Price signaling is a form of implicit collusion in which a firm announces a price increase in the hope that other firms will do likewise. You've probably been surprised when you see an advertisement that an airline fare has been cut drastically, while other companies' fares to the same destination have remained the same. You wait to see whether the other firms will follow suit. Sometimes they do, and sometimes they don't.

When a leading firm regularly advertises a change in price, other firms usually conform to the price. This is known as *price leadership*. This subtle tactic is a way to avoid the legal problems caused by collusion. The informal and tacit nature of price leadership is considered legal by most courts.

> **DEFINITION**
>
> **Price signaling** is a form of implicit collusion in which a firm announces a price increase in the hope that other firms will follow. **Price leadership** is a pattern of pricing in which one firm regularly announces price changes that other firms then match.

The *Cournot model* describes how two firms producing homogeneous products in an oligopoly might make *output* decisions taking their rivals into account. The assumptions are:

- The market demand curve is linear.
- The marginal cost curve is constant.
- Each firm decides its own output.
- Output decisions are made simultaneously and with the knowledge that the competing firm is also making an output decision.
- Each firm treats the output of its competitor as fixed.
- The market price depends on the total output of both firms.

Each firm maximizes its profits at equilibrium in the Cournot model. *Since no firm has an incentive to change its output, they are in Nash equilibrium.* Equilibrium is reached when each firm calculates the quantity its competitor will produce and sets its own output level accordingly. Profits are higher than a firm in perfect competition but are less than they would have been had they colluded.

The *Bertrand model* is similar to the Cournot model but uses *price* as the strategic variable rather than output. Many industries, such as the automobile manufacturing industry, compete on price rather than output.

In this model the firms choose a price (P_A and P_B) simultaneously. The firms' outputs are perfect substitutes. Sales are evenly split if the prices chosen by both competitors are the same. The Nash equilibrium is $P_A = P_B = MC$. Both firms earn zero economic profit. Since this equivalence is the same as it is for a firm in perfect competition, if firm A raises its price, it loses sales to firm B. If firm A lowers its price, it will lose money on each unit sold because it will be selling below its marginal cost.

The *kinked demand curve* is a model that shows how an oligopolistic market has price rigidity when there is tacit collusion to reduce output. In this model the demand curve has an abrupt bend, or kink, that divides demand into a relatively elastic segment (dotted line) for price increases and a relatively inelastic segment for price decreases.

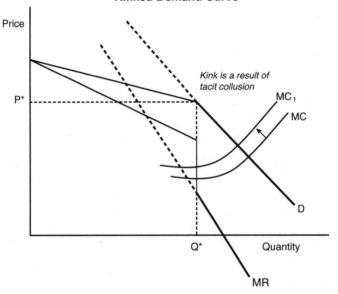

Tacit collusion in oligopolistic firms can lead to price rigidity. In this figure P* is the prevailing price. The dotted portion of the demand curve is elastic above this price because other firms may not follow the firm's lead, resulting in a loss of sales and some market share. If it lowers its price below P*, it runs the risk of triggering a price war. The dotted portion of the MR curve shows discontinuity resulting from the kink in the demand curve. A shift in the MC curve will not affect the price or quantity at which it sells its product. (Source: Microeconomics, 6th ed, Robert S. Pindyck and Daniel L. Rubinfeld, p. 458.)

The marginal revenue curve is discontinuous and gaps at the kink. The gap reflects a firm's uncertainty about how rivals would react if it changed its output quantity after a tacit agreement on a quota. The firm believes it may lose a large number of sales if it reduces output and increases its price (the elastic segment of the demand curve). At the same time, increasing output and lowering price could result in only a slight uptick in sales. The small increase in sales after a price decrease results from a possible price war, as rivals defend their revenues from the firm's lower prices (the inelastic segment of the demand curve). The two MC curves represent two different levels of costs. Whereas MR = MC is the optimal output quantity, in the segment of the MR curve that is discontinuous, there is no change in the output quantity.

To Collude or Not to Collude

That is the question … for firms in an oligopoly.

To answer the question, economists turn to game theory. Game theory aids decision making when there are a small number of firms that are interdependent. Game theory is the study of strategic decision making. We have already seen the strategies used in some decision models. We saw that if collusion is successful, the most profit is made, since the colluding firms behave as a monopoly. The noncooperative competitive models use the Nash equilibrium, where each firm makes the decisions that give it the greatest profit possible, given the actions of its competitors. These firms earn less profit than colluding firms, but more than a firm in perfect competition.

Now the question is how to earn the most profit without resorting to collusion, which is illegal. The firms in an oligopoly need a way to strike a balance between cooperating (effectively colluding) and competing.

The decision-making process of the oligopolists is similar to the quandary of the players in a famous game called the *prisoners' dilemma*. The scenario in the prisoners' dilemma is as follows:

Two suspects, Jack and Jill, are caught by the police for committing a crime. They are now in separate rooms in the police station. They cannot communicate with each other. The prosecutor tries to get each to confess to the crime. The prosecutor tells each prisoner:

- If one of you confesses and implicates the other, but the other does not confess, the one who confesses will get a 1-year sentence and the other will get 10 years in prison.

- If you both confess, you will each get a 5-year sentence.

- If neither of you confesses, each of you will be charged a misdemeanor and the prosecutor will seek a 2-year sentence.

We can compare the choices in a table, or *matrix*.

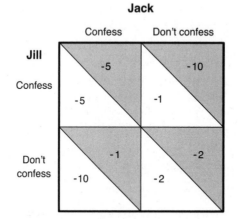

A Payoff Matrix:
Prisoners' Dilemma

In the payoff matrix for Jack and Jill, Jack and Jill both get 5 years in prison if both confess. If neither confesses, they both get 2 years in prison. If Jill doesn't confess, but Jack does and implicates Jill, Jill gets 10 years, and Jack gets 1 year in prison. If Jack doesn't confess, but Jill does and implicates Jack, Jill gets 1 year and Jack gets 10 years in prison. Confession is the dominant strategy for both Jack and Jill.

Jack and Jill face a dilemma: they can decide not to confess and go to jail for 2 years. If Jill does not confess, though, she worries she might be betrayed by Jack and have to serve 10 years in prison. No matter what Jill does, Jack is better off if he confesses. If Jill confesses, Jack gets 5 years if he confesses and 10 years if he does not. If Jill does not confess, Jack gets 1 year if he confesses and 2 years if he does not. Jill is also better off if she confesses, so Jack worries that if he doesn't confess, he will be betrayed by Jill and have to serve 10 years in prison. The best course for each is to confess and each go to jail for 5 years, even though that outcome is worse for both than if neither confessed. Therefore, confession is the *dominant strategy* for both.

DEFINITION

The **payoff** is the reward to a player in game theory. In economics, the payoff is profit. In game theory as used in economics, a **payoff matrix** is a table showing the payoff (profit) to each firm given its decision and the decision of its competitor. A **dominant strategy** is the best choice by a firm in a prisoners' dilemma situation or other game regardless of the action taken by the other firm. Not all games have a dominant strategy.

The lesson of the prisoners' dilemma is that when either behaves to maximize his or her own self-interest, the outcome is worse than choosing to cooperate.

Firms in an oligopoly are often faced with the same dilemma. Should they do whatever it takes to get the greatest market share to the detriment of their competitor, or should they be satisfied with the share they have in order to avoid a price war or other negative consequence?

Let's see how the prisoners' dilemma applies to a *duopoly*, two firms in an oligopoly. Firms A and B are two companies in an industry. They have an implicit agreement to keep prices high to maximize profits. Firm A is considering whether to break the implicit agreement to capture a greater market share. The business manager of Firm A uses the prisoners' dilemma model to see how reducing prices would play out. Knowing the costs, revenues, and demand for his firm and assuming the same information for Firm B, the business manager lists the alternatives as follows:

- If both Firm A and Firm B maintain a high level of prices, the profit for each company increases by $300 million as the firms grow.

- If Firm A lowers prices but Firm B does not, profits increase by $600 million for Firm A, as a result of gaining market share, while Firm B's profits would decrease by $100 million due to loss of market share.

- If both firms reduce prices, the increase in sales offsets the lower price, and profits for each company increase by $200 million instead of $300 million.

If the business manager of Firm A were thinking short-term, he or she would choose to reduce prices. That's because if Firm B chooses to maintain a high level of prices, it would benefit Firm A greatly to reduce prices. If Firm B chooses to reduce prices, Firm A would be better off also reducing prices than maintaining high prices and losing market share.

Reducing prices is the dominant strategy for both firms. The dominant strategy is the best choice regardless of the action taken by the other firm.

However, when both firms reduce prices, they are worse off than when they had the implicit agreement to maintain higher prices. Even if only Firm A reduced prices at first, that reduction could initiate a price war between the firms, to the detriment of both.

This is where implicit collusion strategies, such as price leadership and price signaling, come in. If the firms can figure out a way to maintain their implicit agreement without illegal collusion, they can break out of the prisoners' dilemma.

Implicit collusion is a fragile state and results in *price rigidity* in oligopolies, since firms don't want to disturb their peaceful coexistence with their competitors even when there is a change in their costs or demand. Price rigidity is the basis for the kinked demand curve described earlier.

DEFINITION

Price rigidity occurs when firms are resistant to changing their prices even if there is a change in demand or costs.

Antitrust Legislation and Oligopolists' Response

The antitrust legislation described in Chapter 12 about monopolies is used to attempt to rein in collusive and anticompetitive practices. These laws can be evaded to some extent with tactics such as price leadership and tacit collusion. Operating under a situation of tacit collusion is challenging. Any firm that cheats might instigate a price war.

Product differentiation and advertising are practices a firm can use to increase sales and gain a larger share of the market.

The Least You Need to Know

- An oligopoly is a market structure in which a few firms control all the supply in an industry.
- New firms have difficulty entering an industry dominated by an oligopoly because there are high barriers to entry.
- The firms in an oligopoly are interdependent. This causes them to be wary of each other as they try to maximize their profits. All firms must make decisions considering their competitors' output and pricing decisions.
- Game theory and the Nash equilibrium are used to make strategic decisions for profit maximization.
- Collusion to fix prices and output levels results in the greatest profit, but it is illegal.
- Tacit collusion is common, but fragile. A breakdown can cause a price war. Fear of a price war or losing market share in an attempt to raise prices results in price rigidity in oligopolies.
- Competition and product differentiation are noncollusive ways oligopolists can use to succeed in generating more sales and gaining market share.

CHAPTER 14

Monopolistic Competition

In the spectrum of market structures, monopolistic competition falls between the oligopoly and perfect competition. These are the firms that produce household brands of toothpaste, coffee, cereal, detergents, and many other products. You probably see more advertising by these companies than from any other market form. Without advertising, the companies that make similar products will capture some of their market share.

Let's take a closer look at the characteristics of monopolistic competition and how it compares to other market forms.

In This Chapter

- How monopolistic competition differs from other market structures
- Identifying the inefficiencies in monopolistic competition
- The importance of advertising and brand name recognition in monopolistic competition
- The similarities and differences among market structures

Characteristics of Monopolistic Competition

How does monopolistic competition compare with the polar opposites, perfect competition and the monopoly? Monopolistic competition has some characteristics of both perfect competition and the monopoly. First let's briefly review the main features of perfect competition and the monopoly.

Perfect competition has many thousands of producers. Sellers take the market price, which is equal to the marginal revenue (MR) and marginal cost (MC). In a perfectly competitive market there is zero economic profit in the long run, as firms enter and exit freely.

On the other extreme, a monopolist is the single source of supply in the industry and chooses a price on its downward sloping demand curve that is higher than where MR = MC. As long as that holds true, and average total costs are below the demand curve, a monopolist will make a profit in the short run and in the long run.

With these features in mind, let's see how monopolistic competition compares.

Many Producers and Differentiated Products

Monopolistic competition has many producers, but not as many as you'd find in a perfectly competitive market. No producer dominates. The firms are smaller than those in an oligopoly. As a result, unlike the oligopoly, the firm in the monopolistically competitive market does not usually have to concern itself with the decisions of its competitors. Instead it pours a lot of money into advertising to capture and maintain market share.

The firms in this market compete by selling differentiated products that are easily substituted for similar products, although they are not perfect substitutes. A consumer who is loyal to Crest toothpaste might be disappointed if the brand were out of stock at the local store, or if the price was significantly higher than another brand; but if he needed toothpaste, he would buy a different brand.

Dunkin' Donuts is a household name. It has a strong brand, but it doesn't control the donut industry. It only controls its brand. When Krispy Kreme donuts decided to become a public company in 2000, it got enormous publicity. Dunkin' Donuts had to work hard to retain its share of the donut market.

If you are in the habit of drinking Starbucks coffee, but Starbucks raised its price $2.00 per pound above the average price of the other brands, you might be inclined to lose your habit and try another brand. The same would be true of other branded products.

This is where price elasticity of demand comes into play. If the brand is elastic, demand is sensitive to a change in price. So if Starbucks raises its price, you would switch to another brand. If the price rose sharply in the coffee industry as a whole, you might decide to drink tea.

But we digress … the point is, the monopolistically competitive market features a variety of products and brands. The firms compete by touting the advantages of their brand through advertising.

Free Entry and Exit into the Industry

Unlike the monopoly or the oligopoly, there is free entry and exit into the industry. The firms control their own brand of product but are not the single source of supply to the market. The economies of scale are not formidable, which makes it easier for new firms to try their hand in coffee, toothpaste, soap, sporting goods, or the many other industries structured as monopolistically competitive markets.

Short-Run and Long-Run Equilibrium

The model of the short-run equilibrium of an industry assumes the number of firms is fixed. The long-run equilibrium assumes enough time has elapsed for firms to enter and exit the market, depending on their individual profitability. In the long run, the market returns to an equilibrium condition at zero economic profit. With no profit, there is no incentive to enter or exit. Remember, economic profit includes the opportunity cost of foregoing doing something else, not whether a firm makes an accounting profit.

A firm in a monopolistically competitive market has a downward-sloping demand curve. This implies that it has some market power, since it can set price above its marginal cost. However, the many competing firms put downward pressure on prices. While competition hampers its profits, it is still in a better position than a firm in perfect competition.

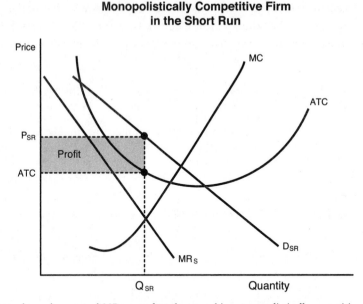

The short-run demand curve and MR curve slope downward in a monopolistically competitive market. The profit-maximizing output, Q_{SR} (SR = short run) is where MR = MC. The ATC is U-shaped and is below the short-run demand curve, so the firm is profitable. The profit is shown by the rectangle.

The marginal revenue (MR) curve is also downward-sloping and remains beneath the demand curve. The profit-maximizing output, Q_{SR} (SR = short run), is where MR = MC. The average total cost (ATC) curve is U-shaped, and the marginal cost (MC) curve slopes upward. As long as the ATC curve remains below the demand curve, the firm is profitable. The price chosen by the producer is on the demand curve at the profit-maximizing output level. The profit is the area of the shaded rectangle.

The long-run equilibrium is established after all unprofitable existing firms have exited the market, and new entrants have entered the market when existing firms are profitable. When firms enter the market, the added supply shifts the demand curve and MR curve to the left. This reduces the price for each unit sold, and profits decline.

When firms make zero profits, no firms will be encouraged to enter the market. When unprofitable firms exit the market in the long run, the demand curve and MR curve shift to the right. The price rises for all units the firm sells, and the firm is profitable. New entrants are attracted to a profitable market, which increases supply. When there is too much supply, the price retreats. In the long run, equilibrium is reached in the industry when there is no entry or exit of firms, which occurs when each firm is earning zero profit. The firms in a monopolistically competitive market earn zero profits when they cover their costs at the profit-maximizing output.

In the following figure, *Monopolistically Competitive Firm in the Long Run,* the demand curve and MR curve slope downward. The average total cost (ATC) curve is tangent to (just touching) the demand curve at the profit-maximizing output quantity. Remember that when the ATC curve is below the demand curve, a firm makes a profit. If the ATC curve is above the demand curve, the firm takes a loss. Either a profit or loss would prevent the industry from reaching a long-run equilibrium, which is when every existing firm makes zero profit at its profit-maximizing output quantity, when marginal revenue equals marginal cost (MR = MC) and price equals the average total cost (P_{LR} = ATC).

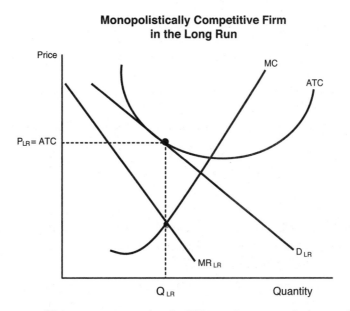

**Monopolistically Competitive Firm
in the Long Run**

The long-run equilibrium output occurs when the ATC curve is tangent to the downward-sloping demand curve at the profit-maximizing quantity of output, which is when MR = MC, P_{LR} = ATC. At this point, no individual firm is making a profit, so it has no incentive to exit or leave the industry.

When we compare the long-run equilibrium of the monopolistically competitive firm to that of the perfectly competitive firm, we find that they are similar in two ways:

1. They both have free entry and exit into and out of the industry.

2. The firms in both cases make zero profits in the long run.

The differences between these market structures highlight the *inefficiencies* of the monopolistically competitive market:

1. The perfectly competitive (PC) firm has equivalences $D = MR = MC = P_{PC}$. The monopolistically competitive (MC) firm has a price (P_{MC}) greater than MC ($P > MC$). This produces a *deadweight loss*. (See accompanying figure.) The monopolistically competitive firm is therefore inefficient.

2. The perfectly competitive market has a horizontal demand curve at long-run equilibrium and zero economic profit. The monopolistically competitive firm's demand curve is downward sloping. The zero-profit point of the monopolistically competitive firm is therefore to the left of the minimum average total cost (ATC) at long-run equilibrium, which causes *excess capacity*. Excess capacity is a sign of inefficiency.

DEFINITION

Excess capacity occurs when actual production is less than what is optimal for the firm.

When we compare the monopolistically competitive market with a monopoly, we find the following similarities and differences:

1. The monopoly makes profits in the short run and the long run.

2. The monopoly has barriers to entry.

3. They both set $MR = MC$ to maximize profits. They both have downward-sloping demand curves and MR curves, so $P > MC$.

4. They both can make profits as long as the ATC curve is below the demand curve, but in the long run at equilibrium and zero profit, the monopolistically competitive firm can only just cover costs. The monopoly makes a profit in the short run and the long run as long as the ATC curve is below the demand curve. It never makes zero profits.

Long-Run Equilibrium in Perfect Competition

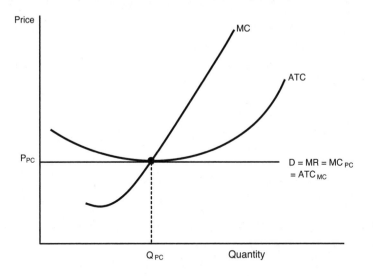

Long-Run Equilibrium in Monopolistic Competition

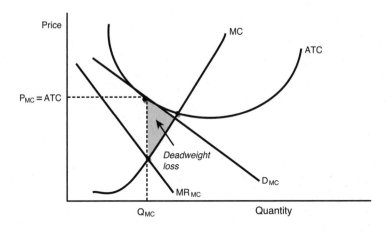

In perfect competition, $P_{PC} = MC = ATC = D = MR$. Since $P = MC$, the perfectly competitive market is efficient.

In the monopolistically competitive market, $P > MC$, generating a deadweight loss—an inefficiency. Since the demand curve and MR curve are downward sloping, the minimum point of the ATC curve is tangent to and on the left side of the demand curve. There is zero economic profit at this point. The firm produces at a quantity below the minimum ATC, so there is excess capacity.

Inefficiency of Monopolistic Competition

As described above, there are two primary inefficiencies in the monopolistically competitive market. The first is that price is greater than marginal cost. This results in a deadweight loss because some mutually beneficial transactions don't take place. A customer might be willing to pay up to the marginal cost, but not beyond.

The other inefficiency is that firms in this market structure operate with excess capacity because they produce less than the output at the minimal average total cost. Consumers appreciate a variety of products. Some economists believe, though, that monopolistically competitive industries have *too* much product diversity; that it is wasteful. They argue that average total costs would decrease with fewer sellers, which would lower prices.

There are no rules about this issue. Think about whether you would be happier with more variety, but a slightly higher price, or less choice at a slightly lower cost. We doubt you have ever contemplated this conundrum!

Advertising and Brand Name Recognition

One thing you *do* know is that you are surrounded by advertising campaigns. If you only get your information and entertainment from the internet, you cannot avoid the advertising. Even the software and big data have become, some might say, a bit like Big Brother following you around. Now the advertisers have got you pegged when you enter a mall if you carry a smartphone. Whether this bothers you or not, advertising is getting personal.

It is impossible to avoid advertising. Take a tour of the big cities in areas like Times Square in New York City, Piccadilly Circus in London, Tokyo in Japan, and many other metropolises—you will be surrounded by enormous electronic billboards. Television, newspapers, spam emails and telephone calls, even sponsoring for high school events—advertising is everywhere.

> **INTERESTING FACT**
>
> Advertising is not a modern phenomenon. As early as 4000 B.C., walls and stones were painted in India. Sales messages were painted onto papyrus and stones in ancient Egypt, Greece, and Rome. Historians tell of Egyptians hanging papyrus notices for runaway slaves. Walls of ancient Pompeii were covered in billboard-type advertising. Some promoted merchandise, while others announced events or political candidates.

The goal of advertising is to persuade you that a company's products, services, and brand are the best. The hope is that you will eventually be a loyal customer. Ads can also be informative. If you aren't told of a new product that you might find useful or attractive, advertising brings it to your attention. A very clever ad might even convince you to change brands.

Did you know, though, that advertising only makes sense in a market structure that sells at a price higher than its marginal cost? Only the firms with market power advertise. Advertising is not necessary when there is perfect competition, because sellers and buyers take the market price.

Firms with market power, especially those in the monopolistically competitive market structure, use branding as a primary method of gaining market share. This makes sense if you think about it. Why would a firm in a perfectly competitive market bother to spend money on marketing when it has no price advantage? Advertising is expensive. Would the extra sales cover the cost? On the other hand, firms with market power can factor in the cost of advertising and choose a sales price accordingly.

Are branding and advertising socially useful? This is a question some economists consider. Whether or not it is socially useful, it is not going away. Advertising is a fact of life.

Comparing Market Structures

Before leaving the subject of market structure, let's do a final comparison of the main features of each form.

Market Structures

Perfect Competition	Monopolistic Competition	Oligopoly	Monopoly
Large number of buyers and sellers	Many sellers	Few sellers; firms are interdependent	Single source of supply
Homogeneous product	Differentiated product	Homogeneous or differentiated product	Unique product
Easy entry and exit	Fairly easy entry and exit	Restricted	Restricted or no entry
Demand curve is horizontal; elastic; P = D = MR = MC	Demand curve is downward sloping; relatively elastic; MR curve is below demand curve	Demand curve is downward sloping; various elasticities; MR curve is below demand curve	Demand curve is downward sloping; various elasticities; MR curve is below demand curve

continues

Market Structures   (continued)

Perfect Competition	Monopolistic Competition	Oligopoly	Monopoly
Price taker P = MC	Price maker, with exceptions P > MC	Price maker P > MC	Price maker P > MC
Small firms	Small/medium-size firms	Large firms	Large firm
Economic profits possible in the short run; zero economic profits in the long run	Economic profits possible in the short run; zero economic profits in the long run	Economic profits possible in the short run and the long run	Economic profits in the short run and the long run

The next time you go shopping or do business with a company, try to identify in which market structure it belongs. See if the comparisons hold up to what has been presented here.

The Least You Need to Know

- There are many monopolistically competitive firms, which are small to medium in size.
- Monopolistically competitive firms compete with product differentiation, branding, and advertising.
- In the short run, the profits of monopolistically competitive firms attract new firms into the market. Short-run losses encourage exit from the market.
- The long-run equilibrium is established at zero economic profit.
- Two inefficiencies of monopolistically competitive firms include selling at a price greater than marginal cost and operating with excess capacity.

PART 4

Macroeconomics

Measuring and managing economic growth, observing the flows of money and goods and services throughout the economic sectors, foreseeing and forestalling the crises of the business cycle, deciding whether and how much government regulation is best—all lie within the realm of macroeconomics. While microeconomics focuses on the individual and firms, macroeconomics takes the wide view, encompassing all businesses, consumers and households, government, labor and unemployment, money, central banks and the banking system, inflation, deflation, recessions, and more.

Macroeconomics came into being largely as a result of the Great Depression of the 1930s. John Maynard Keynes developed a theory that broke from the prevailing classical model of a self-regulating economy in the long run. According to the classicists, no intervention is needed to ameliorate recessions or inflation in the here and now. Keynesian philosophy, on the other hand, proposes that there *is* a role for government and central bank assistance in the short run during such crises. Today policymakers and business leaders keep a watchful eye on the health of the economy. Which ideas will be effective to develop and rebalance the economy when it is out of kilter is an ongoing debate.

Part 4 explains the interrelationship of the many moving parts that make up the economy. Models illustrate how the basic machinery works. Excesses that can wreak periodic havoc are examined, along with how the government and central bank use tools to rein in or repair the damage. The goal is economic progress and growth. Policymakers who are charged with undertaking this task require flexibility, imagination, and determination.

Whether you plan to join other economists in shaping policy, work in the business world, or simply want to have a deeper understanding of where the economy is heading, Part 4 will provide the information you need to know.

CHAPTER 15

Keeping Track of Growth: The National Accounts

If you were in the market to buy a business, the first thing you would do is examine its accounting books. You would want to know its activity, sales, inventory, assets and liabilities, overhead, and other factors that would tell you whether the business was healthy. The same principal is applied to evaluating an economy. The flows of money, goods, and services from one sector of the economy to another can reveal its underlying strengths and weaknesses and whether the economy is in balance.

You would also want to know if the business was growing—how this year's income and profit compares to last year's. What does the trend over several years tell you? In the same way, looking at the growth trajectory of an economy is crucial for policymakers so that any hint of a problem can be addressed before it becomes difficult to manage.

This chapter will outline what the national accounts are and how they work, what is included in the gross domestic product and how it is calculated, and what this information tells us.

In This Chapter

- National income accounting: a measure of the level of economic activity in a given time period
- How money flows through the economy
- A detailed look at the gross domestic product
- How to calculate the GDP

National Income Accounting

National income accounting measures the level of economic activity in a given time period. The data provided give a picture of the health of the economy. The System of National Accounts follows producer sales, business spending on investment, consumer spending, and government purchases.

> **INTERESTING FACT**
>
> Useful data on government activity was hard to come by before the Great Depression of the 1930s. Without this information, it was difficult for economists and government officials to evaluate the state and direction of the economy. As John Maynard Keynes developed his macroeconomic theories, which asserted that government intervention could help to reverse a severe economic contraction, the need for a rigorous national accounting system became evident. A first version was presented to Congress in 1937, and a full report on the gross domestic product was issued in 1942.
>
> Since Keynesian economics developed during the period after the Great Depression, it makes sense that the structure of the accounting system goes hand-in-hand with the dominant models economists use to analyze the economy.

Understanding Output

We know if a country is healthy and growing by judging its *output*. Output is the quantity of goods or services produced in a given time period, by a firm, industry, or country. *Inputs* are used to produce the products. Inputs are the factors of production.

The output of the economy is divided into *production* and *demand*. Under the production column of the accounting ledger, output is distributed as wages to labor, and interest and dividends to owners of capital. Under the demand column, output is invested or consumed by the private sector, and it is also needed for government expenditure and international trade.

On the production side, the study of *growth* and *aggregate supply* focuses on the *factor payments* such as wages, profit, interest, and rent. On the demand side the analysis of *aggregate demand* concentrates on consumption and investment. Demand and production (input and output) should be in equilibrium. Measures of the overall price level are included in the national income accounts.

> **DEFINITION**
>
> **Aggregate supply** is the total supply of goods and services produced within an economy at a given overall price level in a given time period, also called total output. **Aggregate demand** is the total amount of goods and services demanded in the economy at a given overall price level and in a given time period. **Factor payments** are the payments made—wages, interest, rent, and profit payments—to the scarce resources and factors of production (labor, capital, land, and entrepreneurship), in return for productive services.

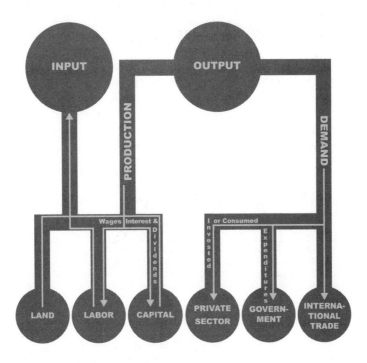

The Flow of Funds Through the Economy

Let's take a small economy, where one couple decides to open a small business. The couple is also a household in our model, which provides the labor, capital, land, and entrepreneurship (factors of production) to open and run the business. In return, the business pays money to the couple, or household, to use the factors of production as follows:

Business Pays to Household per Year

Business	Household
Rent for the building lease	$10,000 per year
Rent for the use of land	10,000 per year
Labor in the form of wages	10,000 per year
Profit as owners, entrepreneurship	?*
Total income to household from business payments	?**
	*, ** We haven't calculated profit yet.

The purpose of starting the business is to provide the couple with food, shelter, and money for other goods and services. So the business is able to sell back to the household goods and services, such as food and renting out property. In this simple example it is the couple's own property. In exchange for the food and shelter provided by the business, the household pays the business as follows:

Household Pays to Business per Year

Household	Business
Food	$20,000
Rent of their house	15,000
Total expenditures of household to business	$35,000

The payment by the household to the business for food and shelter is considered revenue to the business as follows:

Revenue to the Business from the Household per Year

Business	Household
Food	$20,000
Rent of the house	15,000
Total income (revenue) for the business from the household	$35,000

The revenue for the business is $35,000. The expenses for the business—rent for the lease, the land, and labor—are $30,000. The profit for the business is revenue ($35,000) minus expenses ($30,000) leaving $5,000 in profit per year. The profit goes to the couple as owners of the business, so it can be added to the income to the household from the business as follows:

Business Pays to Household per Year

Business	Household
Rent for the building lease	$10,000
Rent for the land	10,000
Labor in the form of wages	10,000
Profit as owners, entrepreneurship	5,000
Total income to household from business payments	$35,000

We see that the total revenue to the business from the household per year ($35,000) equals the total income to the household from business payments ($35,000).

To summarize, the household is providing the business with the factors of production, for which it is paid, and the business provides goods and services, for which it is paid. All of this production is considered the gross domestic product for this small economy.

We can apply the workings of this small economy to the real, complicated economy in which we live. It is not quite as tidy, but it is the same idea. Notice that in the larger economy, below, the government and the outside world are included as major sectors, and the financial markets are added.

The major sectors of the economy are the households, firms, government, and the outside world. Three markets connect these sectors: 1) factor markets, 2) markets for goods and services, and 3) financial markets. The funds flow as follows:

- Firms to households via factor markets as wages, interest, profit, and rent

- Households to government for taxes

- Government to households as *transfers*

- Households to financial markets for savings

- Households to markets for goods and services as consumer spending

- The outside world: private savings and funds via the financial markets including investment and borrowing by firms and governments both foreign and domestic

- Government and households to firms for goods and services

- From the outside world for exports; to the outside world for imports

DEFINITION

Government transfers are payments to individuals without any exchange of goods or services, such as Social Security and welfare.

The Gross Domestic Product

As described above, the basic measure of output is the *gross domestic product (GDP)*. The GDP is also defined as the market value of all final goods and services—including capital goods, new construction, and changes to inventories—produced in the country within a given period, usually a year. Another way to evaluate the GDP is to sum all the factor payments.

GDP Components–United States ($ Billions)

	Line		2009 I	2009 II	2009 III	2009 IV	2010 I
	1	Gross domestic product	14,178.0	14,151.2	14,242.1	14,453.8	14,601.4
C	2	Personal consumption expenditures	9,987.7	9,999.3	10,132.9	10,236.4	10,362.3
	3	Goods	3,197.7	3,193.8	3,292.3	3,337.1	3,406.6
	4	Durable goods	1,025.2	1,011.5	1,051.3	1,052.0	1,072.8
	5	Nondurable goods	2,172.4	2,182.2	2,241.0	2,285.1	2,333.8
	6	Services	6,790.0	6,805.6	6,840.6	6,899.3	6,955.8
I	7	Gross private domestic investment	1,689.9	1,561.5	1,556.1	1,707.8	1,763.8
	8	Fixed investment	1,817.2	1,737.7	1,712.6	1,731.4	1,726.9
	9	Nonresidential	1,442.6	1,391.8	1,353.9	1,366.9	1,371.3
	10	Structures	533.1	494.8	457.9	434.1	417.5
	11	Equipment and software	909.5	897.0	895.9	932.8	953.9
	12	Residential	374.6	345.9	358.8	364.5	355.5
	13	Change in private inventories	-127.4	-176.2	-156.5	-23.6	36.9
X-M	14	Net exports of goods and services	-378.5	-339.1	-402.2	-449.5	-499.4
	15	Exports	1,509.3	1,493.7	1,573.8	1,680.1	1,729.3
	16	Goods	989.5	978.1	1,045.2	1,140.6	1,180.0
	17	Services	519.8	515.6	528.5	539.6	549.3
	18	Imports	1,887.9	1,832.8	1,976.0	2,129.7	2,228.7
	19	Goods	1,508.2	1,461.1	1,592.8	1,739.4	1,827.8
	20	Services	379.6	371.7	383.1	390.3	400.9
G	21	Government consumption expenditures and gross investment	2,879.0	2,929.4	2,955.4	2,959.2	2,974.7
	22	Federal	1,106.7	1,138.3	1,164.3	1,170.1	1,186.4
	23	National defense	750.7	776.2	795.8	793.5	805.6
	24	Nondefense	356.0	362.1	368.5	376.7	380.7
	25	State and local	1,772.3	1,791.2	1,791.1	1,789.0	1,788.3

Source: U.S. Bureau of Economic Analysis

The sum of all the consumer spending, investment spending by firms, government purchases, and the value of exports minus the value of imports in the above flows of money throughout the sectors is the gross domestic product (GDP).

What Is Included in the GDP?

Let's focus on and clarify the GDP defined as "the market value of all final goods and services produced in the country within a given period." The *market value* is the price of each final good or service. This does not include, for example, illegal activity or goods and services produced in the household. If you clean your own house or cook in your home for your own consumption, it would not be included in the GDP. The goods and services have to involve an exchange of payments. The meaning of *final* goods is that the intermediary costs of products used to make the final goods are not included in the GDP because this plus the market value of the final good would total more than 100 percent of the price of the final good.

The last part of the definition of GDP is that it has to be produced within a country. This means that as long as the good is produced within the geographical boundary of the country, it is included in the GDP. The gross national product (GNP) allocates production by ownership rather than geographical location. It is a measure of all income earned by the citizens of a country regardless of where it is made, calculated over a specific period of time, usually one year.

How to Calculate the GDP

Looking again at the small economy in the previous section, we were able to calculate the household *expenditures*, the food and rent, and the *income* to the household from the business for the factors of production; and in exchange for the goods and services from the business, the household has *expenditures* that are *revenue* to the business.

Which should be used to calculate the GDP of this small economy—the household expenditures, the household income, or the business income? The accounting method would have to make sure not to count something twice or even three times. To avoid this, we could measure only the household expenditures, or we could measure only the household income. The business revenue is the same thing as the household expenditures. We want to make sure not to duplicate any categories in our counting. GDP in the small economy would have these equivalences:

GDP = Household Expenses = Business Revenue = [Business Expenses + Profit] = Household Income

There are three methods, then, of calculating GDP:

1. The production, or output, approach

2. The expenditure approach

3. The income approach

The results of each approach should yield the same result. All three methods are used to calculate the GDP.

The production approach. There are two ways to calculate GDP with the production approach. The first is to add up the market values of all final goods and services produced in the country within a given period. Here, the value of intermediate goods at each stage of production are not included in the sum, in order to avoid double-counting. The second is called the *value added* method. With this method, intermediate goods are included; however only the value added of each producer is included in the GDP (value of its sales – value of inputs purchased from other businesses). The production approach, or value added method, can be further broken down into value added to the economy by the major sectors of the economy: government, households, and businesses.

The expenditure approach. We can measure GDP by taking the total, or *aggregate*, spending on domestically produced final goods and services by final buyers.

The GDP, designated in equations as Y, can be described as private consumption (C) plus gross investment (I) plus government spending (G) plus [exports minus imports (X – M)], or

$$\text{GDP (Y)} = C + I + G + (X - M)$$

Consumption, usually the largest component of GDP, is defined as any final domestic spending on newly produced final goods or services by private households. Examples are refrigerators, food, rent, medical expenses, and personal items, but do not include new homes, which are investments.

Investment by businesses include new capital equipment, software, inventory, building structures, or construction of a new mine. For households, an example of investments would include new homes. Investment, when used as part of the GDP, does not refer to an investment in the financial markets. Investment in the financial markets would be classified as *savings*.

Government spending on goods and services includes salaries of government employees and military equipment, but does not include transfer payments, such as Social Security and welfare.

Imports (M) subtracted from *exports (X)*—or net exports (NX)—must also be included because imports represent income spent on goods and services that are not produced domestically.

Also included in the GDP are some goods and services that are part of a country's output but are not sold on the market. They are calculated with *imputed* values. This is done by comparing the market value of similar goods and services or adding up the cost to produce the products. The goods and services in this category include those generated by nonprofit services that are free of charge, goods and services that are produced and used within a business, renovations to a home by the owner and occupier, agricultural production consumed by the producer and household, and bank services that are not charged outright.

The factor income approach. The third method used to calculate GDP is to sum up the payments to factors of production. As shown in the example of the small economy flows, these would include the wages to labor, the rent for leases on land or structures, the interest on capital earned by lending to businesses and the government, and the profit as shareholder dividends.

Real GDP, Nominal GDP, and Per Capita GDP

The goal of comparing the current GDP to the previous year's GDP is to find out the change in output and therefore growth. Over time, a trend can be identified. Getting a clear picture of growth, though, is hampered by the effect of inflation or deflation on the change in GDP for two or more years. To know if an economy is actually growing, the GDP calculation has to be adjusted to account for an increase or decrease in general price level.

To begin the calculation, the *aggregate output* has to be measured in order to obtain the *real GDP*. The *nominal GDP* is the GDP of the current year in current prices. When economists calculate the change in the GDP from one year to the next, they use *chained dollars* in their result. Chained dollars is the method used to calculate the change in real GDP using the average between the growth rate using an early base year and the growth rate calculated using a late base year.

> ### DEFINITION
>
> The **aggregate output** is the total quantity of final goods and services produced by the economy. The **real GDP** is the total value of final goods and services produced by the economy during a given year, calculated using the prices of a base year. The base year is given by the issuing government agency along with the real GDP figure. The **nominal GDP** is the GDP of the current year in current prices. **Chained dollars** is the method used to calculate the change in real GDP using the average between the growth rate using an early base year and the growth rate calculated using a late base year.

To compare the growth within an economy, we can look at the real GDP for each year. If we want to know how the real GDP of one country matches against the real GDP of another country, the aggregate output of a large country will be greater than the aggregate output of a small country. To have an accurate comparison, the size of the population must be included in the calculation. This is accomplished by calculating the *per capita GDP*. The per capita GDP can be obtained by dividing the GDP by the population size of a country. The growth of various countries can now be compared.

GDP Growth and the Standard of Living

An economy that is steadily growing year over year tells us only one thing: the economy is growing year over year. We do not know how that growth is put to use in the country. We do not know what the standard of living is in the country. We do not know whether people are satisfied with their economic lives, or whether the standard of living is uniform among the population sectors. It would be a mistake to assume, then, that a growing economy can be equated with a growing standard of living. When comparing the well-being of people in different countries, be aware that GDP growth does not give us information about the standard of living. Indeed, if the country is growing, but the standard of living is lagging, this is a matter for policymakers.

The real GDP per capita figure, however, *can* tell us something about the standard of living. If there is an increase in population with a stagnant real GDP, each person gets a smaller share of the GDP. This results in a lower standard of living. Conversely, if the real GDP is increasing over time, indicating a growing economy, but the population is stable, the overall standard of living increases. This does not get policymakers off the hook, since how the wealth is distributed is still a factor in the well-being of individuals.

The Least You Need to Know

- National income accounting measures the level of economic activity in a given time period.
- The size of an economy can be measured by its aggregate output.
- The gross domestic product (GDP) is the basic measure of output in an economy.
- Three methods of calculating GDP are the production, expenditure, and factor income approaches.
- The growth of GDP in a country alone does not equate to a rise in the standard of living. The per capita real GDP figure gives us this information.

CHAPTER 16

Unemployment and Inflation

Unemployment and inflation: why are these seemingly unrelated topics paired? What's the connection? You might have heard that, at least in the United States, monetary policy is aimed at keeping unemployment low and prices stable. That gives us a clue that there is a relationship between unemployment and inflation. At a minimum, these are two unloved intruders in economic life.

This chapter will show how unemployment and inflation are related and how policymakers attempt to manage them. Before we discuss how unemployment and inflation are related, let's find out more about each independently.

In This Chapter

- Understanding the unemployment rate
- The natural and actual rate of unemployment
- Categories of unemployment: frictional, structural, and cyclical
- How unemployment and inflation are related
- Factors considered in creating unemployment policy
- Understanding the Phillips Curve

The Unemployment Rate

Getting an accurate figure for *unemployment* is not as straightforward as it may seem. It makes sense that unemployment increases or decreases along with fluctuations in the business cycle, when there are periods of increasing and decreasing demand for goods and services. Nonetheless, as we'll see, people are out of work for other reasons. Identifying the trend in unemployment categories is important in order to diagnose the problem and develop appropriate policies.

DEFINITION

Unemployment is the number of people that are not currently employed but are actively seeking work.

Who Is Counted as Unemployed?

We know that when people are working and earning wages they are employed. In order to evaluate the unemployment picture, get a sense of how the economy is faring, and consider policy, the government keeps track of unemployment figures to see how many people are unemployed, learn which industries are most affected, and identify the unemployment trend.

There are indicators that report the number of people who are employed and others that report the number of unemployed workers. To understand what the unemployment numbers represent, we must first know what groups are *not* counted as unemployed.

The following groups are not counted as unemployed:

Retired workers. Retired workers have completed their working career. In most developed countries, retired workers have some form of ongoing benefits. (A comparison of retirement benefits in 20 countries is compiled in the Melbourne Mercer Global Pension Index: http://www.mercer.us/articles/globalpensionindex2013.)

Workers on disability benefits while they are unable to work.

Children. Sadly, although most agree that children should be in school rather than in the workforce, in some countries they are working, usually in poor conditions. Nevertheless, children are not counted as unemployed if they are not working for wages.

Marginally attached workers. These are workers who are discouraged after being unable to find work for long periods of time but would like to work. Some are working part-time, although they would rather have full-time jobs. This category is described in more detail later in this chapter.

Who is included in the unemployment figure? A person is counted as unemployed if they are not currently employed but have been actively seeking work for some period of time. The duration required to qualify as being unemployed varies by country.

Calculating the Unemployment Rate

To calculate the *unemployment rate*, we first have to define the meaning of the *labor force*. The labor force is the total of all employed and unemployed workers. The unemployment rate is the percentage of the number of people in the labor force who are unemployed. The numbers are usually obtained from a survey of a sampling of the population.

 **DEFINITION**

The **unemployment rate** is the percentage of the total number of individuals in the labor force who are unemployed but are actively seeking jobs. The **labor force** is the total of all employed and unemployed workers.

The unemployment rate reveals the extent of unemployment for workers actively seeking work in a society. The *labor force participation rate* offers another clue to analyze the job market. A decrease in the labor force participation rate will lower the unemployment rate because when people leave the labor force—whether to go back to school, retrain to improve job skills, or because they give up trying to get a job—they are no longer counted as unemployed. The accompanying figure from the St. Louis Federal Reserve/U.S. Department of Labor tells a tale of a drop in labor force participation rate in the United States from a high in the year 2000 until its publication on November 8, 2013.

DEFINITION

The **labor force participation rate** is the percentage of working-age people in the labor force.

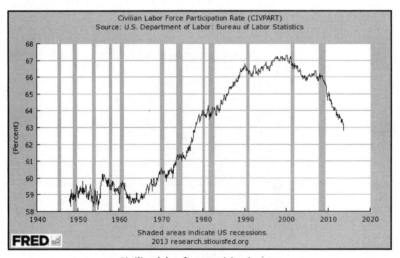

Civilian labor force participation rate
U.S. Department of Labor 11/08/2013
(Courtesy, St. Louis Federal Reserve)

DO THE MATH

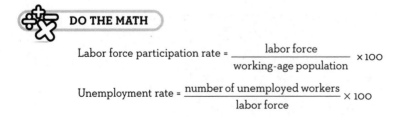

$$\text{Labor force participation rate} = \frac{\text{labor force}}{\text{working-age population}} \times 100$$

$$\text{Unemployment rate} = \frac{\text{number of unemployed workers}}{\text{labor force}} \times 100$$

The unemployment rate does not necessarily give the true picture of the labor situation. Since the definition of unemployment is that the individual must be actively seeking work, people who are discouraged by not being hired after pounding the pavement are not included in the unemployment figure. Another group is working part-time even though they would prefer full-time employment. As an example, a person with special skills, such as a computer programmer who cannot find a job in his or her field, instead settles for a job as a part-time sales representative. This latter group is considered underemployed. *Marginally attached workers* are not counted in the unemployment figure. These are people who have looked for a job and want a job, but have temporarily stopped looking.

These groups are included in the U6 designation of the U.S. Department of Labor statistics for unemployment: total unemployed, plus all persons marginally attached to the labor force, plus total employed part time for economic reasons, as a percent of the civilian labor force plus all persons marginally attached to the labor force. Economists and policymakers must factor the U6 category into their thinking to understand the health of the economy and design appropriate solutions to reduce unemployment.

The Natural Rate of Unemployment

Unemployment ebbs and flows along with the growth rate in the economy. More growth results in lower unemployment; unemployment rises during periods of economic slowdown. The rate of unemployment will never reach zero because there is a continual turnover in jobs. The churn can be caused by industries emerging and declining, people changing jobs or dismissed, individual companies form or go out of business, and young people enter the workforce for the first time. While workers are looking for a new job, they are unemployed. This type of unemployment is known as *frictional unemployment*. Even when jobs are plentiful, there will still be frictional unemployment.

The *natural rate of unemployment* is the normal unemployment rate around which the *actual unemployment* rate fluctuates, calculated as frictional unemployment plus structural unemployment.

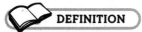 **DEFINITION**

Actual unemployment is the natural unemployment plus the cyclical unemployment. The **natural rate of unemployment** is the normal unemployment rate around which the actual unemployment rate fluctuates. It includes frictional and structural unemployment.

Frictional Unemployment

After leaving a job, either voluntarily or involuntarily, people can take considerable time looking for another that seems attractive and matches their skills. The time between jobs can extend if the job seeker has particular criteria for location, industry, or size of the company. The economy and the individual benefit from a careful job search, since both employer and employee are best served by a good fit. If the economy is doing well, it could take weeks to find a new job. If the economy is slow, and there is a high unemployment rate, the lag between jobs will be longer. Frictional unemployment is not a problem for the economy, since there are as many people job hunting as there are jobs available. There is no imbalance in the number of workers available and the number of job openings.

Structural Unemployment

When there is patchy unemployment because an industry has contracted, a geographical region has an oversupply of workers, or there are enough workers with a specific skill, the term used to define this type of unemployment is *structural unemployment*. Finding a job when there is structural unemployment is more difficult and takes more time than is the case with frictional unemployment. Classical economists believe that—as in other markets—when supply is greater than demand for workers, there are more jobs available *at a given wage rate,* so fewer jobs are offered. This is the supply and demand mechanism at work again. Just as with supply and demand of a good, the labor market will find an equilibrium point at an agreed-upon wage rate when demand for labor at a particular wage rate equals the supply of labor at that wage rate. Stated another way, when the wage rate asked is too high, there is less demand. When the wage rate offered is high enough, more workers apply for the job.

**Labor Supply and Demand Curves
and Real Wage Equilibrium**

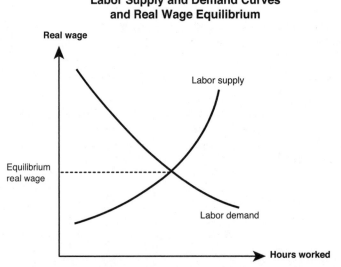

Some economists believe that a minimum wage contributes to structural unemployment. A minimum wage is a price floor established by law. By establishing a minimum wage, the government hopes to increase the income of low-skilled workers. While the concept appears to be fair and helpful, economists using the model of supply and demand of labor and the market equilibrium wage rate believe that raising the minimum wage results in more workers seeking employment at the higher wage than the number of workers demanded at the minimum wage. There is more supply of labor than demand for labor, and this causes structural unemployment. Other economists disagree, saying that employers manipulate the labor market by restricting hiring to keep wages low. A few empirical studies have been done in the United States by comparing neighboring states with and without a minimum wage. In these studies, there was little or no evidence of a drop in employment as a result of the introduction of a minimum wage. However, this issue is still highly controversial.

Structural unemployment is more intransient than frictional unemployment. From a policy perspective, there are few obvious remedies for structural unemployment, although it has been suggested that when there is a mismatch of workers' skills with the skills needed by employers, retraining might help.

Cyclical Unemployment

Cyclical unemployment is related to the business cycle, rising and falling around the natural rate of unemployment. There is also a relationship between cyclical unemployment and the *output gap*. The output gap is the percentage difference between the actual level of real GDP and potential output (GDP). *Potential output* is the output (real GDP) the economy can achieve if it is operating at its most efficient level. When actual aggregate output equals potential output, the actual unemployment rate equals the natural rate of unemployment. When the aggregate output gap is positive, the unemployment rate is below the natural rate. The opposite is true when the output gap is negative. In other words, when the economy's efficiency is below par, there is higher unemployment. When it is operating at full steam, unemployment is lower.

> **DEFINITION**
>
> **Potential output** is the output (real GDP) the economy can achieve when it is most efficient. The **output gap** is the percentage difference between the actual level of real GDP and potential output (GDP).

According to Keynesian theory, cyclical unemployment is caused by a lack of aggregate demand in the economy, which is unable to provide jobs for everyone. Cyclical unemployment is not necessarily benign, since an economic contraction can last a long time. Keynesian economists believe that cyclical unemployment can be helped by policy intervention, such as fiscal or monetary stimulus.

The Relationship Between Unemployment and Inflation

What does inflation have to do with unemployment? Inflation, in particular the inflation rate, has a significant effect on the economy. The general price level may rise without adversely impacting the economy because the *real wage* (wage rate divided by the price level) and the *real income* (income divided by the price level) do not change over time. What does matter is the *rate of inflation*, the percent change in the price level.

A high inflation rate causes purchasing power to deteriorate because the value of the money you hold is eroded by rising prices. Consider the tax effects of a high inflation rate. If you sell your house after having lived there for 20 years, on paper you will have a capital gain, and there will be a substantial capital gains tax. The reality is that adjusted for inflation, your real capital gain, if any, is much less than the taxes you will be paying.

Inflation impacts long-term contracts, since a high rate of inflation lessens the value of money over time. A collective bargaining agreement usually has a cost-of-living adjustment to account for inflationary pressures. The cost-of-living adjustment protects workers from erosion of their purchasing power over time.

Inflation has an impact on lending as well. A loan is calculated using nominal interest rates, which do not adjust for inflation. As a result, a rise in the inflation rate on a long-term loan is to your benefit as the debtor, since as time passes you will be paying with depreciated money. If you are the lender, you stand to lose loan value if the rate of inflation rises because you are being paid in money that is worth less than it was when you initiated the loan. The opposite is true during a deflationary cycle.

Inflation, Unemployment, Policy, and the Phillips Curve

Alban William Phillips—a New Zealand-born economist who studied and taught at the London School of Economics—presented a model in 1958 that showed an inverse relationship between inflation and unemployment.

INTERESTING FACT

If you imagine that economists might be boring, the early life of A. William Phillips might change your mind. As a young man, Phillips moved from New Zealand to Australia to find work. He got jobs as a crocodile hunter and a cinema manager. Phillips traveled to China in 1937 but soon after escaped to Russia after the Japanese invaded China. He then went on to Great Britain, studied electrical engineering, and then joined the Royal Air Force. Phillips fled the Japanese from Singapore to Java, where he learned Chinese while a prisoner of war for three-and-a-half years before returning to Great Britain and to college.

Phillips tracked unemployment rates and wage inflation in the United Kingdom. He plotted them on a graph, which showed the relationship as a curve so that when inflation rose, unemployment decreased; when unemployment rose, inflation fell.

Employers do not have to worry about attracting workers by raising wages if there is high unemployment, so it makes sense that high unemployment results in lower inflation. When they need employees, they would have to advertise a higher wage in order to attract prospects. Other economists applied the concept in their countries and agreed that the relationship bore out.

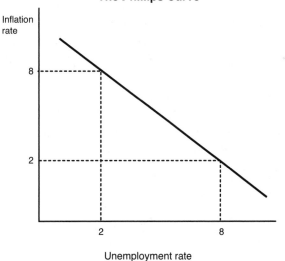

The Phillips Curve

The Phillips model encouraged policymakers to try to moderate unemployment and inflation using fiscal and monetary policy tools to adjust the inflation rate. When the inflation rate is high, the central bank can raise interest rates, causing a tightening in the money supply. When the unemployment rate is high, central banks can increase the supply of money by lowering interest rates. Fiscal measures can also be taken to increase aggregate demand, such as building projects.

The Phillips model was used until the 1970s, when a supply shock—the oil embargo of 1973—caused a surge in the inflation rate as well as unemployment, a combination known as *stagflation*. (See Chapter 17 for more on stagflation.) This simultaneous event invalidated Phillips's model.

Economists Milton Friedman and Edmund Phelps developed a different model for unemployment and inflation based on their belief that wages rise and fall with the demand for labor. Their theory held up during the period of stagflation because their premise was that wage earners and employers used an inflation-adjusted index in their contracts.

The Phillips Curve is still used for short-term policy, which is responsive to shorter duration fluctuations in the rates of inflation and unemployment. It is referred to as the short-run Phillips Curve or the Expectations-Augmented Phillips Curve, which takes inflationary expectations into account by a shift up in the curve.

Edmund Phelps later developed a model for a long-run Phillips Curve. This model was based on the theory that only a single rate of unemployment (the non-accelerating inflation rate of unemployment, NAIRU, also known as the natural rate of unemployment) was consistent with a stable inflation rate. The long-run Phillips Curve is vertical, with no trade-off between inflation and unemployment. This theory also addressed the short run, so that policymakers could still try to manage short-term inflation and unemployment. The short-run Phillips Curve shifts to the right and up when expansionary policy is instituted. The problem with this action is that the new equilibrium would rest at a higher inflation rate than the original equilibrium, thus accelerating inflation. (See Chapter 17 for an example of this model.) Although there are problems with this model, it was able to explain stagflation.

At this time the challenge of managing unemployment and inflation has not been met. Old models are revised, and new models are researched. The economy is very complex, and there are many variables and surprises.

The Least You Need to Know

- In order to be counted as unemployed, a non-employed worker must be actively seeking work for a given period of time.

- A complete picture of the amount of unemployed workers in an economy must account for those who are counted as unemployed as well as those considered underemployed.

- Unemployment can be classified as frictional, structural, and cyclical. Policy choices rely on these categories.

- Inflation affects unemployment because the value of wages decreases unless a work contract includes a cost-of-living adjustment. When wage inflation is high, employers are less likely to hire new workers, contributing to an increase in the unemployment rate in the short run.

CHAPTER 17

Inflation and Deflation

"Consumer prices in the euro zone are rising at the slowest pace since the depths of the global financial crisis, fueling new fears that too little inflation, rather than too much, will threaten Europe's fragile recovery and the world's." So began an article on the front page of the November 1, 2013, *Wall Street Journal.* "So, what's the problem with too little inflation?" you might ask. "I thought inflation was bad for the consumer." You'd be right if there were too much inflation, but like Goldilocks, the economy needs inflation to be "just right." The technical term is price stability.

Keeping inflation and deflation under control is a function of the government and central banks. Either extreme can be problematic for an economy. This chapter will examine inflation and deflation, their causes, how they are measured, and the tools the government and central banks use to manage them.

In This Chapter

- Inflation: the causes, measurement, and cures
- Causes and consequences of deflation
- The causes of hyperinflation
- Stagflation: when unemployment and inflation rise together
- Chronic deflation and the danger of depression

What Is Inflation?

Inflation is the persistent rise in the overall price level of goods and services in an economy. The price level is the total of all previous inflations. As prices rise, the dollar, or other currency in your savings account, buys less over time. In other words, inflation causes a decrease in *purchasing power.*

> **DEFINITION**
>
> **Purchasing power** is the value of a currency expressed in terms of the amount of goods or services that one unit of money can buy. An increase in inflation decreases purchasing power.

If inflation becomes noticeable, not only will it eat into the amount of goods and services you can buy, but it will also erode your confidence in what you can afford in the future. You will be less likely to save and invest your money, because money could lose its current value. More than likely, if inflation is rising quickly, your first thought will be to buy that car, tablet, or pair of good shoes now before the price increases.

There are some positives that come with moderate inflation. Businesses will be encouraged to update their plant and buy new equipment now rather than later. They will also be able to raise their prices and make additional profit if the long-term contracts with their workers don't have an adequate cost-of-living adjustment clause. Of course, this would be a negative for their employees.

Another positive is that central banks will have a tool—adjusting interest rates—to prevent a recession. By having the inflation cushion, there will be leeway to increase interest rates without risking a contraction in the economy. In addition, a low positive inflation rate gives labor wiggle room to adjust to a downturn in the economy.

What Causes Inflation?

As in most of economics, the answer to this question is "it depends," but the finger can usually point to the *money supply.* In order to understand inflation, we have to know how a change in the money supply as well as other dynamics affect the economy in the short run and in the long run. (The expressions *short run* and *long run* in macroeconomics can be somewhat confusing, since microeconomics uses these terms to apply to individual firms.) In macroeconomics the short run refers to the period when wages, prices, and capital—the resource markets—are resistant to change and are not in equilibrium, often measured in months to a few years. The long run refers to the time period when resources become flexible again, and the economy returns to equilibrium. How long this takes depends on the degree of disruption caused by the contraction or negative shock as well as the underlying health of the economy.

> **DEFINITION**
>
> The **money supply,** also known as **money stock,** is the total quantity of account balances at banks and other financial institutions that can easily be accessed to make payments. The standard measure of money stock is M2, which is used to measure inflation.

Inflation in the Short Run

Inflation is generally assumed to fluctuate in relation to the business cycle in the short run. If demand for goods is low, there will be an increase in unemployment and a contraction in the economy, since producers cut back when they can't sell enough products. Prices fall for goods as well as wages because demand shrinks. When the economy is expanding with an increase in the gross domestic product (GDP), the opposite occurs. There is an increased demand for goods and services, employment and wages rise, and the price of products and services increases.

Sometimes, if there is a more serious contraction in the economy, the central bank will step in and stimulate the economy to promote growth. The process involves increasing the money supply by buying bonds from the Treasury, which adds to the amount of funds banks have to lend. When the central bank buys government bonds, the price of the bonds increases and interest rates decline, since interest rates are inversely correlated with bonds prices. With lower interest rates, businesses and consumers are likely to buy more on credit, increasing demand in the economy. When the money supply gets too large, there is a danger of inflation. The central bank will then decrease the money supply by reversing the process.

Economists have noticed that despite the efforts of central banks to increase the money supply during a contraction in the economy in the short run, employers are reluctant to hire workers; unemployment increases, but the wages of those who are employed stay the same. Many economists believe the reason is that wages and prices are *sticky*, or resistant to change. The lag is probably caused by existing labor contracts, lengthy equipment and office leases, price regulations, and other factors.

> **DEFINITION**
>
> Wages and prices are **sticky** when the wage or price levels are resistant to adjustment to their long-run equilibrium level after an economic change. They can remain sticky even when there is significant unemployment, reducing the effectiveness of monetary policy. In better times, wages are slow to rise even when there is a labor shortage.

Inflation in the Long Run

Most economists agree that in the long run overall prices are related to fluctuations in the money supply. An increase in the money supply is usually associated with an increase in the level of prices. A decrease in the money supply can push prices down. In the long run *nominal wages*—the money that is actually paid rather than the *purchasing power*—rise along with prices as resistance to change declines. The GDP does not increase with an increase in the money supply in the long run, as opposed to the short run. Instead, nominal wages and prices remain at higher levels as the money supply increases.

> **DEFINITION**
>
> The **nominal wage** refers to the money paid as opposed to its purchasing power. The **real wage** is adjusted for inflation.

Measuring Inflation

Measuring inflation with indexes plays an important role in the economy, and most countries use price indexes to determine their domestic rate of inflation. Many labor contracts, Social Security benefits, and other programs are tied to an inflation index.

A good example of how significant the inclusion of an inflation index is in labor contracts is seen by comparing wages in the European Union—where a large percentage of labor contracts are indexed to inflation—to wages in the United States, where indexing is rare. In the Eurozone, wages tend to rise along with inflation, but not so much in the United States. The positive for the Eurozone is that workers with indexed contracts are protected from the effects of inflation. The negative is that when prices are rising, indexing induces higher wages so prices of goods increase, perpetuating inflation.

The three main indexes that are used to measure price levels are the GDP deflator, the consumer price index, and the producer price index.

The *GDP deflator* measures the ratio of the nominal gross domestic product (all the goods produced in the economy) of a given year to the real GDP of that year.

Following is a portion of a table containing GDP deflation data from the Treasury department of the United Kingdom. The GOV.UK website also provides an overview of how the GDP and inflation indexes are measured in the UK.

Example of the United Kingdom GDP Deflator for the Years 1971 to 1980

Calendar Year	GDP Deflator at Market Prices	
	2012 = 100	Percent Change on Previous Year
1971	9.889	8.98
1972	10.669	7.88
1973	11.452	7.34
1974	13.131	14.66
1975	16.674	26.98
1976	19.245	15.42
1977	21.875	13.66
1978	24.404	11.56
1979	27.903	14.34
1980	33.322	19.42

Data from GOV.UK (https://www.gov.uk/government/publications/gdp-deflators-at-market-prices-and-money-gdp-march-2013)

In the previous example, notice the large percentage change in the GDP deflator from 1973 to 1974. This was the beginning of a period of high inflation, not only in the UK but in the United States and other countries. In the United States, Federal Reserve Chairman Paul Volcker successfully combatted the high inflation of the 1970s by raising the federal funds rate (the interest rate at which depository institutions trade federal funds with each other overnight) to 19.10 percent in 1981. The outcome of his bold action was to bring inflation down but at the expense of a recession. Nevertheless, the economy stabilized to a mild inflation rate. The following figure illustrates the relationship between the federal funds rate and recessions from 1954 to 2013.

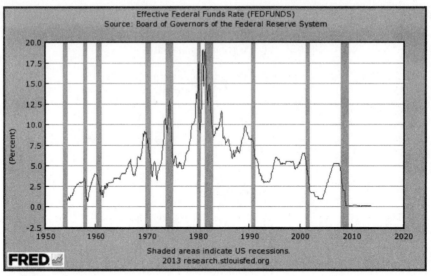

Courtesy of St. Louis Federal Reserve

U.S. Effective Federal Funds Rate from 1954 to 2013 and Recessionary Periods

The *consumer price index (CPI)* gauges the change in prices in a representative fixed basket of consumer goods and services in a typical urban area. It gives a general idea of the trend of price levels in an economy. The CPI differs from the GDP deflator in that the GDP deflator uses a much wider basket of goods than the CPI that changes from year to year to reflect what is produced during the year.

For example, if there is a large component of cars produced, that will be reflected in the GDP deflator. The CPI measures a basket of goods that remains the same every year and includes the prices of imports. The GDP deflator only includes domestic products. To research domestic prices, the government agency sends representatives to retail outlets throughout the country to see what the actual prices of the products are and then puts them into its calculator to come up with the index.

The third index used is the *producer price index (PPI)*. The PPI is an index that includes raw materials and semifinished goods in its basket. The PPI is also known as the Wholesale Price Index because it is measured before products reach retail stores.

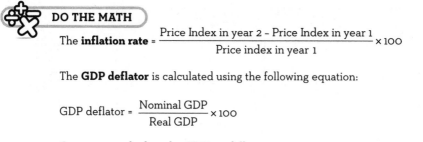

DO THE MATH

The **inflation rate** = $\dfrac{\text{Price Index in year 2} - \text{Price Index in year 1}}{\text{Price index in year 1}} \times 100$

The **GDP deflator** is calculated using the following equation:

GDP deflator = $\dfrac{\text{Nominal GDP}}{\text{Real GDP}} \times 100$

One way to calculate the **CPI** is as follows:

For a single item, CPI = $\dfrac{\text{price in a given year}}{\text{base period cost}} \times 100$

The CPI is usually a calculation of a basket of goods. It is calculated with price data, and the goods categories are weighted.

The **PPI** is calculated by comparing the base period revenue for a set of goods to the current period revenue for the same set of goods.

The government agencies that compile the indexes provide the base period referred to in the calculations. Better yet, they do all the work for you!

Understanding High Inflation and Hyperinflation

Most economists believe that an increase in the money supply in the short run raises the GDP, but in the long run the GDP is left unchanged because the stickiness of nominal wages and prices are relaxed. In the long run the price level rises along with an increase in the money supply.

In an economy with abnormally high inflation, it helps to look at the classical, or pre-Keynesian, model of the price level. Most economists before Keynes believed that the real quantity of money remains at its long-run equilibrium level.

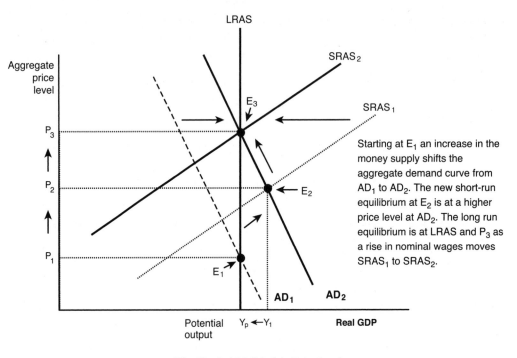

The Classical Model of the Price Level

During periods of high inflation, economists modify their model of the short run by considering the effect of a change in the money supply on the aggregate price level to be immediate. Under this condition, the short-run stickiness of nominal wages and prices disappears quickly, since workers and businesses anticipate higher prices. In response, wages and prices rise rapidly as the money supply increases, despite the shift of the aggregate demand curve to the right initially.

Over time the rise in wages and prices of goods results in a shift of the short-run aggregate supply curve to the left, returning the economy to equilibrium at a higher price level. In the long run, neither the real quantity of money nor the GDP are affected by an increase in money supply. This is effectively a throwback to the classical model of the price level. The result is that increasing the money supply quickly translates to higher inflation.

Government Expenditures and the Printing Press

When governments spend more money than they receive, they run a budget deficit, as does any household. The government has one major advantage: they can pay their bills by printing money. The mechanism is that the Treasury issues bonds, and the central bank *monetizes* the debt by printing money that it uses to buy back the debt from the public on the open market, called an open market operation. The more money printed, the less purchasing power money has, which is inflationary. The difference between the real value and the nominal value is the *inflation tax*. The amount of the inflation tax can be calculated by multiplying the inflation rate times the real money supply. This difference is pocketed by the government to pay its bills.

DO THE MATH

Inflation tax = inflation rate × real money supply. For an individual, a 4% inflation rate on $1,000 held by the public for one year = an inflation tax of $40.

In the United States, the Federal Reserve can use this money to build up its monetary base. Then it can return some funds back to the Treasury. This is called *monetizing the debt*. In the European Union, the Maastricht Treaty forbids the EU central bank from purchasing debt from national governments. Instead, the national governments issue debt on the secondary markets to fund their spending, where the central banks can purchase the debt and hold it until it is due. In either case, the money supply is increased.

DEFINITION

Monetization by a government, including the central bank, is creating, or printing, money. An **inflation tax** is the reduction in the real value of money—e.g., cash and fixed-rate bonds—held by the public resulting from inflation created by the government when it prints money.

While the inflation tax in developed countries under moderate conditions is small, in some countries with unstable economies, such as Zimbabwe and other developing countries, the inflation tax becomes an important way—sometimes the only way when the tax system breaks down—to fund the government. This extreme situation is caused by a feedback loop that begins with the erosion in the value of the money held by the public resulting from money printing to pay for the large government budget deficit. The deficit might have been incurred to pay for war debts, unstable political situations, or economic instability. People do not want to hold currency that is becoming worthless. The government needs money with real value, so it prints even more money to extract additional value from the inflation tax—specifically the *real seigniorage*—the change in the rate of the money supply divided by the price level: $\Delta M/P$. The government continues to print money to pay its bills while the purchasing power of the public dwindles. The end result is hyperinflation. The paper money becomes nearly worthless.

Some economists who study hyperinflation focus on the loss of confidence in the currency once the feedback loop begins. As savings become worthless, capital flight can ensue due to concern that the backer of the currency might not remain solvent. The money supply rapidly increases without a concomitant rise in the GDP. People spend their money quickly before their purchasing power erodes, sometimes within hours of getting paid. In times like this, some firms have been known to give more than one paycheck per day to prevent loss in value. These economists note the *velocity of money* flow—the frequency of spending money in a given period of time—to help project the increase in inflation.

To end the chaotic spiral, the government must come to terms with the negative impact of printing money to pay expenses. Solutions include issuing a new currency after repairing the country's weak or collapsing economic and political structure and perhaps pegging its money to a stable currency.

Does anyone benefit from hyperinflation? The answer is "yes." Those who have taken out loans benefit because they can pay the money back with inflated currency. That includes governments to foreign creditors.

INTERESTING FACT

The countries with the highest historic inflation rates per month to date are listed in the following table.

Countries with the Greatest Monthly Inflation Rate Historically

Country	Date	Daily Equivalent Inflation Rate
Hungary	July 1946	207.19%
Zimbabwe	November 2008	98.01%
Yugoslavia	January 1994	64.63%
Republika Srpska	January 1994	64.3%
Germany	October 1923	20.87%
Greece	October 1944	17.84%

Data courtesy of Steve H. Hanke and Alex K. F. Kwok in Cato Journal, Vol. 29, No. 2 (Spring/Summer 2009)

Inflation Expectations

Inflation expectations are important to businesses, workers, consumers, the financial markets, and the government. If inflation in five years is anticipated to be 4% higher than it is now, wage earners will want to calculate that into their new contracts. For example, if you are deciding whether to accept a certain salary for your new job, it would be helpful to know what the rate of inflation will be over the next few years to know whether you would be losing buying power over time.

Ideally, you would like to have a salary that exceeds what inflation would be by the end of your contract. Inflation expectations give you some idea of what to anticipate.

📖 **DEFINITION**

> **Inflation expectations** is the rate of inflation that workers, businesses, consumers, and investors think will prevail in the future and that they will factor into their decision making.

Consumers shopping for a house will decide the right time to take out a mortgage or refinance their existing mortgage on their house depending on their outlook for future inflation.

Central banks use the inflation expectations to help them form monetary policy. For example, in September of 2013, the Kenyan government decided to keep interest rates the same after learning that inflation had been stable despite an increase in their VAT tax. There had been concern that the central bank would raise interest rates if the added tax raised out-of-pocket costs.

Businesses factor inflation into their purchasing and pricing decisions. In one survey by the Federal Reserve Bank of Atlanta used to determine the inflation expectations of businesses in the area, questions included:

1. How do your current sales levels compare with sales levels during what you consider to be "normal" times?

2. How do your current profit margins compare with "normal" times?

3. Looking back, how do your unit costs compare with this time last year?

Last, but certainly not least, the financial markets will adjust the price of bonds according to the expected inflation rate as well. The bond markets react instantaneously to any change in expectations.

Economists have observed that the expected inflation rate has a one-to-one correlation with a rise in the actual rate of inflation. This can be demonstration in the model of the short-run Phillips Curve, which measures the inverse relationship between the short-run inflation rate and the unemployment rate, discussed in more detail in Chapter 16. An increase in expected inflation shifts the short-run Phillips Curve up. As you can see by the chart below, every percentage point of anticipated inflation increases the inflation rate by one percentage point.

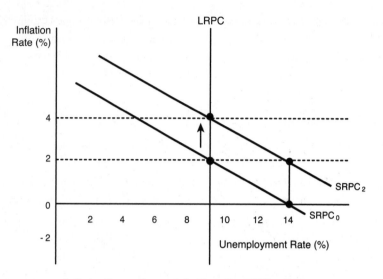

Inflation Expectations and the Short-Run Phillips Curve

Inflation expectations have a one-to-one correlation with the inflation rate, causing a shift up in the short-run Phillips Curve when higher inflation is anticipated at any given unemployment rate. Here SRPC₀ shifts up to SRPC₂.

(Source: frbatlanta.org/research/inflationproject/bie/)

Nominal and Real Interest Rates

The *nominal interest rate* is the rate of interest before adjusting for inflation. The *real interest rate* is the nominal rate of interest minus inflation. In lending, if the rate of inflation is the same rate as the nominal interest rate on the loan, there would be no profit for the lender. As an example, if you took out an equity loan on your home at 4%, but inflation was also 4%, there would be no profit for the lender.

We can summarize the relationship of the nominal interest rate to the real interest rate as:

real interest rate = nominal interest rate − expected inflation.

Deflation

This chapter began by quoting a November 1, 2013, article in the *Wall Street Journal* reporting that the Eurozone had too little inflation, which could negatively affect not only the countries in the Eurozone but the rest of the world. The concern about too little inflation is that it can lead to *deflation*. It is also another piece of evidence that an economy is contracting, especially with increasing unemployment. Where inflation decreases the real value of money, deflation increases its worth. This leads to consumers being reluctant to buy as they wait for prices to go down, causing a contraction in aggregate demand and in the economy.

Debt Deflation

If you recall from our section on inflation, one of the positives of inflation is that borrowers could pay their debt with currency that was worth less than when they took out the loan. This means that the borrower had the advantage and the lender the disadvantage. When there is deflation, the situation is the opposite. Future currency is worth more. This gives the benefit to the lender, since the nominal money he receives in repayment of his loan will be worth more than the money he gave to the debtor. The debtor will be paying the debt with currency that is more valuable as deflation continues.

> **DEFINITION**
>
> **Deflation** is a decrease in the general price level of goods and services; the inflation rate falls below zero percent.

This phenomenon was described by economist Irving Fisher during the Great Depression of the 1930s. He concluded, furthermore, that debtors would cut back on spending as their net worth dwindled. Nor would the lenders spend more, according to Fisher, because the value of the loans they already own continues to grow. The combined effect is to reduce demand in general— aggregate demand—further depressing the economy. This phenomenon is known as *debt deflation*. When collateral is used to support a loan—for example, a home is collateral for a mortgage—if the value of the collateral decreases, this is also debt deflation.

One of the dangers of debt deflation is that the value of the currency will be even greater than anticipated. This can lead to bankruptcy, deleveraging, and selling at any price.

> **DEFINITION**
>
> **Debt deflation** occurs when the aggregate demand decreases as a result of reduced spending by both borrower and lender due to the increasing value of the currency.

Deflation Challenges Central Bank Policy

When inflation expectations result in an increase in the price level, the central bank raises nominal interest rates, which lowers the inflation rate. When expectations are that the price level will drop, central banks lower the interest rates, but take note—*the interest rate cannot be reduced below zero*. Standard monetary policy is ineffective during a deflationary period. This situation is known as a *liquidity trap*. Banks, businesses, and individuals would rather hold cash, which retains its value. There is no incentive for banks to lend, and with no loans available, businesses delay investing in capital equipment and labor. They will likely lay off workers, causing an increase in unemployment. This is how deflation can lead to depression—and did during the 1930s depression.

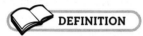 **DEFINITION**

> A **liquidity trap** occurs during a deflationary period when standard monetary policy of adjusting interest is ineffective at a zero nominal interest rate.

The bursting of the housing bubble in the 2007 period resulted in several investment banks and other financial institutions either going bust or needing help from governments to stay afloat. During the thick of the crisis, the stock market collapsed, and the economy—not just in the United States but around the world—was in serious danger of going into a depression. The U.S. Federal Reserve quickly lowered interest rates to prevent a deflationary spiral. When that was ineffective, they instituted extraordinary measures to try to re-inflate the economy. The Federal Reserve introduced a policy of quantitative easing, purchasing assets such as treasury bonds and mortgage debt. While financial assets rose significantly as a result of quantitative easing, interest rates remained anemic. In August and September of 2013 the U.S. Federal Reserve lowered the federal funds rate to 0.08%, and the inflation rate barely budged.

That is where we are as these lines are written. You, the reader, will be able to follow (and understand) the actions of the Federal Reserve and central banks around the world to see what novel approaches they take to stabilize their economies and lay the foundation for future growth.

Hyperinflation, Stagflation, and Chronic Deflation: Three Stories

Now that you are familiar with the concepts of inflation, deflation, and unemployment, let's see how they played out in some of the most significant economic events in history.

Hyperinflation: The German Weimar Republic of 1921 to 1924

The end of World War I left all parties with huge debts incurred to carry out the war, but Germany was also required to pay large reparations to France, Britain, Italy, and Belgium, and some to the United States. Postwar Germany was likewise struggling because of a reduction in prewar industrial exports, inability to obtain supplies and raw materials, an end to industrial production for military supplies, and a loss of its colonies.

Inflation was rising because the German government had been printing money to pay off its war debts. It had suspended the gold backing of its currency when the war began. (In contrast, France initiated an income tax to offset its debts.) After the Treaty of Versailles was signed in 1919, which required Germany to pay hefty reparations in gold and foreign currency, the inflation rate grew rapidly. Germany's gold reserves were depleted, but it continued paying in foreign currency, which it bought with deflating Marks. This escalated its money printing.

Beginning in June 1921, when the first payment of the reparations was made, the German Mark went through a convulsive series of devaluations against foreign currencies. The Mark was so deflated that France and Belgium sent troops to occupy the Ruhr Valley, the industrial region of Germany, to make sure the payments were made in goods instead of Marks. Of course, paying its foreign debt with worthless Marks had been beneficial to Germany, but at great cost to its people and the economy.

It is estimated that the German currency inflated from one to one trillion paper Marks per gold Mark at the height of the hyperinflation.

What was it like to live with hyperinflation? People couldn't spend their Marks fast enough. It was literally better to buy two glasses of beer at once than wait half an hour to buy a second to avoid the higher price. People hoarded goods, savings were depleted, and poverty was widespread. The hyperinflation of the Weimar Republic shocked the German people, who had believed that their country was strong economically before the war.

To stabilize the situation, a series of new currencies were issued, but it was not until the Mark was revalued and the Rentenmark was introduced in November 1923 that the German currency held its value.

Supply Shock and Stagflation: The Oil Embargo of 1973

In October 1973 OAPEC (Organization of Arab Petroleum Exporting Countries) declared an oil embargo in response to the support by the United States of Israel during its defense against a military attack by Egypt and Syria. The embargo caused a sharp reduction in oil supplies mostly to the United States, Europe, and Japan, causing a spike in the price of oil. Oil is used in agriculture and manufacturing, so the supply shock went beyond gasoline. In the United States, consumers were required to ration their oil and gasoline purchases, which resulted in long lines at the gas pump.

The negative supply shock of the reduction in raw materials caused a drop in aggregate output and a higher aggregate price level. The equilibrium of the economy was lower but at the inflated price.

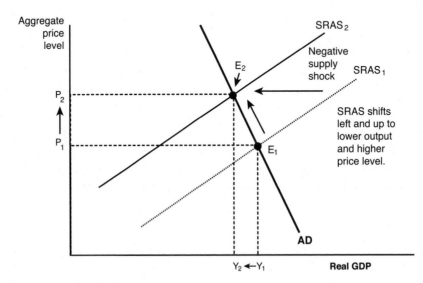

The effect of a negative supply shock on the economy.

The 1973 oil embargo caused a negative supply shock, resulting in lower aggregate output and higher prices.

A new term was coined in 1965 by Iain Macleod of the United Kingdom's Conservative Party to describe the situation in which an economy slows while prices rise—*stagflation*—a combination of economic stagnation and inflation. Standard monetary policy to encourage growth by increasing the money supply cannot work under these conditions because doing so would raise the inflation rate. The central banks were left with a choice: raise the interest rate to bring down inflation or increase the money supply to boost the economy. As described previously, in the United States, the Federal Reserve chose to increase the federal funds rate significantly, which solved the inflation problem but caused a temporary recession.

Chronic Deflation: Japan in the 1990s

Japan's economy was devastated by World War II. The human and material loss was enormous. Hyperinflation caused by debt to pay for the war was an additional burden. After the war Japan was determined to pull itself out of the quagmire and strengthen its economy. With help from the government, a high savings rate, and its own style of capitalism, postwar Japan's growth and development until 1973 was formidable, admired worldwide.

In the 1980s Japanese prosperity was at its peak. Its stock market and real estate markets were booming, but a bubble was forming. In 1990 the Bank of Japan, concerned that the asset bubble would cause instability in the economy, decided to prick the bubble by raising interest rates. The result was the bursting of the bubble and a market crash. The economy did not return to health and stability as the Bank of Japan had expected. Instead, an economic contraction began, and growth slowed steadily and significantly until it reached depression levels.

To reverse the situation, the Bank of Japan and the government instituted the standard stimulus measures of low interest rates and government spending. While each attempt had a burst of positive results, the economy was not able to emerge from its slump. Identifying one problem—that the growth of the retiring population was outstripping the working-age population—the government attempted to reduce the budget deficit by increasing taxes. The outcome was a further recession. More fiscal stimulus was then activated, but to no avail.

Japan has been in a liquidity trap since their economic boom of the 1980s went bust. Despite administering the traditional medicine of fiscal and monetary stimulus, the Japanese economy has remained sluggish at best. In 2012, newly elected Prime Minister Shinzō Abe introduced a program of quantitative easing, fiscal stimulus, and other economic reforms to spark growth. The effectiveness of the policy is unknown two years later. Never having arrived at a positive growth trajectory, Japan is now fighting the same uphill battle as other developed nations in response to the economic collapse of 2008.

The Least You Need to Know

- Inflation causes money to lose its purchasing power.
- Raising interest rates can tame inflation.
- Hyperinflation deflates a currency until it becomes worthless, so that goods become more valuable than savings. Debtors win and lenders lose.
- Deflation causes money to gain purchasing power. Spending is reduced as lower prices are sought. Lenders gain and debtors lose, but both stop spending as currency becomes more valuable. A depression can follow as aggregate demand diminishes.
- Chronic deflation can sometimes be unresponsive to monetary policy and lead to a liquidity trap.

CHAPTER 18

The Business Cycle

The rise of capitalism, characterized by private ownership of the means of production and the market economy, has generated long-term growth. Technology, improved productivity, entrepreneurialism, and the profit motive have been the drivers of economic progress over the past few centuries. Populations expanded as a result of technological improvements in agriculture and with inventions that enabled one worker to produce a thousand widgets in the same time it had previously taken to produce one.

Although economic growth has been rising over the long run, there have been bumps in the road along the way. Years of great prosperity have been interrupted by times of economic contraction: business slumps, unemployment, price declines, and poverty.

This chapter will describe the fluctuations in the short-term growth trend, their causes, and the models economists use to analyze the ups and downs of the economy.

In This Chapter

- Long-run growth and the business cycle
- How the business cycle creates expansions and recessions in the economy
- Unemployment and inflation in the business cycle
- The aggregate supply and demand mode

The Business Cycle: Defining the Short-Run Fluctuations in the Economy

As early as 1819, writer and economist Jean Charles Léonard de Sismondi observed that the economy was subject to periodic crises, later termed cycles. He challenged the predominant theory—that equilibrium leading to full employment is immediately and spontaneously achieved—put forward by the classical economists, J.B. Say and David Ricardo. Sismondi agreed with the classicists that in the long run, the economy would return to its equilibrium price and output level, but that in the interim, there would be a lot of suffering.

Sismondi also noticed that after a sustained increase in manufacturing output by multiple producers, a glut in goods triggered a cutback in production and a reduction in prices and wages. Sismondi and his associate Robert Owen concluded that overproduction led to underconsumption of goods. Their solution was to raise wages to increase aggregate demand. Sismondi advocated government intervention to encourage the process. These ideas were a precursor of Keynesian economics. Other economists refined Sismondi's periodic crises prototype to develop theories of alternating cycles.

Expansions and Recessions

The current macroeconomic model used by central banks identifies fluctuations in the economic equilibrium below and above the economy's potential gross domestic product (GDP) at full employment. The potential GDP or output is sometimes referred to as the *production capacity* of the economy.

⟨✏️ **TAKE AWAY MESSAGE** ⟩

The term **gross domestic product** is interchangeable or closely related to other names, which can be confusing. Gross domestic product is commonly abbreviated as **GDP**. When GDP has been adjusted for inflation, it is called **real GDP**. When referring to GDP that is calculated in current dollars or other currency, it is termed **nominal GDP**.

GDP is also referred to as **total output**, or simply **output**. These terms are also further refined as **real output** and **nominal output**. **Actual GDP** or **actual output** is also used for current output.

Potential GDP or **potential output** or **production capacity** or **natural GDP** refer to the real output of the economy when it is most efficient and prices are fully flexible.

Chapter 16 introduced the *output gap,* the difference between the actual real GDP and potential output (GDP). (Actual real GDP is symbolized by the letter Y, and potential output is symbolized by the letter Y with an asterisk or the subscript p: Y^* or Y_p). This gap, when below potential output at full employment—a negative output gap—coincides with a recessionary period. When the output gap is above potential GDP—a positive output gap—the economy is in an expansionary period. *In short, the output gap is the difference between what an economy is producing and what it can produce.*

The Business Cycle

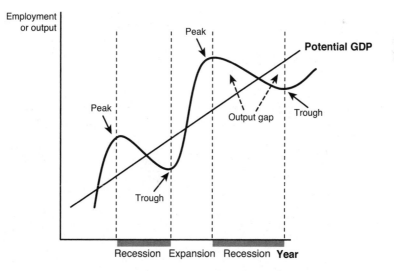

The diagonal line represents the economy's potential real GDP. Deviations from the potential GDP, such as when there is a negative output gap (recessionary) or a positive output gap (expansionary) create the fluctuations in the business cycle. The troughs are the lowest point of the gap, and the peaks are the highest point of the gap.

The accompanying figure shows an idealized *business cycle*, the fluctuations between expansions and recessions in the economy. The vertical axis represents the real GDP, the economy's total output, or employment. Both the actual total output and employment tend to move together. The diagonal line represents the potential real GDP. The actual output of the economy rises and falls in the direction of the longer-term trend. At the point where the actual output reaches a business-cycle *peak* and begins to fall, a recessionary period begins. The point where the actual output is at the lowest point is a business-cycle *trough*, when output increases, and a new expansion starts. Neither extreme is ideal, since the potential output represents the economy operating at its greatest efficiency. When the output gap is positive, the economy is "overheated" because demand is very high. Factories and employees are working above their efficient levels. When the output gap is negative, output is below capacity, indicating that demand is weak. Output gaps in business cycles tell us that the economy is not working efficiently.

    DO THE MATH

The formula for calculating the output gap is:

$Y - Y_P$, where Y is the actual output (real GDP), and Y_P is the potential output (real GDP).

The percentage GDP gap is the actual GDP minus the potential GDP divided by the potential GDP.

$$\frac{GDP_{actual} - GDP_{potential}}{GDP_{potential}}$$

The Business Cycle and Employment

The vertical axis on the accompanying figure of the business cycle can represent either the real GDP or employment. The reason we can interchange these and get the same information from the graph is that a negative output gap is associated with lower employment, since less demand than would occur at full capacity requires fewer workers. A positive output gap means more workers are needed because the economy is working above capacity. Another way to look at it is that when the economy is operating below capacity, unemployment is high, and when the economy is "overheated," unemployment is low.

Another relationship that economists use to judge the efficiency of the market is the unemployment gap, which is related to the output gap. Economists track the *non-accelerating inflation rate of unemployment (NAIRU),* which is the unemployment rate at a constant rate of inflation. (NAIRU was mentioned in Chapter 16 in relation to the long-run Phillips Curve.) Movements of the unemployment rate away from the NAIRU are associated with an output gap. Tracking this relationship can alert economists to the effectiveness of their policy because when the unemployment level equals the NAIRU, the output will also be at its most efficient level, and at the same time, there is no inflationary pressure. So, no output gap and no inflationary pressure would be the ideal outcome for policymakers. Since the dual mandate of the U.S. Federal Reserve is to keep unemployment in check as well as to stabilize the inflation rate, the correlation between the unemployment rate and the output gap is a helpful indicator.

 **DEFINITION**

> The **non-accelerating inflation rate of unemployment (NAIRU)** is) the unemployment rate at a constant rate of inflation. Frictional and structural, but not cyclical, unemployment are included in the NAIRU.

The "booms and busts" of the business cycle are unpredictable, and so are the durations of the expansions and contractions. The severity of the recessions is difficult to predict as well, although the Great Depression of the 1930s and the Great Recession of 2008-2009 were marked by a *liquidity crisis*. Recessions that occur in the aftermath of a liquidity crisis have been especially deep and prolonged. A liquidity crisis involves the inability to get cash, when interbank lending has frozen, banks stop making loans, or it is not possible to find a buyer for a security. A liquidity crisis causes panic and runs on the banks. (Runs on the bank will be covered in more detail in Chapter 21.)

DEFINITION

> A **liquidity crisis** occurs when there is a lack of cash flow; banks stop lending to businesses, consumers, or other banks.

Aggregate Demand and Aggregate Supply

What exactly causes the short-term fluctuations in the economy? Economists have varying opinions, but in the 1930s during the Great Depression, John Maynard Keynes developed a model that is currently accepted by most mainstream (Keynesian-oriented) economists and that is used to try to moderate the booms and the busts of the business cycle. Disciples of Keynes further refined the model. As you read about how the model works, it might help to think of it as a little machine, where a movement in one part causes a change in other parts.

The mechanism underlying the business cycle, or the short-run fluctuations in the economy, involves the relationship between the total quantity of finished goods and services demanded in the economy—the *aggregate demand*—with the total output, or the supply of goods and services produced within an economy—the *aggregate supply* at a given price level and in a given time period.

By now you should be somewhat familiar with the terms aggregate demand and aggregate supply, as they have been occasionally mentioned in preceding chapters. You might have concluded that they play an indispensable role in analyzing economics. You would be right. In fact, the relationship between aggregate demand and aggregate supply is a cornerstone of macroeconomic analysis, according to the Keynesian model. Since key institutions, like central banks and the International Monetary Fund, apply the Keynesian model to formulate monetary policy, we will use it to explain the dynamics of the economy.

Aggregate Demand

Aggregate demand is the total amount of goods and services demanded in the economy at a given overall price level and in a given time period. When the economy is humming along, there is plenty of aggregate demand. When the economy is sluggish or worse, it is usually because there is not enough aggregate demand.

The *aggregate demand curve* is a graphic model that shows the relationship between the aggregate price level and the quantity of aggregate output demanded. The aggregate demand curve is downward sloping. Simply put, if the general price level in the economy is high, the real output of the economy will contract. If the general price level in the economy is low, the real GDP of the economy will expand.

> **DEFINITION**
>
> The **aggregate demand curve** shows the relationship between the aggregate price level and the quantity of aggregate output (real GDP) demanded by the economy.

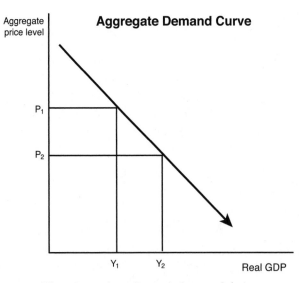

The aggregate demand curve is downward sloping.

The reason for the downward slope of the aggregate demand curve is not the same as the reason for the downward slope of the demand curve for the individual consumer. As you have read, microeconomics theory asserts that the individual consumer's demand curve for a good—holding the price of the other goods and services constant—slopes downward as well. The demand curve slopes downward because people can substitute a different good if the price of the original good is too high.

Let's say you are a coffee drinker. You can't be fully awake until you've had your morning cup. One morning you run out of coffee and go to the store to get a bag. You soon find out that the price of coffee has skyrocketed because of a coffee bean disease. Dismayed, you decide to buy a box of tea instead. Because you were able to substitute tea for coffee, the quantity of coffee you bought declined. This causes the downward slope of your demand curve for coffee.

The aggregate demand curve does *not* slope downward because of the law of demand. Now we are concerned with the entire economy, not just one consumer. The aggregate demand curve represents a change in the prices of *all final goods and services in any combination in the economy as a whole.* There are two reasons for the downward slope, all things being equal (*ceteris paribus*): the *wealth effect* and the *savings and interest rate effect.*

In an imaginary scenario, if you were to pick up the newspaper one morning and read that there was a sudden drop in the price of everything, the first thing you would probably do is to go shopping. This is a fantasy, of course, but the idea is that a drop in the aggregate price level—all other things remaining the same, *ceteris paribus*—would encourage households and businesses to spend because their purchasing power would be increased. All that spending would cause an expansion in the real GDP of the economy. Likewise, a higher aggregate price level causes households to lose purchasing power. As a result, consumers' spending on all goods and services is reduced. The real GDP in the economy would then contract. This relationship is called the *wealth effect* of a change in the aggregate price level.

The *interest rate effect* of changes in the aggregate price level works as follows. If the aggregate price goes down, everything is less expensive, and households and businesses can save more because they are spending less. This savings goes into the banks, which make loans to businesses for investment. As more loans are made, the cost of borrowing money—interest rates—declines. Since it becomes less expensive to borrow money, more investments are made in business and on the part of households. This increases the real GDP of the economy. Likewise, if the aggregate prices level goes up, people have to spend more of their money on things they need to survive, they save less, and less money is loaned, causing interest rates to rise. Investment declines, and, as a result, the real GDP of the economy goes down.

> **DEFINITION**
>
> The **wealth effect,** caused by a change in the aggregate price level, is the effect on consumer spending resulting from a rise in the aggregate price level that reduces the purchasing power of consumers' assets. The **interest rate effect** is the effect on consumer and investment spending on real production caused by the effect of a change in the aggregate price level that alters the interest rate. The higher interest rate affects the cost of borrowing for household and business sectors and lending by banks.

Shifts in the Aggregate Demand Curve

What would cause an overall increase or decrease in aggregate demand? To follow this line of thought, we re-introduce the components of the GDP:

GDP (Y) = C + I + G + NX

C: Consumption

I: Investment

G: Government spending

NX: Net exports

When we think about what could shift the aggregate demand curve, imagine what would affect the components of GDP. Taking them one at a time, what could affect consumption?

Consumption. Changes in expectations, such as changes in consumer and business optimism and changes in wealth not caused by the aggregate price level, shift the aggregate demand curve to the right or left. Tax increases or decreases either encourage or discourage spending by consumers, since they would have more or less money left over after taxes for spending. A tax cut would create more consumer demand and would shift the aggregate demand curve to the right, if all other components of GDP remained the same. An increase in taxes would reduce consumer demand and would cause a shift of the aggregate demand curve to the left.

Investment. An increase in investment, whether because of an act by government that encourages investment, the development of a new technological industry, or investment in natural resources, would increase aggregate demand and cause the aggregate demand curve to shift to the right. The size of the existing stock of physical capital, such as plant equipment and housing affect investment and shift the aggregate demand curve to the right or left. If the existing stock of physical capital is relatively small, aggregate demand increases; if it is relatively large, aggregate demand decreases.

Government. If government spending goes up, the aggregate demand curve would shift to the right, whereas if government spending goes down, the aggregate demand curve would shift to the left. Fiscal policy causes a shift in the aggregate demand because stimulative fiscal policy involves government spending or lowering taxes, either of which would shift the aggregate demand to the right. A policy of government spending is considered *direct* because the government is included in the aggregate demand. A change in tax rates or government transfers, such as unemployment insurance, is considered *indirect* because it affects disposable income. A cutback in government spending would shift the aggregate demand to the left.

Net exports. If a country increases its net exports, possibly because its currency is low in relation to other currencies, or it manufactures a product that is in great demand, or it has a natural resource that other countries need, aggregate demand would increase, and the aggregate demand curve would shift to the right. Conversely, if the currency in this country were to appreciate significantly against other currencies, aggregate demand would go down, and the aggregate demand curve would shift to the left.

Monetary policy. Last, but certainly not least, is monetary policy, when central banks increase and decrease the money supply to reduce inflation or mitigate a recession. An increase in the quantity of money increases the aggregate demand and shifts the aggregate demand curve to the right. A decrease in the quantity of money decreases aggregate demand and shifts the aggregate demand curve to the left. Fiscal policy was listed in the government component of GDP.

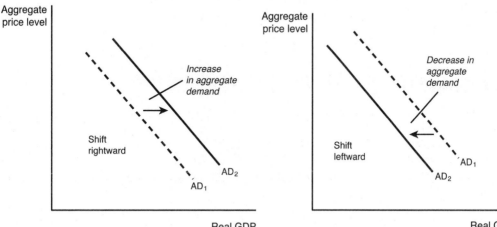

Shifts in the Aggregate Demand Curve

Aggregate Supply

Aggregate supply is the total supply of goods and services produced within an economy at a given overall price level in a given time period. It is also called the total, or aggregate, output and the real GDP. The *aggregate supply curve* shows the relationship between the aggregate price level and the quantity of aggregate output supplied in the economy.

Aggregate supply will be discussed in two timeframes: the short run and the long run. The reason these timeframes are examined independently is that the short-run aggregate supply curve and the long-run aggregate supply curve have different slopes. We'll discuss these differences as we study each independently.

The short-run aggregate supply curve (SRAS) has a positive slope. If the aggregate price level rises, the total output, or real GDP, will rise. Conversely, if the aggregate price level declines, the total output will decline as well. The accompanying figure shows the aggregate price level rising from P_1 to P_2, causing an increase in the real GDP from Y_1 to Y_2.

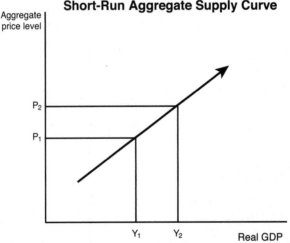

Short-Run Aggregate Supply Curve

During a deflationary period, such as during the Great Depression from 1929 to 1933, there is a movement downward in the short-run aggregate supply curve, resulting in less aggregate output at a lower aggregate price level.

One of the primary reasons the short-run aggregate supply curve is upward sloping is because in the short-term, many of the costs, including nominal wages, are taken as fixed. The reason they are assumed to be fixed is because contracts have already been signed for limited periods of time, such as labor contracts, leases, and so on. The rigidity in nominal wages in the short-run is dubbed "sticky," because they don't readily respond to an increase or decrease in employment levels in the economy. ("Sticky wages" and prices were explained in Chapter 17.) When the aggregate price level rises, more aggregate output is generated because with fixed costs, producers' profits increase, since costs remain stable.

Let's say a baker is buying flour for her cakes for the next month. She already negotiated a contract with her supplier for 5,000 pounds of flour at a cost of $1,300. Since the contract was signed, the aggregate price level in the economy rose by 3%. Now her cakes have risen in value by 3%, but the contract for the flour, which was not adjusted for inflation, stays the same. The baker pockets the additional profit.

Shifts in the short-run aggregate supply curve: an external change in circumstances for the producer that causes either an increase or decrease in profits will shift the short-run aggregate supply curve at every aggregate price level. The short-run aggregate supply curve will shift to the right if an event is increasing the producer's profits, resulting in an increase in real GDP. The short-run aggregate supply curve will shift to the left if an event is increasing the producer's profits, resulting in a decrease in real GDP.

Shifts in the Short-Run Aggregate Supply Curve

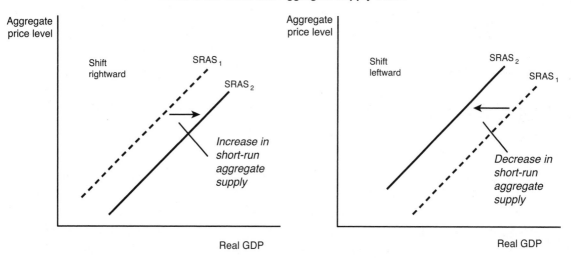

A few of the circumstances that would cause a shift in the short-run aggregate supply curve are:

Changes in commodity prices. The oil shock of the early 1970s caused by the OAPEC (Organization of Arab Petroleum Exporting Countries) oil embargo (see Chapter 17) was a supply shock. The embargo cut oil supplies to customers, which raised the price of oil dramatically. Plotting the effect of this event on a chart would involve shifting the supply curve to the left at every aggregate price level, showing a higher aggregate price level and a reduction in real GDP of the economy, as you can see in the accompanying figure.

Changes in nominal wages. Although nominal wages are sticky in the short-term because of standing contracts, eventually the contracts will expire, and a new contract will be negotiated at the expected inflation rate. Depending on where the parties see inflation headed over the term of the new contract, the nominal wage for the next period can rise or fall. The short-term aggregate supply curve will shift to the right or left to reflect the new wage agreement. If there are any benefits, like health insurance benefits included in the contract, any changes in the benefits will act as a decrease or increase in the nominal wage. This will also shift the short-term aggregate supply curve to the right or the left.

Changes in productivity. An increase in productivity, where there is more production for the same number of workers, will increase the profit margin of the producer. New technology, for instance, can allow workers to produce more goods in the same amount of time. Think about the change in productivity as a result of the development of the internet. This positive change will shift the short-run aggregate supply curve to the right. Conversely, any decrease in productivity, for example, new regulations, will decrease productivity, and the short-term aggregate supply curve will shift to the left.

While in the short run, wages, prices, and costs are sticky because of contracts, leases, and other agreements established before there was a change in the aggregate price level, in the long run, these agreements end, and the stickiness disappears when new contracts are renegotiated that incorporate the new aggregate price level. In the *long run*, with flexible costs, the aggregate price level has no effect on the quantity of aggregate output supplied.

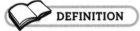 **DEFINITION**

The **long run** is the period of time over which all prices are fully flexible.

Keep in mind that the aggregate price level affects all prices in the economy—the producer's costs as well as the price of the final goods or services. To take the example of the baker, suppose the baker woke up one morning to learn the aggregate price level in the economy was cut in half because there was a sudden negative shock causing all prices to fall. Would her profit go up as a result? The answer is "no" because, although her costs would be cut in half, so would the price of the cake, all else being equal (assuming she does not adjust the price as an individual baker). Likewise, if the aggregate price level of the economy doubled, she would still be making the same profit because the price of the cake would double as well.

TAKE-AWAY MESSAGE

A change of the aggregate price level in the long run has no effect on the quantity of aggregate output supplied.

The *long-run aggregate supply curve* (LRAS) reflects the fact that the aggregate price level does not affect the quantity of aggregate output supplied. It is therefore vertical. The position of the long-run aggregate supply curve on the horizontal axis is also significant because it is at the point of *potential output*, where the economy is producing output at maximum efficiency—that is, all prices are fully flexible. In the broadest sense, if the country's economy or even the world economy continues to experience growth over time, the vertical long-run aggregate supply curve will continue to shift to the right, as it has thus far.

Long-Run Aggregate Supply Curve

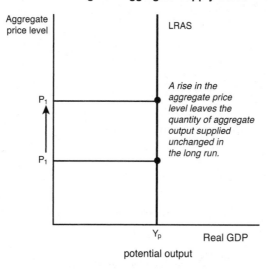

Despite the fact that there are short-run fluctuations in the economy—which can be painful or exuberant—in the long run, the world economy has been growing. As we saw in the section on the business cycle, where the output gaps continually crisscross the trend line of potential GDP, the economy ultimately adjusts back to the potential output.

The fluctuations in the short-run aggregate supply curve adjustments around the long-run aggregate supply curve are depicted in the accompanying figure as a rise in nominal wages shifts the SRAS to the left. At the aggregate price level, P_1, the quantity of aggregate output supplied is greater than the potential output. However, the low unemployment caused by the increased output at P_1 causes nominal wages to rise. As a result, the short-run aggregate supply curve adjusts by shifting from $SRAS_1$ to $SRAS_2$, the long-run aggregate supply curve at potential output.

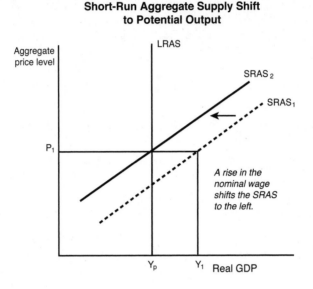

**Short-Run Aggregate Supply Shift
to Potential Output**

A rise in the nominal wage shifts the SRAS to the left.

The AD-AS Model

The culmination of our study of aggregate demand and aggregate supply is a model that attempts to depict the short-run state of the economy—the *short-run macroeconomic equilibrium*. The equilibrium is the point at which the quantity of aggregate output demanded is equal to the quantity of aggregate output supplied.

When the short-run aggregate supply curve is plotted on a chart along with the aggregate demand curve, the point at which they intersect is the short-run macroeconomic equilibrium. The horizontal axis represents the short-run equilibrium level of aggregate output, Y_E and the vertical axis represents the short-run equilibrium price level, P_E.

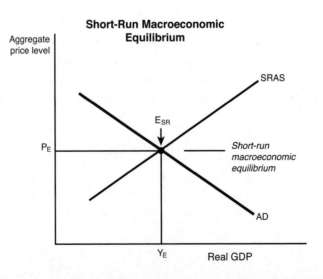

Short-Run Macroeconomic Equilibrium

Short-run macroeconomic equilibrium

The short-run macroeconomic equilibrium can be disturbed by external shocks to the economy. This can be either a negative or positive shock to aggregate demand or a negative or positive shock to aggregate supply. When these shocks occur, they shift the aggregate demand curve and the aggregate supply curve to the left or right. These shifts move the short-run macroeconomic equilibrium to a new aggregate price level and real GDP level.

A negative demand shock shifts the aggregate demand curve down and to the left. Since there will be less aggregate demand, the aggregate price level will go down as well. At the same time, the aggregate output is reduced. Conversely, a positive demand shock shifts the aggregate demand curve to the right, and the aggregate price level and aggregate output increase.

By the same token, *a negative supply shock will shift the short-run aggregate supply curve to the left and up the aggregate demand curve*, resulting in lower aggregate output and a higher aggregate price level at the new short-run macroeconomic equilibrium. This situation is exactly what took place during the 1973 oil embargo. The negative supply shock caused a drop in real GDP as well as an increase in the aggregate price level. So voilà—*stagflation!* The AD-AS model accurately accounted for the conundrum of inflation *with* unemployment.

To round out the effects of a shift in the short-run aggregate supply curve, *a positive shock shifts the short-run aggregate supply curve to the right and down the aggregate demand curve*, resulting in a higher aggregate output and a lower aggregate price level. This best of all worlds is what occurred in the 1990s, and the economy experienced more output at a low aggregate price level. This was the period of the growth of technology and the internet.

INTERESTING FACT

Because the short-run aggregate supply curve is upward sloping, a shock, whether negative or positive, causes the aggregate price level and aggregate output to move in opposite directions. This is not the case with a shift in the aggregate demand curve. When there is a negative aggregate supply shock, monetary and fiscal policy is a challenge. The aggregate price level is already too high, and the output is too low. Policymakers have to make tough choices in this situation.

The short-run macroeconomic equilibrium tells us what is going on in the economy during the ups and downs of the business cycle. What about the *long-run macroeconomic equilibrium?* The long-run macroeconomic equilibrium is the point where the short-run macroeconomic equilibrium meets the long-run aggregate supply curve. At this point, short-run equilibrium aggregate output is equal to potential output—the economy is producing at the most efficient level.

DEFINITION

The **long-run macroeconomic equilibrium** is the point where the short-run macroeconomic equilibrium meets the long-run aggregate supply curve.

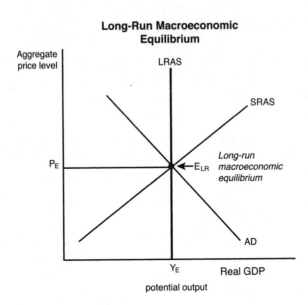

Long-Run Macroeconomic Equilibrium

A demand shock in the economy affects the short-run demand curve, as described in the section on shifts in the aggregate demand curve. What happens to the long-run macroeconomic equilibrium when there is a demand shock? Let's go through this step by step.

1. A *negative demand shock* shifts the aggregate demand curve to the left and down, causing a decrease in the aggregate price level and aggregate output, which leads to higher unemployment.

2. The short-run macroeconomic equilibrium moves down the short-run aggregate supply curve and away from the original long-run macroeconomic equilibrium. This event corresponds to the negative output gap covered at the beginning of this chapter.

3. With high unemployment, nominal wages *in the long run* are low enough for producers to start hiring again. Remember, only in the short-run are wages and prices sticky.

4. There is now a positive shift of the short-run aggregate supply curve to the right and down, returning the economy to a new long-run equilibrium at a lower aggregate price level.

In the long run, the economy is self-correcting, according to current theories. In the short-run, negative demand shocks can cause undesirable unemployment and output levels. For this reason, economists in the Keynesian and New-Keynesian schools recommend monetary and fiscal intervention to hasten the return of the short-run macroeconomic equilibrium to the long-run macroeconomic equilibrium, when the economy is producing at its most efficient level. The neo-classical economists believe the market is efficient, and no intervention is necessary. They are in the minority, however.

The Least You Need to Know

- The business cycle describes the short-run difference between the actual total output and the long-run potential output.
- A trough in the business cycle output gap, when the actual total output is below the long-run potential output, coincides with an economic contraction.
- A peak in the business cycle output gap, when the actual total output is above the long-run potential output, coincides with an economic expansion.
- The AD-AS (aggregate supply and aggregate demand) model combines the aggregate supply curve and the aggregate demand curve to locate the short-run equilibrium point of the economy.
- The long-run macroeconomic equilibrium, when the economy is most efficient, occurs when the short-run equilibrium aggregate output is equal to potential output.

CHAPTER 19

Recessions and Depressions

Booms and busts, or economic expansions and contractions, are the hallmark of the business cycle. While the booms will inevitably end—sometimes painfully when sudden and unexpected—living through a boom is not all bad, since they are accompanied by low unemployment and high output. If they spark inflation, the central bank can usually increase interest rates to control the rise in prices. The aftermath—the bust—is the topic of this chapter.

The busts are more troublesome and cause hardships, especially for those who were not in a position to profit from the boom times. This chapter takes a closer look at recessions and prolonged and deep recessions called depressions.

In This Chapter

- How recessions affect the economy
- Deleveraging debt
- The causes and characteristics of recessions
- Major schools of thought on the business cycle and recessions

Effects of Recessions

Recessions can have a damaging, sometimes long-lasting effect on working people as well as businesses. Unemployment increases to unacceptable levels, wages are often cut, and the consumer is less likely to buy anything but the essentials. This reluctance or inability to spend hurts businesses, and they end up with more inventory than they can sell, causing them to cut prices, sometimes below cost. The result is a downward spiral.

In severe recessions, a large number of workers who are laid off or lose their jobs are unable to find work for more than six months. The longer people are not in the workforce, the harder it is to be hired. There is debate about whether this is caused by loss of their skills, falling into the category of structural unemployment, or whether there is bias against those who are unemployed for long periods of time. Eventually their unemployment benefits end, and they can lose self-respect and become psychologically depressed and impoverished. People who live in countries with generous unemployment benefits and other social safety nets can ride out the recessionary period with less misery than in other countries. Nevertheless, people are happier when they are being productive and don't have to rely on others for their survival.

Businesses suffer from a drop in productivity at the early stages of recessions, and the weaker businesses can go bankrupt. In order to preserve their liquid capital, businesses cut costs wherever they can. Public companies are more likely to show a profit by cutting costs than by selling their wares.

The living standards of households with wage earners drop as a result of the depressed economy, since workers depend on a paycheck, which might be cut if they are lucky enough to stay employed. People on a fixed income, such as Social Security recipients, are in a more stable situation.

Many economists believe that prolonged recessions can have an adverse effect on longer-term growth. Some of the reasons are …

- The economy will have to make up for the lack of growth in the short term in order to stay on track.

- A decline or halt in capital investment can leave businesses with outmoded equipment.

- Long-run growth can be hampered by a lack of investment in research and development.

- A long and deep recession can cut the labor force that will be needed when the economy turns around.

- The long-term unemployed may be considered unemployable.

- There is a lack of incentive to start a new business.

- The decreased output during the recession eventually affects tax revenues for many years.

The Paradox of Thrift and Deleveraging

The paradox of thrift, an observation made centuries ago and popularized by John Maynard Keynes, is the irony that if everyone individually cuts spending to increase his or her own saving, aggregate saving will eventually fall because one person's spending is someone else's income. During the Great Depression of the 1930s, Keynes concluded that the economy was suffering from the paradox of thrift. He advocated an increase in government spending to replace the lack of demand from the private sector to boost the economy. The paradox of thrift is associated with recessions that are caused or exacerbated by a lack of aggregate demand for goods and services in the economy, which is true of most recessions.

DEFINITION

A **paradox of thrift** occurs when, during a recession, an increase in planned savings can cause actual savings and investment to decrease.

According to economist Paul Krugman in an article titled "Debt, Deleveraging, and the Liquidity Trap," (www.princeton.edu/~pkrugman/debt_deleveraging_ge_pk.pdf and www.voxeu.org/article/debt-deleveraging-and-liquidity-trap-new-model) the increase in household debt rose from 96 percent of personal income in 2000 to 128 percent in 2008 in the U.S., in the UK from 105 percent to 160 percent, and in Spain from 69 percent to 130 percent. The enormous debt was considered by many to be a major cause of the 2008 financial crisis, and some believe it is a drag on recovery.

 DO THE MATH

The macroeconomic basis for the paradox of thrift lies with the relationships:

Consumption + savings = disposable income.

The marginal propensity to consume (MPC) + the marginal propensity to save (MPS) = 1.

(MPC is the proportion of the disposable income that individuals would like to spend on consumption. MPS is the proportion of each additional dollar of household income that is used for saving.)

Under normal conditions, a decrease in consumption at a given level of disposable income means that savings will increase. When there is a recession, disposable income goes down, and MPS decreases, so the expected increase in savings will not occur. The drop in disposable income could fall to the point where a planned increase in savings can actually reduce savings, paradoxically.

Deleveraging of debt occurs during and after most financial crises. Deleveraging of debt is the simultaneous reduction of leverage in multiple private and public sectors, which lowers the total debt-to-nominal GDP ratio of the economy.

📖 **DEFINITION**

Deleveraging of debt is the simultaneous reduction of leverage in multiple private and public sectors, which lowers the total debt-to-nominal GDP ratio of the economy.

Deleveraging can be achieved in the following ways:

1. Imposition of austerity, where spending is cut and savings are increased.

2. Encouraging high inflation, which reduces the value of the nominal currency, increases nominal GDP growth, and reduces the debt-to-GDP ratio.

3. Default on the debt.

4. Growth of real GDP, when the economy grows out of its debt naturally.

During and after the freezing up of the financial system during the 2008 financial crisis, global response to the enormous public and private debt, including leverage in the financial sector, involved all of the above methods of deleveraging. In Europe, the policy pursued by the European Central Bank and the Economic and Monetary Union (EMU) has been one of loans, but with severe austerity measures as a condition for the loans. These austerity measures caused a further contraction in the countries already suffering from a depression brought about by the 2008 crisis.

As a policy response, central banks, concerned with debt as well as with the possibility of deflation, instituted policies of near zero or zero interest rates, and central banks of some countries—notably the United States and Japan—have been buying assets to re-inflate their economies, as of this writing.

Thus far, no country has defaulted on its debt in this crisis, but there were some close calls. Some cities in the United States defaulted. In 1998, Russia defaulted on its debt during the Russian financial crisis. Russia had suffered from a chronic fiscal deficit and kept a high fixed exchange rate, which some consider to be the reason it chose to default on its debts.

Finally, growth as a way of decreasing debt is certainly on every country's wish list, and monetary—and in some countries fiscal—policies are aimed at growth and stabilization.

The Great Recession beginning in 2008 was set off by the bursting of a housing bubble made worse by extreme leverage used by the financial sector. Paul Krugman's article, cited previously, describes the 2008 crisis as "a *deleveraging shock*, a sudden downward revision of acceptable debt levels," forcing debtors to sharply reduce their spending. This is called a *Minsky moment*—a sudden major collapse of asset values caused by long periods of prosperity and increasing value of investments that lead to increasing speculation using borrowed money. Hyman Minsky was an economist and professor at Washington University in St. Louis whose work linked periodic economic crises of the business cycle to financial speculation and bubbles.

A deleveraging shock can push the economy into a liquidity trap, according to Krugman. As discussed in Chapter 17, a liquidity trap occurs when the monetary policy is impotent because the economy is depressed, but interest rates are already at the zero lower bound.

A liquidity trap causes debt deflation, identified by Irving Fisher in his theory of economic cycles. Fisher developed his idea after the 1929 stock market crash and subsequent Great Depression. His theory portrays a cascade of events set off by the bursting of a debt bubble. The bursting of the bubble causes forced liquidation; a contraction in the deposit currency; a fall in the level of prices; a fall in the net worth of businesses precipitating bankruptcies; a decline in profits; a reduction in trade, output, and employment; pessimism and loss of confidence; hoarding; and slowing down the velocity of circulation, leading to a fall in the nominal, or money, rates and a rise in the real, or commodity, rates of interest.

Fisher's theory accurately predicted the sequence of events that followed the bursting of the housing bubble in 2008, as is evident by a speech by current Chair of the Federal Reserve Janet Yellen on April 16, 2009, when she was President of the San Francisco Federal Reserve Bank:

"The recession, in turn, deepened the credit crunch as demand and employment fell, and credit losses of financial institutions surged. Indeed, we have been in the grips of precisely this adverse feedback loop for more than a year. A process of balance sheet deleveraging has spread to nearly every corner of the economy. Consumers are pulling back on purchases, especially on durable goods, to build their savings. Businesses are cancelling planned investments and laying off workers to preserve cash. And financial institutions are shrinking assets to bolster capital and improve their chances of weathering the current storm. Once again, Minsky understood this dynamic. He spoke of the paradox of deleveraging, in which precautions that may be smart for individuals and firms—and indeed essential to return the economy to a normal state—nevertheless magnify the distress of the economy as a whole."

Defining a Recession

A downturn in economic activity can be called a recession, according to the U.S. National Bureau of Economic Research, when there is a significant decline in economic activity across the economy that lasts more than a few months and can be measured in the real GDP, real income, employment, industrial production, and wholesale-retail sales numbers. The United Kingdom and the European Union define a recession as two consecutive quarters of negative economic growth, as measured by the seasonally adjusted quarter-on-quarter figures for real GDP.

Causes of Recessions

Recessions can be precipitated by a number of factors, as has been outlined in preceding chapters. One that was not named is the *balance sheet recession*.

A balance sheet recession, described by economist Richard Koo in reference to Japan's recession that started in 1990, is triggered by the collapse of an asset or real estate bubble. This leads to assets that are less than liabilities on corporate balance sheets. Japanese corporations chose to pay down their debt rather than borrow, which made them net savers. The Japanese government's fiscal policy of massive spending offset the corporations' saving, resulting in a stable GDP for the Japanese economy. The question of whether monetary policy is effective in a balance sheet recession is still debated. Koo believes that there is a limited demand for funds while firms pay down debt. Krugman disagrees, saying that inflation expectations induced by monetary easing could help raise real GDP.

📖 **DEFINITION**

A **balance sheet recession** occurs when assets are less than liabilities on corporate balance sheets, caused by the bursting of a financial asset or housing bubble.

A balance sheet recession occurred after the bursting of the 2008 housing bubble as well. In this case, consumer demand and employment are determined by household leverage levels. Consumption declined as households deleveraged when property values fell during the subprime mortgage crisis.

As described in Chapter 18, recessions are usually precipitated by a demand shock or a supply shock. The mechanism for how the negative demand shock plays out according to the AD-AS model is also covered in Chapter 18. Supply shocks, the most infamous of which is the oil embargo shock of 1973, are caused by a sudden drop in supply that leads to a decline in output and an increase in inflation. Most recessions are caused by a general decrease in demand in the economy for all goods and services.

Let's review the mechanism of a recession caused by a lack of aggregate demand, or negative demand shock. As an example, a financial asset bubble bursts, such as the 1929 stock market crash. Since the rise in stock prices had been fueled by borrowing, called *margin,* there was forced selling of stocks caused by margin calls. Margin calls occur when investors are forced to give more cash to their brokers in order to own stocks on margin. Investors sold their shares as quickly as possible, since stock prices decline rapidly during a forced liquidation. The stock market crash shocked the nation and the world, and fear was widespread. People held on to whatever money and assets they had, so there was little spending. In "econospeak," there was a lack of aggregate demand. The absence of demand caused prices to fall. The economy was gripped by deflation and massive unemployment.

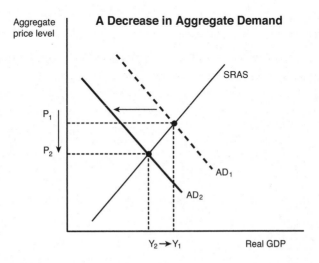

Economic Theories of Recessions

While the causes of the business cycle have been analyzed by all the economic schools of thought, the most influential are the Keynesian/neo-Keynesian and the classical/neo-classical/real business cycle schools. The mainstream policy debates about how to respond to the aftermath of the 2008 recession involve economists who adhere to these two models, although new theories from the monetarist school are emerging and gaining acceptance. Most central banks and the International Monetary Fund follow the Keynesian/neo-Keynesian models in that they come to the aid of economies when necessary. The debates are ongoing among policymakers in government and policy institutes, also called "think tanks."

Keynesian Theory

The **Keynesian and neo-Keynesian** models hold that the short-run aggregate supply curve slopes upward, as opposed to being vertical, as in the classical model. Keynesians believe most short-run fluctuations in the business cycle are caused by a change in business confidence and a change in the aggregate demand. A reduction in aggregate demand caused by a negative shock results in the actual output of the economy falling below the potential output, as described in Chapter 18. An increase in aggregate demand caused by positive influences, such as a technology boom, causes the real output to rise above potential output. The Keynesian theory states that while, in the long run, potential GDP is unaffected by the aggregate price level and market inefficiencies self-correct, in the short-run the fluctuations around the long-term trend can and should be smoothed out. Keynes famously said, "In the long run we are all dead."

As a result, this model advocates *an active government and central bank role to smooth out the business cycle using fiscal and monetary policy.* The interventions would moderate the fluctuations in the business cycle and, especially, avoid the negative impact of recessions.

Policy actions have to be tailored to the causes of individual recessions.

- The depression of 1929 to 1933 was caused by a fall in consumer and investment spending accompanied by deflation. The policy of choice was to increase the money supply and fiscal stimulus.

- The recessions sparked by the high price of oil as characterized by both unemployment and inflation during the 1970s put central banks in a quandary: which should be fixed first, inflation or unemployment? The U.S. Federal Reserve opted to bring down soaring inflation and worry about unemployment later. This dual goal was achieved.

- The 2008 Great Recession has challenged monetary policy. At zero lower bound interest rates, central banks are trying to re-inflate the economy to increase real GDP by using various measures. These include asset purchases, interest rate guidance, and possibly a negative interest rate policy on bank deposits at the central bank. The latter would encourage banks to lend out money rather than keeping it at the central bank to earn interest.

These are some of the ways Keynesians use the AD-AS model to design fiscal and monetary response. The coming chapters will explain the models in more detail.

Classical Theory

The **classical school** is commonly associated with a *laissez-faire* approach to the economy. This model sees the contractions and expansions in the economy as efficient reactions to external events in the real economy. Economists supporting this model say that the output of an economy maximizes *expected* utility. The economy is self-correcting in the long run, and they are not concerned with the short run.

The classical school believes that prices are flexible, resulting in vertical short-run and long-run supply curves. This implies that monetary policy only affects the price level. The stated belief of the classical school was that an increase in the money supply increased the price level proportionally. The result would be inflation, but the output would not be affected.

Nevertheless, some classical school economists were aware of the business cycle and even considered whether policy intervention could alter short-term fluctuations.

Two **neo-classical models**, **rational expectations** and **real business cycle theory**, have added new ideas to the classical model.

Adherents of the rational expectations model believe that firms and individuals use all available information to make decisions, which are optimal. They believe the information is incorporated into the expectations of agents immediately. For example, if the central bank signals that higher inflation is expected, businesses and labor will negotiate their contracts under this assumption. In addition, rational expectations theory holds that expected changes in monetary policy only affect the price level and not output nor unemployment, but unexpected changes can affect aggregate output and employment.

Proponents of real business cycle theory believe that the business cycle is affected by fluctuations in the total factor productivity. Since productivity is tied to technological advances, technological shocks cause the fluctuations, rather than monetary in origin. Critics of this idea point out that a slowdown in the economy might be the cause, rather than the effect, of a decline in productivity.

The real business cycle theorists believe that the role of policymakers is to concentrate on long-term structural policy. They hold that business cycles do not represent an inability of the markets to "clear." On the contrary, they think the business cycle represents the most efficient possible operation of the economy.

Proponents of the classical and neo-classical models *oppose any policy intervention, such as fiscal or monetary stimulus, to smooth out the short-term fluctuations in the business cycle.*

Monetarist Theory

Monetarist theory focuses on the macroeconomic effects of money supply and central banks. Milton Friedman is associated with developing the monetarist model. He believed that nothing was as important to the economic system as the quantity of money. Friedman also held that central banks could not manage the money supply in the short run because the information they needed to calculate the correct amount would not be available in a timely fashion, that data could be ambiguous, and that policymakers would be dug into their long-held beliefs. He advocated that the supply of money should be expanded by a fixed percentage geared to the long-term growth of the country's output rather than an interest rate target. Friedman thought this mechanism would rein in the economy when it got overheated and nudge the economy when it was contracting. The percentage increase in the supply of money should follow the natural rate of long-run economic growth, according to Friedman. He was not able to identify the natural rate of long-run growth, however. Friedman further believed that fiscal policy was ineffectual and could possibly do more harm than good.

Modern versions of monetarist theory still promote the idea that money supply is the only cure for short-run economic problems, and that there is no place for fiscal stimulus.

Market monetarism theory, a recent concept espoused by Lars Christensen and Scott Sumner, among others, holds that central banks should target the nominal GDP (NGDP)—the sum of all current-dollar non-inflation-adjusted spending in an economy—instead of inflation or unemployment. The theory holds that targeting the NGDP would be most effective because shocks to the economy are in nominal terms. They believe the government should seek a steady level of nominal GDP growth rather than targeting inflation. This concept has gained credence even with some prominent new Keynesian economists.

Modern monetary theory (MMT), which is as much Keynesian as it is monetarist, espouses the idea that money enters the economy through government spending. The government creates the *fiat* money, and taxation legitimizes it as a currency. Fiat money is currency that is not backed by gold or any other physical commodity. The theory states that fiscal stimulus is fundamental to spark growth in an economy, especially during a recession. MMT advocates allowing government budget deficits to exist as a vehicle for money to be available to the private sector. They also say that as long as a nation uses fiat money that is exchanged freely, it can never default. (Recall that Russia defaulted on its debt because it had a fixed exchange rate.) The government can print unlimited amounts of money to pay for spending until the economy is at full employment. MMT proponents claim that the level of taxation relative to government spending is a way to regulate unemployment and inflation.

These diametrically opposed theories and prescriptions for policy show how difficult it is to analyze a complex economy. Empirical observation of how the economy responds to policy is a good way to evaluate what works and what does not work. You might even be inspired to go further in your study of economics to join in the research and debate!

The Least You Need to Know

- Recessions are characterized by a decrease in spending, causing businesses to cut back or go bankrupt, high unemployment, and in severe cases, deflation.
- Deleveraging of debt can occur via austerity, high inflation, default, or growth.
- A paradox of thrift occurs when, during a recession, an increase in planned savings can cause actual savings and investment to decrease.
- Recessions usually occur when there is a lack of aggregate demand in the economy as a result of a negative demand shock and sometimes by a negative supply shock.
- Predominant economic theories about recessions include those of the Keynesian and neo-Keynesian schools; the Classical, neo-Classical, and Real Business Theory schools; and the Monetarist school.

CHAPTER 20

Money

From the earliest days of barter more than 10,000 years ago to the complexity of our modern economy, with its need to manage a nation's money supply, humans are clearly an enterprising species. We have been clever in fulfilling the necessities of our survival, devising all manner of instruments and mechanisms to achieve our individual and collective goals.

This chapter begins by discovering the earliest forms of exchange and how money became a vital part of the development of economies over time. The significance of gold, still a matter of interest and debate, will be explored. The chapter concludes with an examination of the role of money in our modern economy. We will look at how central banks work with the private banking system to maintain the right balance of money supply so the economy remains stable and how new money is created.

In This Chapter

- From barter to bills: the evolution of money
- What happened to the gold standard?
- Understanding the money supply
- How money is created

A Brief History of Money

Some form of exchange has existed for tens of thousands of years. In early communities of hunters and gatherers, anthropologists have identified societies that engaged in gift giving, whereby items were freely given without any obvious expectation of getting something in return. There is still uncertainty about how the gift economy functioned.

The use of an object representing value, making trade viable, began thousands of years ago. Archeologists have unearthed obsidian in Anatolia used to make tools dating from 12000 B.C. Trade in obsidian took place from 9000 B.C. Silver and copper came into use soon after.

The manner in which goods and services were exchanged evolved over thousands of years. Development correlated with the size and geographical range of societies.

Barter

Trade began with the system of *barter*, exchange of one item or service for another of similar value. Archaeologists excavating a pre-agricultural site dating back to 19400 B.C., called **Ohalo II** near the Sea of Galilee, discovered grains that are believed to have been used in some form of barter. Grain as well as cattle, sheep, camels, and other livestock, were used in barter as early as 9000 B.C.

Later, agricultural societies chose objects that were sturdy enough to remain intact through multiple exchanges. As these early economies established a division of labor, objects that represented value, which we can now call money, were more widely used. When skills advanced in the production of original goods that could be traded, a universal form of money was necessary. Cowrie shells, the shells of a mollusk, were popular in China and the Pacific region as well as Africa starting in about 1200 B.C.

Barter had its limitations, as perishable items were not reliable. In order to be useful, barter is dependent on a *double coincidence of wants*—each person would need what the other is offering within a time constraint. These restrictions on the ease of trade made barter an inconvenient system.

> **DEFINITION**
>
> A **double coincidence of wants** describes the requirements for a successful barter: each person wants what the other is offering within the same timeframe.

Commodity Money

Commodity money developed as a store of value and medium of exchange. The money itself—gold and silver coins, for example—had intrinsic value. Commodity money facilitated trade by assuring that producers would always be able to sell their products. A double coincidence of wants was no longer a barrier.

Metal money and coins, usually bronze and copper, were first used in China about 1000 B.C. Outside of China, in about 500 B.C., silver coins came into use. Lydia, located in modern Turkey, is thought to be the first place to mint these coins, but their use soon spread throughout the region. Unlike China, which used base metals for their coins, communities in the Lydia region used precious metals. King Pheidon of Argos, Greece, was the first to set official standards of weight for coins in the seventh century B.C.

The introduction of the *touchstone* to determine the amount of gold or silver contained in a coin advanced the acceptance of these coins as commodity money. Once weight and value were obtainable, precious metal coins could become a standard means of exchange.

> **DEFINITION**
>
> A **touchstone** is a slate or fieldstone tablet used to determine the purity of a gold or silver coin. The soft metal leaves a colored streak on the tablet that can be matched to the known colors of other gold and silver alloys.

Precious metal coins became the most prevalent form of money for thousands of years. Some wrinkles had to be ironed out from time to time, such as the usual suspects trimming bits of coins off for safe keeping, governments stamping a value on coins that was less than accurate, and a difference in preference of metals among countries for a time. Eventually, national governments guaranteed to exchange money into gold at a published rate.

Once coins became a unit of value rather than a unit of weight, it was possible to calculate the difference in price between value and weight, called *seigniorage*. (If you recall in Chapter 17, seigniorage was used by governments to extract value from money during hyperinflation.)

Representative Money

Representative money was the next innovation to facilitate trade. Instead of using the gold or silver directly, the coins or bars were stored in bank vaults, and the depositor received a certificate that could be returned to the bank to collect the silver or gold. The goldsmiths in England during the sixteenth century turned this activity into an early banking business. More broadly, representative money is any money that is backed by a commodity.

Fiat Money

Fiat money, the money we use today, has no commodity backing or intrinsic value. It is declared legal tender by a government and can be exchanged for goods, services, or money in other currencies. Fiat money, you might say, is "backed" by trust in the government's ability to stand behind the value of money because it is legal tender. All else being equal, you will accept the money in exchange for your services or a product that you want to sell.

Paper Money

Paper money can either be representative or fiat money. Under the gold standard, paper money could be brought to the bank in exchange for gold in the denomination printed on the face of the paper money. Fiat money cannot be exchanged for gold, unless you are buying gold.

Paper money first appeared in China about A.D. 800 and lasted until about 1455 until the overprinting of money caused massive inflation. The Ming Dynasty stopped printing money as a result.

Paper money was not used in Europe until about 1600. Bank notes came into use at this time. These notes were paper and could be exchanged for silver or gold coins by the banks or other private institutions that issued them. Governments began issuing paper money in the late 1600s.

The Function of Money

The introduction of money has advanced the evolution and growth of economies by simplifying trade, which in turn provided a fertile environment for businesses and the opportunity to work for income.

More efficient than barter, money provides us with a …

- *Store of value.* You can work for a month, put your earnings in the bank, and, all else equal, the value of your money will remain the same as when you deposited it in the bank. Over a long time frame inflation will begin to decrease the value.

- *Unit of account.* Money has a recognizable, standard and acceptable value. This facilitates transactions if you want to buy something. It would be much more cumbersome to buy a tablet with your guitar, for example.

- *Medium of exchange.* Money is legal tender and accepted everywhere. The value of the money is printed on the currency and can be exchanged for a product or service of equal value.

Gold and the Gold Standard

People have long sought gold for its striking color, malleability for jewelry, density, and scarcity. Civilizations throughout history fortunate enough to evolve in locations rich in gold and silver deposits were able to amass great wealth. If they were not so lucky, they had to search for gold outside their territory. In the fifteenth century, the European countries that explored west to the Americas were amply rewarded. The search for gold and silver continued, and other areas abundant in the metals were later found in Australia and South Africa.

The Origin and History of the Gold Standard

In the 1600s, paper money became a favored alternative to carrying gold and silver coins in Europe. For the most part, paper was redeemable for gold in most European countries. The United States waffled between money backed by gold or silver, but after briefly choosing silver after 1780, it eventually decided on gold.

The gold standard is a monetary system where the value of currency is fixed in terms of the weight of gold. Since the price is fixed at a specific weight, for example, $20.67 per ounce, it is a factor in setting the price level in an economy.

The gold standard began with a gold *specie* standard, based on the amount of gold coins in circulation. Another category was the gold *exchange* standard, based on a fixed exchange rate with a foreign country that used a gold standard. The gold *bullion* standard was a system where the government would hold gold, which could be exchanged for paper money at a fixed rate.

The height of the gold standard was the period from 1871 to 1914. This was a time of political tranquility among nations. The calm was replaced by instability and turmoil as World War I broke out.

The underlying problems of the gold standard became visible as the belligerent governments accumulated enormous deficits to carry out the war. While the United States reaped benefits by selling war supplies to the European countries in conflict, Germany was punished by its war debt and reparations after the war was over.

INTERESTING FACT

Important dates in the history of gold:

1377. Great Britain shifts to a monetary system based on gold and silver.

1792. The Coinage Act places the United States on a silver-gold standard.

1900. The Gold Standard Act puts the United States on the gold standard.

1913. The Federal Reserve Act specifies that Federal Reserve Notes be backed 40 percent in gold.

1931. Great Britain gets off the gold bullion standard.

1933-1934. President Roosevelt prohibits private holdings of gold. The Gold Reserve Act of 1934 gives the U.S. government title to all monetary gold and halts the minting of gold coins. It also raises the price of gold to $35 per ounce.

1944. The Bretton Woods agreement is ratified by the U.S. Congress.

1961. Americans are forbidden to own gold.

1971. The United States terminates gold sales or purchases.

1982. The U.S. Gold Commission report recommends no new monetary role for gold.

Source: The History of Gold. National Mining Association.

As gold reserves became depleted in the United Kingdom, gold had little influence on money. Germany ended the gold standard at the beginning of World War I. Inflation shot up throughout Europe. The destabilization of European economies and their monetary systems did not fully recover before the 1929 stock market crash—a major shock to world economies.

The United Kingdom ended the gold standard in 1931. The Bank of England, like other central banks, only kept a fraction of the gold needed to back their money supply. At one point, speculators lost confidence in the bank's ability to exchange paper for gold. When the rumor spread that there was not enough gold to back the paper money, there was a run on the bank. The bank's gold reserves were soon depleted. Great Britain was forced to abandon the gold standard. Australia, New Zealand, and Canada followed.

In 1933 President Franklin D. Roosevelt prohibited the private holding of gold, and in 1934 the U.S. government enacted the Gold Reserve Act of 1934, giving the government permanent title to all monetary gold and halting the minting of gold coins. The United States adopted a limited gold bullion standard, restricting redemption of gold to dollars held by foreign central banks and licensed private users. President Roosevelt increased the price of gold to $35 per ounce from $20.67 per ounce, reducing the value of the U.S. dollar.

INTERESTING FACT

During the Great Depression, countries tried to improve their economies by erecting foreign trade barriers. They devalued their currencies to improve their exports and prohibited citizens from holding foreign exchange. These measures, called *beggar-thy-neighbor* policies in economic parlance, resulted in a plunge in international trade and an exacerbation of the world depression.

The Bretton Woods agreement, forged in 1944 at the United Nations Monetary and Financial Conference, aimed to reverse the beggar-thy-neighbor policies of the Great Depression and promote cooperation among nations. The agreement established the structure for the global currency markets as an adjustable foreign exchange rate system pegged to the U.S. dollar, which was then fixed to the price of gold. It also established the International Monetary Fund and the World Bank. Member countries agreed to convert foreign official holdings of their currencies into gold at an established par value.

In 1971, U.S. President Richard Nixon ended all gold sales and purchases and devalued the dollar by raising the official dollar price of gold to $38 per ounce and then again in 1973 to $42.22 per ounce. Gold could then trade freely.

Currently, no currency is on the gold standard, although some countries and organizations hold gold in reserves.

Advantages and Disadvantages of the Gold Standard

Advocates of the gold standard—such as the Austrian School of economics, some objectivists, and others who are against fiat currency—hold that the gold standard reduces the risk of inflation, hyperinflation, and credit expansion, since the money supply is tied to the gold supply. Some advocates maintain that long-term price stability can be obtained with a gold standard. The Mises Institute believes that a gold standard would eliminate the political business cycle they contend is caused by monetary policy determined by the politics of the day. (Expansionary policy would help an incumbent candidate.) They also contend that fixed international exchange rates reduce uncertainty in trade.

Most economists today do not favor a gold standard. Maintaining a gold standard prevents central banks from supporting growth during a recession. When Great Britain got off the gold standard in 1931, they were able to mitigate the effects of their recession because the central bank had the flexibility to increase the money supply. Students of the 1930s Great Depression, such as Ben Bernanke, believe that had the United States not been on the gold standard, the Federal Reserve would have had the flexibility it needed to prevent the worst of the depression and speed up recovery. When the money supply cannot be increased during a recession, there is no way to re-inflate the economy to encourage growth, resulting in the danger of deflation.

Another negative cited by economists is that it causes short-term volatility in the economy's output and inflation, although there is stability in the long term. For example, a gold discovery can cause inflation because more gold is added to the supply. In the short run, gold-mining strikes can decrease the supply of gold. A shortage in gold when the economy is growing can cause short-term deflation. This is a problem for farmers and other producers who must make fixed payments but cannot get a good price for their products. Before 1913 this was one of the main motivations for the passage of the Federal Reserve Act, which created the Federal Reserve. One of the functions of the Federal Reserve was to manage the gold standard.

Another disadvantage of the gold standard is that the countries on the gold standard have fixed exchange rates, since they are all fixed to the price of gold. This means that if one country instituted a monetary policy for a domestic situation, the effects of the policy would be transferred to the other countries on the gold standard. During the Great Depression, the U.S. Federal Reserve carried out a contractionary monetary policy rather than an expansionary policy. The policy intensified the depression. Since there was a fixed exchange rate because of the gold standard, the negative effects of the U.S. monetary policy spread to all countries on the gold standard.

The gold standard is inherently unfair to countries that do not have adequate or any gold stocks, since possession of physical gold is required to back up paper currency.

Some think the gold standard hinders the growth of the economy because the money supply should grow along with the economy. By having a finite amount of gold stock, this is not possible.

These are just some of the disadvantages raised by critics of the gold standard. The main issues revolve around the constraints put on policymakers and the necessity of having physical gold.

The Money Supply

A stable currency generates confidence and trust that the value of money will not change for the foreseeable future. Businesses are willing to take your money in exchange for something you want to buy. You know that your paycheck will meet your budget requirements each month. You are confident that putting money aside as savings will still be worth what it was when you deposited it in the bank.

As we've seen in preceding chapters, this is not always the case because of the ups and downs of the business cycle. That is where the central bank comes into the picture. Central bank policy might increase or decrease the money supply to smooth out the business cycle. How is this accomplished? Where does the money come from to increase the money supply, and where does it go when monetary policy calls for tightening the money supply during an inflationary period? The process involves the relationship between the central bank, the commercial banks, and you.

Classification of Money

One of the most important roles of central banks is to manage an economy's *money supply*. Since modern economies use fiat money, the central banks and the treasury do not have to keep a stock of gold and silver for redemption by a bearer of paper money. They can create as much fiat money as necessary so that economic activity can continue with a stable currency.

The money supply is divided and categorized into *monetary aggregates,* which are categories of money that make up the money supply. By having the ability to measure the monetary aggregates, the central bank can monitor their growth and compute the total money supply. This information is used by the central banks to track the health of the economy and design monetary policy. It is possible, for example, to recognize a budding increase in inflation by noting that the monetary aggregates are growing too fast. The central bank might decide to raise interest rates to stave off inflation. (Chapter 21 addresses monetary policy.)

In the United States the most important monetary aggregates are MB, M1, and M2. MB is the monetary base. M1 includes the currency in circulation, traveler's checks, and checkable bank deposits. M2 includes assets that can be easily converted into cash or checkable bank deposits. This includes CDs, savings deposits, money market accounts, and similar instruments. Bank deposits are a big part of both M1 and M2 and therefore make up a large portion of the money supply. Other countries define monetary aggregates according to their own conventions, which are similar.

DEFINITION

The **money supply** is the currency in circulation plus the checkable bank deposits (ability to write checks against deposits). A **monetary aggregate** is a category of money that is part of an overall measure of the money supply.

The Role of Banks in Creating Money

Banks have an important function in the process of increasing or decreasing the money supply. *Fractional reserve banking* is a mechanism by which a quantity of newly printed money by the central bank is multiplied via bank lending, increasing the supply of money in the economy.

The bank retains only a fraction of the money deposited in its bank and loans out the rest. By repeating this process, the money originally received from the central bank multiplies and circulates in the economy.

INTERESTING FACT

Fractional reserve banking began with the goldsmiths of sixteenth-century England. The goldsmiths had vaults used to store their gold. After King Charles I of England confiscated the gold from the Royal Mint in 1640, traders and merchants took their gold out of the Royal Mint and stored it in the locked vaults of the goldsmiths for a fee. The goldsmiths set up a system that became a precursor to the modern banking system. As the system became more sophisticated, the goldsmiths issued receipts to the owners for the deposited gold. Realizing that the deposits were not redeemed all at once, the goldsmiths made loans to other customers using the receipts, for which they were paid interest. They were, in fact, using the deposited gold as a form of reserves. The notes held by the owners of the gold were payable on demand. This, then, was an early form of fractional reserve banking.

The *monetary base*, also called *high-powered money*, includes the currency in circulation and the deposits of banks held at the central bank. The currency not in circulation that is in the vaults of private banks plus the banks' deposits held at the central bank are used as *reserves* to back the deposits made at private banks by individuals and businesses. The *reserve ratio* is the fraction of bank deposits that a bank must hold in cash as reserves. The reserve ratio is determined by the central bank.

Here are the steps involved in adding money to the money supply:

1. The central bank creates money by printing it or, more likely, electronically. Central bank policy determines the quantity. How does the money get into the economy?

2. The central bank buys securities on the open market, commonly government bonds, from you. You have the central bank's money in exchange for the bonds, which puts the money into circulation. The bonds are now owned by the central bank.

3. You now have money that can either be spent or put into a checkable deposit account in a private bank. The private bank now has whatever money you deposited with them. These deposits, plus the banks' deposits held at the central bank, are called *bank reserves*.

> **DEFINITION**
>
> **Fractional reserve banking** is a process by which a quantity of newly printed money by the central bank is multiplied by means of bank lending, increasing the supply of money in the economy. The **reserve ratio** is the fraction of bank deposits that a bank must hold in cash as reserves. **Bank reserves** are the currency banks keep in their vaults and their deposits at the central bank.

4. The bank may now lend out most of your money but must keep a *fraction* of your money, which is part of their reserves, within the bank. The fraction to be kept as reserves is determined by the central bank. You are able to take money out of the bank and write checks against all the money you deposited. You might be wondering how this is possible if the bank lends out most of your money.

5. Before we answer that question, what happens to the money—*your money*—loaned to someone else by your bank? Those bank customers either spend the money or deposit it into another private bank. Keep in mind that they are borrowing a portion of the money you deposited in the bank, since the bank must retain a fraction of your money as bank reserves. Repeating the process, a fraction of the money deposited in the second bank is loaned to someone else, and the procedure continues. Each time the bank lends the money to another customer who deposits it into another bank, which lends part of it out, more money is put in circulation.

Fractional Reserve Banking

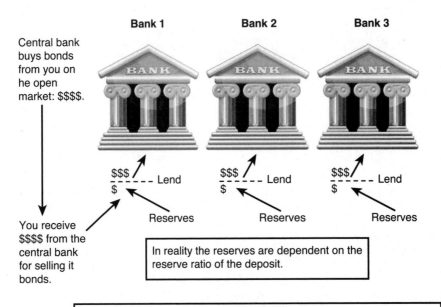

In reality the reserves are dependent on the reserve ratio of the deposit.

How Money Is Multiplied

The central bank buys bonds from you for $$$$. You deposit $$$$ in Bank 1. Bank 1 keeps $ as reserves (The reserves are dependent on the reserve ratio of the deposit.) and lends out $$$. The recipient puts $$$ in Bank 2. Bank 2 puts $ in reserves and $$ are lent out. This process continues.

The original $$$$ are subject to the multiplier effect, as 9$ are created as of Bank 3. As the process continues, more money is added to the money supply. You still have the rights to all your deposits.

Despite the fact that your bank has lent out most of your money, you can write checks against the balance in your checking account. The person who received a loan from your bank can write checks against his bank balance, and so on. This is how money is created.

Let's see how this works if you sell $10,000 of treasury bonds to the central bank. *Remember, the money supply is defined as currency in circulation plus checkable bank deposits.*

IMPORTANT: Let's assume the reserve ratio is 10 percent.

How Money Is Added to the Money Supply

	Currency in Circulation	Checkable Bank Deposits	Money Supply
You have **$10,000** from selling bonds to the central bank.	$10,000	$0	$10,000
You deposit $10,000 in Bank 1, which lends **$9,000** to John. [$10,000 − (.10 × $10,000) = $9,000]	$9,000	**$10,000**	**$19,000** ($9,000 + $10,000 = $19,000)
John deposits $9,000 into Bank 2, which lends **$8,100** to Anne. [$9,000 − (.10 × $9,000) = $8,100]	$8,100	**$19,000**	**$27,100** ($8,100 + $19,000 = $27,100)

By this *money multiplier effect,* the central bank accomplished its goal of taking a small amount of money, in this case $10,000, and increasing its size to $27,100, increasing the monetary supply.

DO THE MATH

The **money multiplier** is the ratio of the **money supply** (currency in circulation + checkable bank deposits) to the **monetary base** (bank reserves + money in circulation).

Money supply (M) = currency (CU) + deposits (D)

Monetary base (MB) = currency (CU) + reserves

The money multiplier (mm) = $\dfrac{\text{money supply} = CU + D}{\text{monetary base} = CU + \text{reserves}}$

The money multiplier is also the inverse of the *reserve requirement* (R): mm = $\dfrac{1}{R}$

To find the increase in checkable bank deposits if the bank has excess reserves (actual reserves minus required reserves), divide the excess reserves by the reserve ratio (rr) (stipulated by the central bank).

Example: If a bank has $2,000 in excess reserves, and the reserve ratio is 20%, the increase in checkable bank deposits is:

$$\$2,000/rr = \$2,000/0.20 = \$10,000.$$

From $2,000 in excess reserves, the increase in checkable bank deposits is $10,000, so $10,000 is added to the money supply.

If the central bank wants to *reduce* the amount of money in circulation, it sells the bonds it holds to you and puts the money from the sale of the bonds into its vaults or takes it out of circulation.

How Deposits Are Protected

Fractional reserve banking relies on the assumption that all depositors will not need their money at the same time, since most of the deposits have been lent out. A lack of confidence in the bank could cause a bank run. In order to protect against this possibility, the government insures deposits up to a certain amount of money, which varies by country. In the United States, the insurance comes from the Federal Deposit Insurance Corporation (FDIC). Other precautions include governments' modifying the amount of reserves banks must maintain and regulating the banks to prevent risky behavior.

The central bank is also the lender of last resort. If there is a bank run or if there is a financial crisis, so that banks are unable to carry out their normal activities, the central bank will provide money—liquidity—to the banks. Without the help of the central bank, the bank could go bankrupt.

The central bank clearly plays a key role in the economy. The next chapter will describe how central banks came about, more on the functions of the central bank, and how the central bank conducts monetary policy.

The Least You Need to Know

- Barter was an early form of trade. The system was limited by the inconvenience of each person's needing what the other person was offering to trade. Commodity money was more convenient than barter and facilitated trade because it had an intrinsic value and was portable and durable.

- Representative money had no intrinsic value but had commodity backing. Fiat money, used today, is not backed by a commodity. It is accepted because the government has declared it legal tender.

- The function of money is as a store of value, a unit of account, and a medium of exchange.

- The height of the gold standard, which pegged currencies to gold prices, was between 1871 and 1914. Some argue that adherence to the gold standard prolonged the Great Depression because central banks could not use monetary policy. The United States was the last country to abandon the gold standard in 1971.

- Fractional reserve banking, where banks lend a portion of their deposits but depositors have the right to write checks against their entire deposit, creates new money through the multiplier effect. The central bank increases and decreases the money supply using the bank as an intermediary.

CHAPTER 21

The Central Banks and Macroeconomic Policy

The central bank plays the principal role in the monetary and financial realm of an economy. While private banks had an early part in supporting economies, population growth outstripped the ability of small entities to provide sufficient support. Central banks were established to fill this need in growing economies.

This chapter describes the origins and history of the central banks, their modern functions, how macroeconomic policy can affect the economy, and the tools used to reduce the large swings of the business cycle. The chapter will also describe the extreme situations of financial crises and how economic theory can make or break an economy.

In This Chapter

- The history of central banking
- Bank runs and financial panics
- Macroeconomics and the lessons of the Great Depression
- The role of the central banks in the economy
- The 2008 financial crisis and the response by central banks

Origins of Central Banks

The Riksbank of Sweden is the oldest central bank, dating from 1668. It was originally established as a joint stock bank by the Swedish Parliament, which was composed of nobles, clergy, and burghers. One of the first tasks of the new central bank was to fund Sweden's war against Denmark. It also served as a clearing house for commerce.

The Bank of England was established in 1694 as a joint stock bank and was the dominant central bank for many years. The bank functioned at first as the English government's banker to purchase government debt. It was not brought under public ownership until 1946.

The remaining central banks in Europe were formed after the 1600s. Napoleon established the Bank of France in 1800. These banks also served as repositories for other domestic banks and were connected to the individual banks in the nation's banking system. As a result of their key role in the economy and their gold and silver reserves, they served as lender of last resort in a liquidity crisis.

In Asia the Bank of Japan was founded in 1882. The People's Bank of China (PBC) was established in 1948 and became legally confirmed in 1995. In 2003 the PBC was given the role of forming and implementing monetary policy. It is the largest central bank in the world by asset value.

Financial Panics

In Chapter 20 we pointed out that the fractional reserve banking system was based on the assumption that not everyone would want to withdraw their bank deposits at the same time. Most of the deposits are long-term loans, perhaps for businesses or machinery. Depositors, on the other hand, have the rights to all their money. Confidence in the bank's ability to return cash to depositors on demand is what allows the banking system to function. If there is any suggestion that a bank might fail, depositors will demand their money before the bank is insolvent.

Bank runs do, in fact, occur. There were four important bank runs in the 1700s and 11 in the 1800s. Many of them began with an overexpansion of credit, resulting in too much financial speculation that ended in a bust followed by a recession. Panics were also set off by the inability of a bank to exchange paper money for silver or gold.

In 1893 in the United States, speculation in railroads went too far, as an overexpansion of railroads caused expenses to exceed income. The mining rush in silver was overdone, resulting in a drop in silver prices. At the same time, farmers were losing money on their agricultural products because prices were falling. A panic and run on the banks was triggered by the collapse of the Philadelphia and Reading Railroad. The fear spread to England and Europe, where stock speculators sold U.S. stocks in exchange for money backed by gold. More than 500 banks and 15,000 businesses failed in the United States, as well as many farms. Unemployment was in the high double digits.

The Panic of 1907 saw a 50 percent fall in the U.S. stock market. Initiated by a too-clever effort to corner the United Copper Company by Charles Morse, the failed attempt rippled across financial companies. As the situation worsened, J.P. Morgan, one of the wealthiest and savviest bankers in New York, gathered other wealthy bankers and business leaders, including John D. Rockefeller, to put an end to the run on banks and brokerage houses. They hoped to assuage the public by plowing funds into salvageable businesses.

One of the largest brokerages in New York was heavily in debt. The debt was backed by shares in the Tennessee Coal, Iron and Railroad Company (TC&I). A collapse in the brokerage would have forced it to sell its shares in TC&I, which meant its shares would plunge, and further panic would follow. If U.S. Steel were able to buy TC&I, that would save both TC&I and the brokerage. The deal couldn't be accomplished without the government's permission to waive the Sherman Antitrust Act, since U.S. Steel already owned 60 percent of the firm.

The end of the crisis came from Washington, when President Theodore Roosevelt agreed to set aside the Sherman Antitrust Act to prevent a complete collapse of the banking system. With the government finally involved, confidence was restored in the financial system, and the panic ended.

The Establishment of the U.S. Federal Reserve Bank

One thing was clear—private wealthy individuals were not the solution to salvaging a growing country's financial system. After a thorough study on the feasibility of establishing a central bank to handle financial panics, the Federal Reserve Act was passed by Congress in 1913 under President Woodrow Wilson. The Act established the Federal Reserve Bank in 1914 as the central bank of the United States, after another financial panic.

The Federal Reserve's initial mandate was to be the lender of last resort in light of the recurrent panics and bank runs. It also was tasked with managing the gold standard. The monetary system backed by gold had been creating volatility in interest rates, deflation, and inflation. Congress also wanted to prevent a speculative attack on the dollar that could drive the United States off the gold standard. (See Chapter 20.)

In establishing the Federal Reserve Bank, President Wilson avoided the issue that caused the failure of the second attempt at establishing a central bank in the United States: farmers and others who lived far from Washington and New York were wary of a central bank located in the capitol. People living away from Washington wanted their interests represented. Sensitive to their needs, and for the good of the country, President Wilson created 12 Federal Reserve located in major cities throughout the country and a Board of Governors in Washington. This structure remains today.

European Central Banks

Early on, central banks in Europe were primarily concerned with maintaining the availability of gold for conversion of bank notes. This was important because the money supply of an economy depended on the gold stores, which could be affected by a balance-of-payments deficit, and the aggregate price level of an economy was determined by the value of gold. Price stability was the major concern of central banks under the gold standard.

The other function of the central banks in Europe was to be the lender of last resort. Depositors would commonly want access to their cash if there were crop failures, wars, or bankruptcies. At first, the banks would try to protect their own gold reserves and turn away depositors, sparking panics.

To stem these panics, economist and writer Walter Bagehot in the mid-1800s proposed that the Bank of England provide liquidity by lending freely, provided the loan was backed by collateral and with the stipulation that there be a penalty rate on the loan to prevent moral hazard. This successful policy is now known as *Bagehot's rule*.

> **DEFINITION**
>
> **Bagehot's rule**, used by central banks during a financial crisis, advises to lend freely, add a penalty to the loan, and require collateral that is good in normal times. Banks that are unlikely to survive should go bankrupt, be dissolved, or be purchased.

The modern European Central Bank (ECB) was established in a decade-long process starting in 1990 to permanently end antagonisms among nations in Europe by facilitating trade, commerce, and individual mobility throughout the Eurozone. Each country still has a central bank. The ECB can now conduct monetary policy for the entire Eurozone.

On January 1, 1999, fixed exchange rates were a prelude to the euro's becoming the currency of ~st European Union members. It did not go into circulation until January 1, 2002. The Euro is ~l currency of 17 of the 28 member states as of this writing.

˜epression

˜he 1930s—caused by the aftermath of World War I, panic caused by
˜rcent in 1929, and complications with the gold standard—was a
˜heory and policy.

The Effect of Policy on the Crisis

In the United States, a Liquidationist theory held sway over those responsible for monetary policy, led by Treasury Secretary Mellon. This theory posited that the excesses of the 1920s, including the stock market bubble, had to be wrung out of the system so the economy could return to a healthy state. As a result, during the Great Depression, the Federal Reserve tightened monetary policy in order to rein in financial speculation and support the gold standard. This resulted in rapid deflation, further contraction in the economy, and a spike in unemployment.

DEFINITION

Liquidationist theory holds that there should be no intervention by the government or central bank to help end recessions but that the pain of the bankruptcies was the best medicine.

When the Federal Reserve did not serve as lender of last resort as bank runs caused multiple panics from 1930 to 1933, the economy went into a tailspin. Almost 10,000 banks failed during the crisis.

The Federal Reserve was also concerned about the potential for an attack on the dollar, which had recently occurred in Great Britain on the pound. If speculators sensed a weakness in the dollar, an attack could cause a mass redemption of dollars for gold. Great Britain had been forced to abandon the gold standard, and the Federal Reserve wanted to protect against that possibility. The Federal Reserve chose to raise interest rates to make U.S. investments attractive and encourage money to remain in the United States. An increase in interest rates is the opposite remedy for an economy suffering from deflation and contraction, according to most economists.

International trade fell, in part hurt by the American Smoot-Hawley Tariff Act of 1930 that raised tariffs on imports. Retaliatory tariffs were imposed by other countries, exacerbating the depression.

It was during the Great Depression that John Maynard Keynes published his classic work *The General Theory of Employment, Interest, and Money* in 1936. Keynes's ideas provided the basis for macroeconomic theory. Keynes identified the cause of the Great Depression as a lack of aggregate demand, which resulted in deflation, a fall in output, and extreme unemployment. His remedy was to increase demand to replace the lack of spending by the private sector even if it involved deficit spending. His ideas began to percolate among some economists as the depression intensified.

The Recovery

Gradually, policies initially taken were reversed. Internationally, countries were ending the gold standard. Great Britain, the Scandinavian countries, and Japan left the gold standard in 1931. The United States, under President Franklin Roosevelt, forbade the hoarding of gold in 1933.

Analysis of the relationship between ending the gold standard and recovering from the depression showed a clear correlation—the countries that left the gold standard first recovered first. As soon as the currencies were no longer pegged to gold, monetary policy could provide support by lowering interest rates and increasing the money supply to reverse the deflationary spiral.

In 1934, the United States established the Federal Deposit Insurance Corporation, FDIC, which guaranteed depositors return of capital up to a certain amount. This measure stopped the bank runs. The Smoot-Hawley Act was ended by President Roosevelt in 1934. His New Deal fiscal policies included the 1938 Works Progress Administration (renamed in 1939 as the Work Projects Administration), which provided employment to millions of the unemployed.

Economies slowly began to recover. The recovery accelerated when rumor of another world war became a reality. Men were employed by the military, manufacture of war supplies ramped up, and women started to work in industry as the men went off to war. The massive war spending is assumed by most economists to have been the needed increase in aggregate demand (fiscal stimulus) by the government described by Keynes.

Lessons of the Great Depression

The Great Depression provided a laboratory in which economic theories could be tested, if only by witnessing the response of the economy to policies applied before and during the onset of the Great Depression. The accompanying table compares the problems identified by policymakers at the time, the policy measures taken, the results of the policy, and what policies might be taken today.

For most observers of the policies used during the rise and fall of the stock market and the subsequent depression, the weight of evidence does not seem to support the Liquidationist measures. Future central bank policies would be forged in light of the lessons of the Great Depression.

Government and Central Bank Policies from 1928-1932, Policy Results, and What Policies Would Be Enacted Today

Identified Problem	Policy	Policy Results	Today's Likely Policies
Excesses should be wrung out of heated economies by raising interest rates	Raise interest rates; decrease money supply; balance the budget	Deflation and depression	Decrease interest rates; increase money supply and fiscal spending
The gold standard provides price stability	Gold standard maintained	Deflation	Abandon gold policy
Protect the domestic currency pegged to gold	Raise interest rates	Deflation	Lower interest rates
Businesses and financial institutions should operate in an unregulated environment	Few regulations or oversight	Bank failures, bank runs, and panic	Regulate financial institutions; central bank should be the lender of last resort

Functions of the Central Banks

The goals of modern central banks are to maintain macroeconomic and financial stability, and in the United States to also foster maximum employment.

Macroeconomic stability includes (1) *stabilizing growth* by smoothing out the swings of the business cycle, in particular reducing or eliminating recessions, and (2) *stabilizing inflation* at a low—but not zero—level.

Maintaining financial stability means trying to reduce or eliminate financial panics and crises.

Monetary policy is the tool used to preserve macroeconomic stability. This includes raising and lowering short-term interest rates to adjust the money supply. Monetary policy can cool down an overheated economy or stimulate a slow economy.

To maintain financial stability, one of the tools central banks can provide is *liquidity* to banks during a panic. As the lender of last resort, the central bank can make short-term loans to financial institutions to remove the depositors' fears of not having access to their money.

Another tool to sustain financial stability is regulation and supervision of the banking system. The central banks, as well as other government agencies, review the books and portfolios of banks to make sure their operations are well maintained and their risk levels are moderate. Ideally, this action would prevent a situation that could cause a panic.

Read on for more details about central bank macroeconomic policies.

An Independent Central Bank

First, it is important to understand the value of having a central bank that is independent from the politics of government. Originally, central banks were private and independent, so they could make their own policy decisions. In the twentieth century, they were nationalized and no longer independent. Now most central banks in developed countries are able to make their own policy decisions. In 1951 the Federal Reserve gained independence from the Treasury to carry out the goals of Congress. Congress still has the authority to change the Federal Reserve Act to reverse this arrangement. The European central banks became independent in the 1990s.

An independent central bank is in a better position to construct policy that it believes will benefit the economy. Often given long tenures, members and officials of central banks are sheltered from political forces that can pressure monetary policymakers to design policy for the sake of political gain rather than the long-term health of the economy.

Maintaining Macroeconomic Stability

How do central banks maintain macroeconomic stability? In Chapter 18 on the business cycle, we noted that the long-run GDP trend, or potential output, has an upward slope, indicating that the economy has been in a steady climb to this point. There are short-run fluctuations around the long-run GDP trend, or potential output. The difference between the economy at the potential output and a trough is a negative, or recessionary, output gap. The difference between the economy at the potential output and the peak is a positive, or expansionary, output gap. Macroeconomic policy is aimed at reducing the gaps around the potential output so that the actual output equals the potential output.

A central bank uses tools to manage the short-run contractions and expansions in the economy to carry out its monetary policy. The main tool used by central banks is changing the short-term interest rate to increase or decrease the money supply. An increase in the money supply (expansion) will stimulate a slow economy. A decrease in the money supply will slow down an overheated economy. An increase in the money supply shifts the aggregate demand curve to the right, increasing output. A decrease (contraction) in the money supply shifts the aggregate demand curve to the left, decreasing output.

Chapter 20 covered how the central bank increases and decreases the money supply via *open market operations*. As a review, to increase the money supply, the central bank buys treasury bonds from you on the open market. You deposit this money into the checking account of your bank. Although you have access to your deposits, the bank will lend out most of your money. The fractional reserve banking system process continues, and through this multiplier effect, the money supply increases.

To decrease the money supply in order to cool an overheated economy, the procedure is reversed. The central bank sells you some assets from its portfolio, such as bonds. You pay with the money deposited in your bank. The bank has less money to lend, and the money supply contracts.

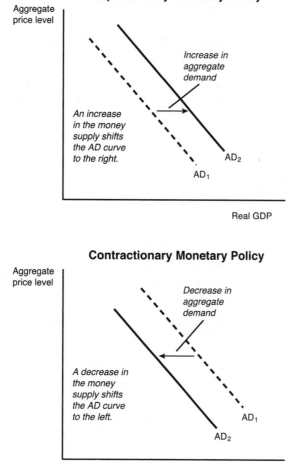

This process controls the supply of money. How does this affect interest rates, or, alternatively, how do interest rates affect the money supply?

If the central bank wants to stimulate the economy, it will lower the short-term *federal funds rate*. When the central bank, in this case the Federal Reserve, raises the federal funds rate, other short-term interest rates will also decline. The lowered interest rate filters through the economy by encouraging borrowing, which promotes spending for goods and housing. An improvement in housing sales can increase construction and jobs. The boost in demand stimulates growth.

If the central bank wants to cool off the economy, it will raise the short-term interest rate, which will discourage lending and borrowing, resulting in less spending and a slowing down of the economy.

Monetary policy to stimulate the economy is less effective during a severe recession, when the economy is so depressed that interest rates reach the zero lower bound because interest rates cannot go lower than zero. In this situation, the central bank initiates *extraordinary monetary policy* to attempt to reinflate the economy. This might include buying assets, such as long-term treasury bonds, mortgage-backed securities, or other assets in the central bank's portfolio or in the market.

The Bank of Japan (BOJ) instituted quantitative easing in the early 2000s because the economy was in protracted deflation. The goal was to nudge the economy out of this hole. It was no longer possible to use ordinary monetary policy, since the BOJ had lowered interest rates to the zero lower bound. The BOJ proceeded to purchase large quantities of bonds, asset-backed securities, and even equities.

Quantitative easing has been a major tool used by the Federal Reserve Bank of the United States since the end of 2008 in response to the Great Recession, which is still in place as of this writing in 2014.

The Federal Reserve initiated three separate quantitative easing programs over this time by purchasing large amounts of long-term treasury bonds and mortgage-backed securities in an attempt to lower the long-term interest rate and mortgage rates to boost housing sales and the economy. The results so far have been muted. The greatest impact of the quantitative easing program has been to inflate the stock, bond, high-yield bonds (for income to savers because treasury yields are so low), and initially, the precious metals and other commodity markets. Commodities and precious metals rose in anticipation of high inflation because of the bond buying, but deflationary pressures ruled that out. Commodity prices dropped and remain subdued. Dubbed "the Fed trade" by traders or "Don't fight the Fed," the markets have been sensitive and reactive to any whiff of central bank policy change.

A similar reaction from the markets occurred in Japan in 2012, when the BOJ under Prime Minister Shinzō Abe instituted a new round of quantitative easing. The Japanese yen plunged, and the stock market surged. The impact on the real economy of Japan thus far has been minimal.

The jury is still out as to the effectiveness of quantitative easing, especially since unwinding the programs has its own challenges. The balance sheets of the central banks that have instituted these policies have grown enormously—a potentially destabilizing situation. Some economists, financial experts, and central bankers fear the policies have created new asset bubbles. Yet, reducing and eventually stopping the policy has unknown consequences. Since this quantity of asset purchases has never been attempted, the results of the effort will not be known for some time to come.

Inflation is sensitive to interest rates, as discussed in Chapter 17. Raising the interest rate will cause a decrease in the inflation rate, and lowering the interest rate will increase the inflation rate in most cases.

Some central banks use the *Taylor rule* for controlling interest rates. The Taylor rule stipulates that for each 1-percent increase in inflation, the central bank should raise the nominal interest rate by more than one percentage point. Other central banks set an inflation target, which can be a range that they believe is consistent with stable growth.

> **DEFINITION**
>
> The **federal funds rate** is the interest rate at which a depository institution lends funds that are immediately available to another depository institution overnight. The **Taylor rule** is a method used by some central banks to control inflation using a change in interest rates. The Taylor rule advocates a 1.5-percent increasein the nominal interest rate for every 1-percent increase in inflation.

Maintaining Financial Stability: Lender of Last Resort

One of the most important functions of central banks throughout history has been lender of last resort. Inevitably, some banks will run into trouble, or the financial system will overheat and then break down, resulting in panics that feed on themselves. In these situations, the central bank provides immediate loans to troubled banks so depositors can recoup their money. Central banks rely on Bagehot's rule of providing lending if the banks have collateral to back the loan and pay a penalty charge to prevent *moral hazard*, the temptation by banks to continue to engage in risky behavior because they know they will be bailed out by the government. This measure usually calms depositors and the financial markets.

One of the avenues of lending to banks is the *discount window*. Banks borrow directly from the central bank, but pay a penalty, as per Bagehot's rule. The interest rate including the penalty is the *discount rate*. Without the central bank's lender-of-last-resort function, bank runs could turn into major panics and threaten the entire financial system.

> **DEFINITION**
>
> The **discount window** is a monetary policy allowing banks to borrow short-term cash loans against collateral at the discount rate as a liquidity measure when the bank or banking system is in trouble. The **discount rate** (also called **base rate** or **repo rate**) is the interest rate charged by the Federal Reserve to banks for loans obtained through the central bank's discount window, which includes a penalty fee.

In extreme cases—as when major investment banks went under or nearly so in 2008, there was a freeze in banks' lending to each other, and a too-close-for-comfort collapse in the financial system—the central bank can provide massive liquidity by buying up troubled assets. Other extraordinary measures include nationalizing banks and businesses temporarily or managing controlled bankruptcies.

As told by former Federal Reserve Chair, Ben Bernanke, in his lectures to students in April 2012 (reprinted by Princeton University Press in 2013 as *The Federal Reserve and the Financial Crisis*), during the height of the 2008 financial crisis, on October 10, 2008, the Federal Reserve and the central bank governors and finance ministers of the G7, the largest industrial countries, met in Washington. They agreed to …

- Work together to prevent the failure of systemically important financial institutions.

- Provide banks and other financial institutions access to funding from central banks and capital from governments.

- Restore depositor and investor confidence.

- Cooperate to normalize credit markets.

The Federal Reserve embarked on an emergency program to shore up the financial system. It provided extra liquidity to banks through the discount window by extending the terms of loans, and instituted auctions of discount window funds where banks could bid on how much interest they would pay.

In addition, liquidity and credit facilities were established to give cash and short-term loans to larger financial institutions, such as broker-dealers. Commercial paper borrowers and money market funds were also supported, as well as financial instruments that are usually available to the public but had dried up during the panic. More liquidity was added to the financial system in various ways until the fear subsided.

The next challenge was to reverse the course of the economic downdraft. As described earlier, the Federal Reserve took the unusual step of deploying the first leg of quantitative easing from December 2008 to 2010. The stock market began to turn around and eventually reached all-time highs starting in March 2009. Other central banks, notably the ECB and the Bank of Japan, have pledged to support the financial markets and their economies and have taken various measures to accomplish this goal. However, the economies of all countries are still sluggish at this writing.

Maintaining Financial Stability: Regulation of the Banking Industry

Financial protection became paramount to central banks after witnessing the devastation wrought by the Great Depression. Central banks concluded that financial institutions cannot be given free rein to conduct business without accountability or regulation. Protective measures for depositors were put in place.

In the United States these included the Federal Deposit Insurance Act, the Securities Act of 1933, the Glass-Steagall Act, the Securities Exchange Act of 1934, and the Investment Company Act of 1940, among others. These Acts provided the following protections:

- Deposit insurance that guaranteed the government would return deposits up to a certain limit.

- Commercial banks and investment companies could not be mingled. This would prevent risky behavior by bankers and financial institutions.

- Interest rate ceilings were imposed to prevent banks from paying interest on bank deposits for the purpose of luring depositors away from riskier investments.

Some of these regulations were in place from 1933 to 2011. As a result of these measures, there were no banking crises from the late 1930s to the 1970s.

The "Great Inflation" of the 1970s caused by the oil embargo shock reversed some of these protections. Consequently, risky behavior re-emerged, which destabilized the financial sector and lead to bank failures and the Savings and Loan Crisis of the 1980s. The government bailed out banks that were too big to fail to prevent a banking system collapse.

Interest rate ceilings were eliminated in order to carry out contractionary monetary policy to bring down the high inflation of that period. Central banks later required banks to hold more capital as a cushion against failure.

In 1999 Congress passed the Gramm–Leach–Bliley Act (GLBA), which repealed the two provisions of the Glass-Steagall Act that restricted connections between banks and securities firms. The GLBA arguably gave a blank check to the financial industry to re-engage in risky behavior, which it did.

The Response by Central Banks to the 2008 Financial Crisis

The financial industry, released from the restrictions of the Glass-Steagall Act, devised complex low-quality *structured products* to take advantage of a bubble in housing. The structured products were sold to investors globally. (Structured products can be likened to a computer Trojan, a malware program that, when executed, causes damage to computers once inside.) To maximize gains, investment banks and divisions of commercial banks that were involved in trading used extraordinary *leverage*. This combination of risky financial products and massive leverage at the top of a housing bubble caused the near collapse of the financial system in October of 2008.

> **DEFINITION**
>
> **Structured products** are synthetic investment instruments that use derivatives of an underlying asset class to increase gains or mitigate risk. The underlying asset can be bonds, mortgages, stock indexes, or other assets. **Leverage** is the use of various financial instruments or borrowed capital, such as margin, to increase the potential return of an investment.

Since the 2008 crisis, new regulations are being designed to prevent the excesses of the financial industry. In the United States the Dodd-Frank Wall Street Reform and Consumer Protection Act was enacted on July 21, 2010.

The European Union is in the process of designing its *Basel III Accord* to regulate the financial industry, which can be adopted by any nation. The purpose of Basel III is to prevent a repeat of the banking industry collapse. It calls for higher capital requirements, reduced leverage used by banks, and increased liquidity ratios. These measures are being put in place to cushion banks and protect depositors in the event of another financial crisis.

The U.S. Federal Reserve will also implement its version of the Basel III rules. The rules will apply both to the commercial banking industry and to any financial institution holding more than $50 billion in assets.

Macroeconomic policy used by most central banks has been expansionary in the aftermath of the 2008 crisis. In all cases, interest rates have been lowered to induce growth. In many situations, quantitative easing—buying assets such as long-term treasury bonds and mortgage-backed securities—has been used to further reinflate the economy.

The Mandate to Foster Maximum Employment (United States)

All countries would like to maximize employment, but in the United States it is one of the mandates of the Federal Reserve stipulated by Congress.

The Great Recession starting in 2008 has been characterized by stubbornly low employment rates and long-term unemployment. The Federal Reserve has declared that it will keep interest rates low and use other accommodative measures until the unemployment rate reaches 6.5 percent as of this writing. Policy is being re-evaluated continually.

Central bank economists hold the stability of the economic system in their hands. Their creativity and adept handling of ever-challenging situations provide the environment necessary for economic growth.

The Least You Need to Know

- Central banks are responsible for macroeconomic policy to provide stability and foster growth in the economy.
- Recurrent banking panics that could cause systemic economic collapse convinced governments that a central bank was necessary. The Federal Reserve of the United States was formed in 1914 after the 1907 panic.
- The Great Depression of the 1930s provided lessons for economists on the importance of correct monetary policy.
- The functions of a central bank are to provide macroeconomic and financial stability, including playing the role of lender of last resort and regulating the banking and financial systems.
- The Federal Reserve is also responsible for maximizing employment.

CHAPTER 222

Using Government Fiscal Policy to Influence the Economy

Governments have a lot of spending power because of their ability to tax. How to allocate spending and how much to tax is what keeps politicians busy. The philosophical differences are fairly universal. They are not so different from the debates that might take place in your own household.

This chapter is *not* about how to allocate the mandated expenses of governments, which differ from country to country. Instead, we will explore how the government stabilizes the economy through fiscal policy and regulation. The goal of fiscal policy is to mitigate recessions and inflation. The government also regulates businesses and the financial industry to protect the economy.

In This Chapter

- The government budget: deficits and debt
- Fiscal stabilization policy
- How expansionary and contractionary fiscal policy is implemented
- How the government uses regulation to protect consumers and the economy

Establishing a Budget

Any government will have ongoing expenses. Typical categories include national defense, education, health care for some or all of the population, social security or pension and other welfare benefits (transfers), and general goods and services.

The income side of the balance sheet includes various kinds of taxes, depending on the country. These are personal income taxes, social insurance taxes, corporate profit taxes, property taxes, and sales taxes or VAT.

This is our starting point. Now that we have an idea about government expenses and income, we can use this information to see how the government (**G**) portion of the GDP impacts the other components of the GDP, namely, consumption (**C**), investment (**I**), and net exports (**NX**) [exports (**X**) – imports (**IM**)].

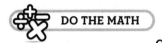

DO THE MATH

$$\textbf{GDP} \;=\; \textbf{C + I + G + (X - IM)}$$

value of all final goods	aggregate spending on
and services produced	final goods and services
in the economy	produced in the economy

Focusing on the equation **GDP = C+I+G+(X – IM)**, you can see that an increase in **G**, government spending, will also increase **GDP**. The government also influences consumption (**C**), since it can raise and lower taxes and increase or decrease *transfers*, which are also part of disposable income.

The government can affect investing (**I**) by offering tax incentives to businesses to invest. With tax policy, the government can nudge consumer and investment spending in one direction or the other, depending on its fiscal policy goal.

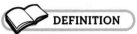

DEFINITION

A **transfer**, referring to the government, is a payment made by the government to households without receiving a good or service in return. This includes Social Security, Medicare, Medicaid, unemployment insurance, and food stamps.

Balancing the Budget and the Business Cycle

The government budget—income and expenditures—is affected by fluctuations in the business cycle. When the economy is expanding beyond potential output, there will be more income from taxes. Although spending might rise because of inflation, the increase in income and reduction in transfers has been observed to offset the cost increase, so there is a net gain in the real GDP. Any *budget deficit* will decrease, and it is even possible that there could be a *surplus*. In the 1990s, a rising stock market and expansion of technology resulted in a budget surplus in the United States. During a recession, there is often a budget deficit because tax revenues fall due to a decrease in incomes, and transfers are increased.

> **DEFINITION**
>
> The **budget deficit (or surplus)** is a periodic, usually yearly, accounting of the difference between income and expenditures.

In order to know whether the government budget is within reason in the long run, the effects of the business cycle have to be taken into account. This is done in some countries by using a cyclically adjusted budget balance, which assumes the economy is at potential output in the long run. Discretionary fiscal policy affects the budget independently of the cyclical budget. Keep in mind that the long-run budget deficit or surplus should coincide with the long-run potential output. The purpose of discretionary fiscal policy is to moderate the short-run swings in the economy.

Should a Balanced Budget Be Mandated?

Should balancing the budget be required by law? Requiring the budget to be balanced every year ignores the short-run fluctuations in the business cycle, which can be partially offset by the *automatic stabilizers*. If there are extremes in the fluctuations, such as a severe recession, government spending to end the recession can have a beneficial long-term effect by reducing what could be a deep and prolonged downturn. Even if the government runs a bigger deficit in the short run, to try to balance the budget during a recession could be penny wise and pound foolish.

> **DEFINITION**
>
> **Automatic stabilizers,** such as income taxes and transfers, reduce the impact of an economic shock without requiring intervention.

Public Debt (Government Debt)

What about *public debt?* A continual build up of the budget deficit can mount up, which increases government debt; but note that a budget deficit is not the same as government debt. The deficit is an accounting of the difference in income and expense over a period of time, usually one year. The public debt is the total debt of a country.

Historical war debts are a major factor in the accumulation of public debt. The U.S. debt started with the American Revolution and has been carried on the books by the United States government since it formed in 1789. The highest debt level in the United States was during and just after World War II.

> **DEFINITION**
>
> **Public debt** (government debt) is the total debt owed by the government.

United States Federal Debt Held by the Public 1790 - 2013

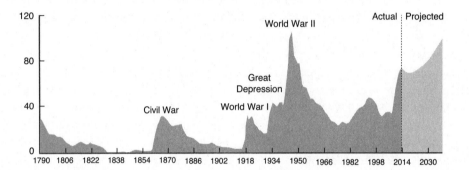

Recessions are also a major contributor to government debt. The Greek sovereign debt crisis is an extreme example of how public debt can mount up. Greece amassed huge fiscal imbalances from 2004 to 2009, with expenditures more than twice its income. The government failed to reduce its debt during the years of expansion, and the 2008 crisis that led to a deep depression made matters worse. Greece has not cracked down on pervasive tax evasion. The adoption of the euro eliminated flexibility in devaluing its currency to improve exports, which is hampering Greece's recovery.

A useful way to understand and analyze a country's debt is by comparing its debt-to-GDP ratio. This ratio gives a truer picture of the extent to which debt is hampering the economy. If the debt-to-GDP ratio declines over time, the economy might be healthier than it seems just from the absolute debt figure. A cautionary note is in order when using this ratio because implicit liabilities, such as future social welfare payments, can be obscured by a positive trend in the debt-to-GDP ratio. Governments are working on ways to handle the long-term obligations of social welfare.

Using Fiscal Policy to Expand or Contract the Economy

Chapter 21 described how monetary policy was able to shift the aggregate demand curve to the right by increasing the money supply, which in turn increases output during a recession. To rein in an overheated economy with a high rate of inflation, the money supply is reduced. This shifts the aggregate demand curve to the left, decreasing output and lowering the aggregate price level, which reduces inflation.

Fiscal policy can also be used to shift the aggregate demand curve to control output and the aggregate price level. The government uses changes in spending and taxes to achieve its goals. To picture how this works, we will look at the aggregate market using the *AD-AS model* discussed in Chapter 18. The AD-AS model depicts in graph form the interaction between aggregate demand and short-run (SRAS) and long-run aggregate supply (LRAS).

Implementing a Contractionary Fiscal Policy

If the economy is experiencing high inflation, a fiscal policy can be constructed to rein in the inflation rate. Since government spending increases output, the government can reduce spending to decrease inflation and an overheated economy. It can also put a damper on the economy by increasing taxes, since consumers will spend less if their disposable income is reduced. Government transfers can be decreased as well.

DEFINITION

The **AD-AS model** depicts in graph form the interaction between aggregate demand and short-run (SRAS) and long-run aggregate supply (LRAS).

We can see how this works using the AD-AS model. When the economy is producing more output than would occur at potential output (or full employment), there is an inflationary gap. An overheated economy is in macroeconomic equilibrium to the right of potential output at point E_1, which is the inflationary gap. To bring the economy back to equilibrium at the potential output, the government can institute a contractionary fiscal policy. When the government decreases spending, increases taxes, and reduces transfers (or any combination of these measures), there is a decrease in aggregate demand.

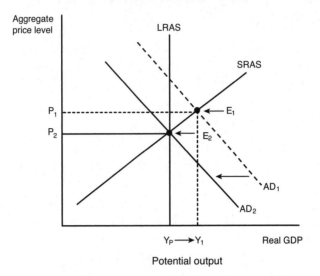

Contractionary Fiscal Policy

Contractionary fiscal policy shifts the aggregate demand curve from AD₁ to AD₂ along the short-run aggregate supply curve (SRAS). The economy moves from the short-run macroeconomic equilibrium point E₁ to E₂ at potential output, closing the inflationary output gap.

In the AD-AS model, a decrease in aggregate demand shifts the aggregate demand curve to the left from AD₁ to AD₂. This moves the short-run macroeconomic equilibrium from point E₁ to a new macroeconomic equilibrium at point E₂ at potential output, eliminating the inflationary output gap. The economy is now in equilibrium at potential output.

Implementing an Expansionary Fiscal Policy

If the economy is in a recession, the government can construct an expansionary fiscal policy to boost growth. In this case, the government wants to increase output to close a recessionary output gap. To raise output, the government can augment spending. It can also decrease taxes and increase transfers, since consumers will spend more if their disposable income is increased.

When the economy is producing less than would occur at potential output (or full employment), there is a recessionary gap. A slow economy is in macroeconomic equilibrium to the left of potential output at point E₁, creating a recessionary output gap. The expansionary fiscal policy that increases spending and transfers and/or decreases taxes brings the economy back to equilibrium at potential output.

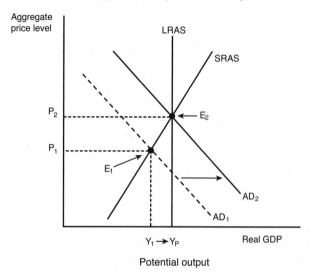

Expansionary Fiscal Policy

Expansionary fiscal policy shifts the aggregate demand curve from AD₁ to AD₂ along the short-run aggregate supply curve (SRAS). The economy moves from the short-run macroeconomic equilibrium point E₁ to E₂ at potential output, closing the recessionary output gap. LRAS is the long-run aggregate supply curve.

In the AD-AS model, the aggregate demand curve shifts to the right from AD₁ to AD₂. The short-run macroeconomic equilibrium moves from point E₁ to a new macroeconomic equilibrium at point E₂, which is also at potential output. The move eliminates the recessionary output gap. The economy is now in equilibrium at potential output.

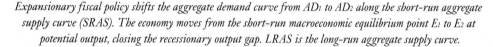 **TAKE-AWAY MESSAGE**

A **contractionary fiscal policy,** which *decreases* aggregate demand, can close an inflationary output gap and return the economy to long-run macroeconomic equilibrium at potential output.

An **expansionary fiscal policy,** which *increases* aggregate demand, can close a recessionary output gap and return the economy to long-run macroeconomic equilibrium at potential output.

Shortcomings of an Expansionary Fiscal Policy

Fiscal policy is especially effective during recessions, when expansionary monetary policy is impotent because interest rates are already at zero. On the other hand, there is a downside to using fiscal policy in other circumstances that should be considered when deciding whether fiscal policy is applicable in a particular situation.

When a large fiscal stimulus is enacted, some economists believe the increased spending raises the interest rate, which *crowds out* private investment. The high interest rate discourages investors from taking out loans. Crowding out does not occur if monetary policy reduces the interest rate to zero. Also, if the money supply is increased while the government is implementing its expansionary fiscal policy, the interest rate will be repressed, and little-to-no crowding out takes place.

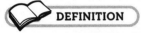 **DEFINITION**

Crowding out occurs when increased public sector spending replaces, or drives down, private sector spending.

Another concern is the lag in time from enacting legislation to implementation. Crafting legislation is time consuming. Politicians often disagree about how the legislation should be shaped. After the legislation is passed, spending that involves construction, for example, needs to be put to work on "shovel-ready" projects. Even if funds are allocated by the government for construction of highways or bridges, the local governments must have ready plans, or else they have to start from scratch. They first have to decide what work is needed and who should be hired to carry out the work, and then start the designs and blueprints for the project before they can begin to hire workers to dig the first hole.

A time lag was a problem in the United States in the immediate aftermath of the 2008 financial crisis, when the economy was hemorrhaging jobs. Congress allocated spending, but there were no "shovel-ready" projects. When the economy needs a shot of adrenaline, fiscal policy is not necessarily an immediate fix. Monetary policy is generally quicker, but there is a lag there as well.

During the 1990s deflation and recession in Japan, the government used extensive fiscal policy. Japan turned to fiscal policy to revive its economy after having lowered interest rates to zero with no effect on their depressed economy.

Japan spent hundreds of billions of dollars on infrastructure construction. The results have been somewhat disappointing. As mentioned in Chapter 21, in 2012 Prime Minister Shinzō Abe initiated another stimulus program in the form of quantitative easing—a monetary policy. This policy involves the Bank of Japan's buying assets on the open market, such as stocks and bonds. The result of this measure has been a rise in the stock market and a decline in the Japanese yen, its currency. In theory, the decline in the yen should boost exports.

The results are not in as to the effectiveness of Prime Minister Abe's efforts. The rise in the aging population means Japan must increase its transfer payments. This requires raising taxes, which is, in turn, a contractionary fiscal policy. As a result, the impact of the expansionary monetary policy is reduced. At the same time, the monetary policy, economic slowdown, and support of an aging population add to the nation's debt burden. The International Monetary Fund projects a stunning 242 percent debt-to-GDP ratio in 2014 for Japan.

How Fiscal Policy Filters Through the Economy

In a depressed economy, where people window shop but do not buy, or only buy what they absolutely need; where employers do not hire and probably lay off workers; and where businesses do not invest in new capital equipment because—why bother?—no one is buying, the spending has to start somewhere to get the ball rolling.

Only the government, for the sake of the economy, can spend when no one else will. Whether the government spends on direct purchases or increases transfers, or whether household consumers get a tax break so they have more money as disposable income, the government can play a decisive role in jump-starting the economy.

If the government decides to fund a major project, such as repairing all near-failing bridges as well as roads, the funds may be given to a local government or governments. The local governments hire professionals to evaluate the bridges and roads. Once that is accomplished, an architectural firm draws the plans. Finally, workers are hired to build the bridges and repair the roads. Construction companies buy building materials. They need more workers to fulfill the order, and so on.

At each step, the original money allocated by the government is given to the people hired and the businesses who sell their goods and services. They, in turn, are able to go to the store and buy what they could not afford before because they have more disposable income. Every business that receives some of the government's funding spends it somewhere in the economy. The money flows from the government to businesses to households, which increases consumer spending. This flow of money throughout the economy has a *multiplier effect*. The fiscal multiplier effect occurs when an initial injection of stimulus causes a greater increase in the national income than the cost of the initial injection.

Fiscal Stimulus

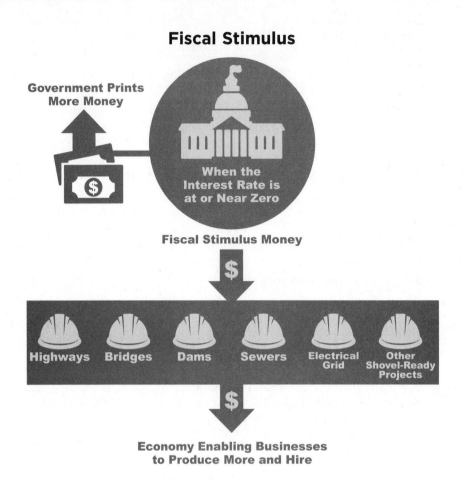

Government Prints More Money

When the Interest Rate is at or Near Zero

Fiscal Stimulus Money

$

Highways   Bridges   Dams   Sewers   Electrical Grid   Other Shovel-Ready Projects

$

Economy Enabling Businesses to Produce More and Hire

Measuring the Effect of Fiscal Stimulus

When deciding the kind of fiscal stimulus package to construct, government policymakers would like to get an estimate of the effects of each spending category available to stimulate the economy—direct spending, taxes, and transfers. They would like to know how much "bank for the buck" they will get. The size of the *fiscal multiplier* determines the impact the stimulus will have on the output of the economy. This, in turn, is a function of the *marginal propensity to consume (MPC)*. The MPC is how much of that extra dollar the government is giving out you will spend. Will you spend 50 percent? 60 percent? That is your MPC.

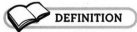 **DEFINITION**

The **fiscal multiplier** is a change in real GDP (Y) divided by the change in the government spending (injection). The **marginal propensity to consume (MPC)** is the proportion of each additional dollar of household income that is used for consumption expenditures.

So this makes sense. The government is putting together a fiscal stimulus package, and it wants to get as much additional output as possible. The more people and businesses spend of the fiscal stimulus they get, the more the stimulus measure will percolate through the economy in order to foster growth.

To reduce an overheated economy, the government will reverse the process.

 DO THE MATH

To calculate how much additional output the economy gets from the fiscal policy, we need to know the fiscal multiplier and the marginal propensity to consume (MPC). For example, if you are given an extra dollar by the government to help the economy, you might only spend 60% or 0.60 of that dollar. That would be your individual marginal propensity to consume (MPC).

The multiplier depends on the marginal propensity to consume. It is related to the MPC as $\dfrac{1}{1-\text{MPC}}$

If households spend a large percent of the extra income given to them by the government, which means their MPC is large, the multiplier effect will be greater. Said another way, the greater the marginal propensity to consume, the greater the multiplier effect.

As a hypothetical example, let's say the central government agrees to spend $100 million to repair bridges and roads. If the MPC is 0.6, the multiplier is 1/(1−0.6) = 1/0.4 = 2.5. The initial injection by the government into the economy is $100 million. Since the multiplier is 2.5, another $150 million was added to the economy via consumer spending.

Conducting Fiscal Policy with Taxes and Transfers

The government can design a fiscal policy that is based on a change in direct spending, taxes, transfers, or some combination. Direct spending, such as funding improvements in bridges, has the biggest impact on expansionary fiscal policy because it has a large multiplier.

Reducing taxes to stimulate the economy has a smaller multiplier. It has less impact on real GDP because households and businesses are likely to hold on to some of the tax savings rather than spend it. The portion that is saved reduces the disposable income that feeds the multiplier effect. The MPC might be 0.5 instead of 0.8, for example. *Since the greater the MPC, the greater the multiplier effect, reducing taxes is less effective than direct spending.*

The government can also decide who gets a tax cut (or increase, depending on the fiscal goal) and what taxes to cut. The debate is whether households with low incomes are more likely to spend their newfound money from an income tax cut than are wealthy individuals who get a capital gains tax cut.

A fiscal policy that increases transfers, such as unemployment and welfare benefits, will increase consumer spending, but much less than direct government spending. The multiplier, which depends on the MPC, is variable. Also, the increase in the amount of the transfer is relatively small, which reduces its impact on aggregate demand.

The Effect of Taxes and Transfers on the Multiplier

"Nothing is certain but death and taxes," the saying goes. Income taxes reduce our disposable income. The government's direct-spending fiscal package is included in income and is therefore taxed, reducing the disposable income. The reduction in disposable income reduces the multiplier, since they are positively correlated. The result is that the effect of fiscal policy is reduced by paying taxes. Just as the government's direct spending propagated throughout the economy via the multiplier effect, paying income taxes lessens the impact of fiscal policy by reducing the multiplier effect.

Taxes that are not based on income, called lump-sum taxes, do not reduce the multiplier.

Taxes and Transfers as Automatic Stabilizers

Taxes mitigate the effects of inflationary and recessionary output gaps of the business cycle. When the economy is expanding, income expands. The tax is a percentage of income, so it reduces the real GDP, countering the inflationary pressures. When the economy is in a recession, income declines, and the taxes produce less revenue for the government. This boosts the economy. Also, during recessions more transfers are usually allocated to the unemployed and poor because the slowdown in the economy causes more unemployment or difficulty in finding a job, which in turn increases poverty. When people spend this additional income, real GDP is increased. During inflationary times, fewer transfers are given, decreasing real GDP. These are automatic stabilizers. The government does not have to take any action to affect the fluctuations in the business cycle.

Government Regulation

The government is a policymaker, a regulator, and an enforcer of the law. Each country designs regulations for its businesses and its financial industry. International rules and regulations are agreed upon by governments and international agencies. The government enacts regulations to protect its public against illegal or unfavorable business practices.

Governments establish agencies to follow through on the regulations that are approved by lawmakers. The agencies establish and enforce rules that businesses must follow. Some examples are:

- Federal Deposit Insurance Corporation (U.S.)
- Interstate Commerce Commission (U.S.)
- Securities and Exchange Commission (U.S.)
- Federal Trade Commission (U.S.)
- The European Securities and Markets Authority (E.U.)
- European Shadow Financial Regulatory Committee (E.U.)
- European Systemic Risk Board (E.U.)
- European Banking Authority (E.U.)

How much regulation is sufficient, but not restrictive, is always in dispute. One philosophy is that businesses and markets should be free to operate without government interference. The belief is that less regulation is necessary to encourage innovation and growth. The other viewpoint is that regulation is needed to prevent excesses on the part of business to ensure that products are safe, to prevent illegal activities, and to ensure fair competition.

Judging from the historical examples that have been presented in these chapters, there seems to be a pattern, logically, of more regulations being enacted after there has been excessive speculation leading to a financial crisis and recession. After a period of calm, the pendulum swings in the opposite direction. The most recent crisis of 2008 is a case in point. As described in Chapter 21, the Glass–Steagall Act, put in place as a result of the 1929 stock market crash, was dismantled during the exuberant period of the 1990s stock market bubble. That led to a housing bubble and the engineering of highly leveraged financial instruments sold throughout the world.

When the housing bubble burst, the subsequent banking crisis nearly brought down the financial system and led to a deep recession. This disaster generated new enthusiasm for global government regulation of the financial industry. Yet the debate about the worthiness of regulation in a free-market society continues. It is up to you to weigh the facts and form your own opinion on the proper role and extent of government regulation.

The Least You Need to Know

- When a government balances its budget, the cyclical nature of the business cycle must be taken into account. Budget deficits during an economic downturn are not a cause for alarm.
- An expansionary period is a good time to pay for deficits.
- Fiscal policy is used to expand the economy during recessionary phases of the business cycle and rein in the economy during inflationary phases.
- Fiscal policy can affect the economy by adding or reducing government discretionary spending, increasing or decreasing taxes, and increasing or decreasing transfers. Direct spending has the greatest impact of these choices.
- Governments use regulatory policy to protect consumers, the economy, and the financial system. There is a long-standing debate concerning the degree of regulation governments should pursue.

Glossary

absolute advantage   When an individual or country is better at producing something than its trading partner.

accounting profit   The revenue of a business minus the explicit costs and depreciation.

actual unemployment   Natural unemployment plus the cyclical unemployment.

aggregate demand   The total amount of goods and services demanded in the economy at a given overall price level and in a given time period.

aggregate demand curve   A curve on a graph that shows the relationship between the aggregate price level and the quantity of aggregate output demanded by households, businesses, the government, and the rest of the world.

aggregate supply   The total supply of goods and services produced within an economy at a given overall price level in a given time period; also called total output.

allocative efficiency   When capital is allocated so that all participants in a society benefit.

automatic stabilizer   A policy that reduces the impact of an economic shock without requiring intervention; examples are income taxes and transfers (welfare benefits).

Bagehot's rule   Used by central banks during a financial crisis, advises to lend freely, add a penalty to the loan, and require collateral that is good in normal times. Banks that are unlikely to survive should go bankrupt, be dissolved, or be purchased.

balance sheet recession   Occurs when assets are less than liabilities on corporate balance sheets, caused by the bursting of a financial asset or housing bubble.

bank reserves   The currency banks keep in their vaults and their deposits at the central bank.

budget constraint   The combinations of goods and services that a consumer may purchase given current prices within his or her given income.

budget deficit (or surplus)   A periodic, usually yearly, accounting of the difference between income and expenditures.

budget line   The line that depicts all the possible combinations of quantities of goods and services a consumer can make if all income is spent.

business cycle   The fluctuations between expansions and recessions in the economy.

cartel   In an oligopoly, an agreement among competing firms to fix prices, set output quotas, allocate territories, and other methods of limiting competition.

ceteris paribus   Latin for "holding other things constant." In economics this refers to evaluating the effect of one variable against the other while the effect of other variables are held constant.

collusion   An agreement by two or more firms in an oligopoly, usually illegal and secret, to limit open competition in order to raise profits for their mutual benefit.

comparative advantage   Producing a good with a lower opportunity cost than the opportunity cost of its trading partner for that good.

complements   Two goods are complements if a fall (or rise) in the price of one good makes people more (or less) willing to buy the other good.

consumer surplus   Occurs when the consumer is willing to pay more for a given product than the current market price. It is calculated by the area above the market price and below the demand curve.

consumption bundle   The set of all goods and services consumed by an individual.

consumption possibilities   The set of all affordable consumption bundles.

cross-price elasticity of demand   The effect of change in one good's price on the quantity demanded of the other good.

crowding out   When increased public sector spending replaces, or drives down, private sector spending.

curve   In economics, a curve is a line on a graph that shows the relationship between two variables.

deadweight loss   The cost to society of inefficiency created by price controls and taxes.

deflation   A decrease in the general price level of goods and services; the inflation rate falls below zero percent.

deleveraging of debt   The simultaneous reduction of leverage in multiple private and public sectors, which lowers the total debt-to-nominal GDP ratio of the economy.

demand curve   The graphical representation of the demand schedule showing the quantity demanded by a consumer at any given price.

demand schedule   A table of data that shows how much of a good or service a consumer wants to buy at different prices.

dependent variable   The variable determined by the independent variable in a causal relationship.

depreciation   In a business, the reduction in value for use over time.

dominant strategy   The best choice by a firm in a prisoners' dilemma situation or other game regardless of the action taken by the other firm. Not all games have a dominant strategy.

duopoly   Two firms in an oligopoly.

economic profit   The revenue of a business minus the explicit and implicit costs and depreciation.

efficiency   (1) When there are no missed opportunities, and resources are used with little or no waste. (2) There is no way to make some people better off without making someone else worse off. (3) There is no way to produce more of one good without producing less of another good.

excess capacity   When actual production is less than what is optimal for the firm.

exchange-traded fund (ETF)   A security which represents a market sector, commodity, or stock index and trades like a stock.

explicit cost   The expenses of a business that are paid outright with money.

factor mobility   The degree to which a factor of production, such as labor, capital, or land, is able to move among industries or countries or be put to a different use in response to a change in market conditions.

factor payments   The payments made (wages, interest, rent, and profit payments) to the scarce resources and factors of production in return for productive services.

factors of production   Labor, land, and capital are the three main factors that are used in production. Entrepreneurship is a fourth.

financial intermediary   An institution that transforms the funds it gathers from many individuals into financial assets.

fixed input   An input whose quantity is fixed and cannot be varied in the time period considered, usually the short run. Capital is a fixed input.

fractional reserve banking   A process by which a quantity of newly printed money by the central bank is multiplied by means of bank lending, increasing the supply of money in the economy.

gains from trade   The increase in consumption in each nation resulting from specialization in production and trading.

game theory   The study of strategic decision making.

government transfers   Payments to individuals without any exchange of goods or services, such as Social Security and welfare.

gross domestic product   The total value of all final goods and services produced in the economy during a given year.

human capital   The educated workforce.

implicit cost   The opportunity costs representing the value, in dollar terms or other currency, of benefits lost by not doing something else.

income elasticity of demand   The percent change in quantity demanded divided by the percent change in income.

independent variable   In a causal relationship, a mathematical variable that is independent of the other variables.

inferior good   A good that experiences a decrease in demand when income rises.

inflation expectations   The rate of inflation that workers, businesses, consumers, and investors think will prevail in the future and that they will factor into their decision making.

inflation tax   The reduction in the real value of money, e.g., cash and fixed-rate bonds, held by the public resulting from inflation created by the government when it prints money.

inputs   The resources or factors of production.

interdependence   The few firms in an oligopoly are mutually dependent on one another to make pricing and output decisions.

interest rate effect   The effect on consumer and investment spending on real production caused by the effect of a change in the aggregate price level that alters the interest rate. The higher interest rate affects the cost of borrowing for household and business sectors and lending by banks.

labor force   The total of all employed and unemployed workers.

labor force participation rate   The percentage of working-age people in the labor force.

law of demand   The quantity demanded is related to the price, such that as price increases, quantity decreases, all else being equal.

law of diminishing marginal returns to an input   Describes the decline in the marginal product of that input when the quantity of the input increases, if levels of all other inputs are fixed.

law of supply   As the price of a good or service increases, the quantity of goods or services offered by suppliers increases, and vice versa.

leverage   The use of various financial instruments or borrowed capital, such as margin, to increase the potential return of an investment.

long run   In regard to aggregate supply, the long run is the period of time over which all prices are fully flexible.

macroeconomics   The study of the entire economy.

marginal analysis   An analytic method of decision making by measuring the incremental changes in the variables.

marginal product of labor   The additional quantity of output that is produced using one more unit of labor.

marginal propensity to consume   Illustrates the concept that the increase in personal consumer spending (consumption) occurs with an increase in disposable income. It is the proportion of additional disposable income that is spent on consumption.

marginal utility   The change in utility generated by consuming one additional unit of the good or service.

market power   The ability of a firm to raise prices.

microeconomics   The branch of economics that analyzes the market behavior of individual consumers and firms.

minimum-cost output   The quantity of output at which average total cost is the lowest—when marginal cost equals the average total cost—MC = ATC.

model   A model is a simplified version of a complex idea that can be used to predict outcomes in theory or in the real world. In economics models are often illustrated in graph form.

monetary aggregate   A category of money that is part of an overall measure of the money supply.

monetary base   The monetary base is the sum of the domestic currency and the bank reserves held at the central bank.

monetization   Creating money (coinage and bank notes), usually by the government and central bank.

money multiplier   The ratio of the **money supply** (currency in circulation + checkable bank deposits) to the **monetary base** (bank reserves + money in circulation).

money stock or money supply   The money stock or money supply is the currency in circulation plus the checkable bank deposits. The standard measure of money stock is M2.

monopolist   A firm that is the sole producer of a good with no substitutes.

monopoly   An industry that controls the entire source for a good.

mutual fund   A financial intermediary that creates a stock portfolio and sells shares of the portfolio to individual investors.

Nash equilibrium   An equilibrium where no firm has an incentive to deviate from its chosen strategy after considering its competitor's decision.

nominal interest rate   The rate of interest before adjusting for inflation.

normal good   A good that experiences an increase in demand when income rises.

normal profit   An economic profit of zero: total revenue minus total explicit and implicit costs. It is the minimum amount of profit needed for the firm to be competitive in the market.

opportunity cost   The real cost of an item—what must be given up in order to do something else or get something else.

payoff   The reward to a player in game theory. In economics, the payoff is profit.

perfect elasticity of demand   An elasticity in which infinitesimally small changes in price cause infinitely large changes in quantity.

perfect price discrimination   The ideal form of price discrimination whereby every consumer pays the monopolist the price he or she is willing to pay.

price discrimination   A pricing strategy by a monopolist that aims to get the most consumer surplus possible by charging different prices to different customers depending on the consumer's willingness to pay.

price elasticity of demand   A measure of the relationship between a change in the quantity demanded of a particular good and a change in its price. Calculated by the %change in quantity demanded/%change in price.

price leadership   A pattern of pricing in which one firm regularly announces price changes that other firms then match.

price rigidity   When firms are resistant to changing their prices even if there is a change in demand or costs.

price signaling   A form of implicit collusion in which a firm announces a price increase in the hope that other firms will follow.

producer surplus   The difference between the market price, or price received, and the price the producer is willing to receive for the good. The difference is the benefit to the producer by his selling the good in the market.

production function   The relationship between the quantity of inputs a firm uses and the quantity of outputs it produces.

production possibility frontier   A graph, usually a curve, portraying the trade-offs facing an economy that produces only two goods. It shows the maximum quantity of one good that can be produced for any given quantity produced of the other.

productive efficiency   When the least amount of resources are used to produce a good.

productivity   The measure of the amount of output per unit of input.

public debt   The total debt owed by the government.

nominal wages   The wages that are actually paid as opposed to their purchasing power with inflation taken into consideration.

optimal consumption bundle   The consumption bundle that maximizes a consumer's total utility given his or her budget line.

output   The quantity of goods or services produced in a given time period, by a firm, industry, or country.

output gap   The percentage difference between the actual level of real GDP and potential output (GDP).

paradox of thrift   Occurs when, during a recession, an increase in planned savings can cause actual savings and investment to decrease.

potential output   The output (real GDP) the economy can achieve when it is most efficient.

principle of diminishing marginal utility   Each successive unit of a good or service consumed adds less to total utility than the previous unit.

production capacity   Another name for the potential output of an economy.

purchasing power   The value of a currency expressed in terms of the amount of goods or services that one unit of money can buy. An increase in inflation decreases the amount of goods and services that can be bought.

real GDP   The total value of all final goods and services produced in the economy during a given year calculated using a given base year.

real interest rate   The nominal rate of interest minus inflation.

real wages   Wages that have been adjusted for inflation and that reflect the purchasing power of the money received by the worker.

recession   A significant decline in economic activity spread across the economy, lasting more than a few months, normally visible in real GDP, real income, employment, industrial production, and wholesale-retail sales.

reservation price   The maximum price that a customer is willing to pay for a good.

reserve ratio   The fraction of bank deposits that a bank must hold in cash as reserves.

schedule   A table containing variables that are used to create a curve, such as in a supply curve or a demand curve.

shift (in a curve)   A *shift* in the demand curve or the supply curve represents a change in demand (or supply) caused by an external event.

shortage   Occurs when the market price is below the equilibrium price.

slope   The measure of the direction and steepness of a curve.

stagflation   When inflation and falling aggregate output occur simultaneously.

sticky   Used to describe wage or price levels that are resistant to change and do not immediately adjust to their long-run level because of long-term leases, contracts, or other factors. This can be true even with an increase in money supply.

structured products   Synthetic investment instruments that use derivatives of an underlying asset class to increase gains or mitigate risk. The underlying asset can be bonds, mortgages, stock indexes, or other assets.

substitutes   Comparing two goods, when a fall (or rise) in the price of one of the goods makes consumers less (or more) willing to buy the other good.

surplus   Occurs when the market price is *above* the equilibrium price.

Taylor rule   A method to control inflation using a change in interest rates. The Taylor rule prescribes a 1.5 percent increase in interest rates for every 1 percent increase in inflation.

total product curve   Shows how the quantity of output depends on the quantity of the variable input for a given quantity of the fixed input.

total utility   The aggregate amount of satisfaction received from a good or service.

touchstone   A slate or fieldstone tablet used to determine the purity of a gold or silver coin.

transfer   A payment made by the government to households without receiving a good or service in return.

unemployment   The number of people who are not currently employed and are actively seeking work.

util   A unit of utility.

utility   A measure of the satisfaction the consumer derives from the consumption of goods and services.

utility function   The total utility generated by a consumption bundle.

variable   A symbol in mathematics that can change in value within a problem set.

variable input   An input whose quantity the firm can vary. Labor is a variable input.

velocity of money   The frequency of spending money in a given period of time.

wealth effect (in relation to aggregate demand)   Caused by a change in the aggregate price level, the effect on consumer spending resulting from a rise in the aggregate price level that reduces the purchasing power of consumers' assets.

Recommended Reading

Ahamed, Liaquat. *Lords of Finance: The Bankers Who Broke the World* (New York: Penguin Press, 2009).

Akerlof, George A., and Robert J. Shiller. *Animal Spirits: How Human Psychology Drives the Economy, and Why It Matters for Global Capitalism* (Princeton, NJ: Princeton University Press, 2009).

Bernanke, Ben. *The Federal Reserve and the Financial Crisis* (Princeton, NJ: Princeton University Press), 2013.

Ferguson, Niall. *The Ascent of Money: A Financial History of the World* (New York: Allen Lane/ Penguin Group, 2008).

Friedman, Milton, and Anna Jacobson Schwartz. *A Monetary History of the United States, 1867–1960* (Princeton, NJ: Princeton University Press, 1971).

Galbraith, John Kenneth. *The Great Crash of 1929* (New York: Houghton Mifflin Harcourt Publishing Company, 2009).

Hayek, F. A. *The Road to Serfdom: Fiftieth Anniversary Edition* (Chicago: Chicago University Press, 1994).

Heilbroner, Robert L. *The Making of Economic Society* (Englewood Cliffs, NJ: Prentice Hall, 1989).

———. *The Worldly Philosophers: The Lives, Times and Ideas of the Great Economic Thinkers* (New York: Touchstone/Simon and Schuster, 1999).

Karabell, Zachary. *The Leading Indicators: A Short History of the Numbers That Rule Our World* (New York, NY: Simon & Schuster, 2014).

Keen, Steve. *Debunking Economics—Revised and Expanded Edition: The Naked Emperor Dethroned? 2nd edition* (New York/London: Zed Books, 2011).

Keynes, John Maynard. *The General Theory of Employment, Interest, and Money* (Kissimmee, FL: Signalman Publishing, 2009.)

Krugman, Paul. *End This Depression Now!* (New York: W.W. Norton & Company, 2012).

———. *The Return of Depression Economics and the Crisis of 2008* (New York: W.W. Norton & Company, 2009).

Marx, Karl. *Capital: A Critique of Political Economy (3 volumes)* (New York: Penguin Classics, 1992).

Smith, Adam. *An Inquiry into the Nature and Causes of the Wealth of Nations* (New York: Bantam Classics, 2003 or New York: Oxford University Press, 2008).

Smith, David. *Free Lunch: Easily Digestible Economics, Served on a Plate* (London: Profile Books, 2003).

Stiglitz, Joseph E. *Freefall: America, Free Markets, and the Sinking of the World Economy* (New York: W.W. Norton & Company, 2010).

Wapshott, Nicholas. *Keynes Hayek: The Clash That Defined Modern Economics* (New York: W.W. Norton & Company, 2011).

Index

C

D

J-K

L

M

Q-R

V

W-X-Y-Z